A G Spelding

Spalding's official base ball guide

A G Spelding

Spalding's official base ball guide

ISBN/EAN: 9783741176371

Manufactured in Europe, USA, Canada, Australia, Japa

Cover: Foto ©Stingray / pixelio.de

Manufactured and distributed by brebook publishing software (www.brebook.com)

A G Spelding

Spalding's official base ball guide

Spalding's Trade Marked Base Balls.

Our line of Base Balls is now so well known to the trade, and they are so thoroughly appreciated by the base ball players of the country, that it seems almost unnecessary to call special attention to their superior merits. Spalding's League Ball, having stood the severe test of the National League for the last seven years, and having again been adopted as the official ball of that leading organization for 1886, as well as most of the other prominent associations, gives it a reputation and sale unequaled by any other ball on the market. It is made of the very best material, in accordance with the latest League requirements, and with every League Ball sold is given a guarantee that it will stand a full game without ripping or losing its shape. *Beware of cheap imitations;* no League Ball is genuine without our trade mark on each box and ball, and the autograph of

A. G. Spalding

on each label. To further protect ourselves and customers from the impositions of certain unprincipled manufacturers, and for the better protection of the balls, we have this season adopted a new feature of sealing each of our trade marked balls (from the $1.50 "League Ball" to the 25c. "Boys' Favorite") in a separate box, and purchasers of our goods will serve their own interest by noticing that the seals are not broken or the balls tampered with.

With the general improvement made in the quality of our full line of balls, and the new and valuable feature of putting up all our trade marked balls in separate boxes, sealed and labeled to prevent counterfeiting, together with the extremely low price made on some of the goods, especially on the cheaper grades, we believe we are offering the best line of base balls now on the market.

Special trade prices quoted to dealers on application.

A. G. SPALDING & BROS.,
108 Madison St., CHICAGO.   241 Broadway, NEW YORK.

SPALDING'S
BASE BALL GUIDE

—AND—

Official League Book for 1886.

A COMPLETE HAND BOOK OF THE NATIONAL
GAME OF BASE BALL.

CONTAINING REVIEWS OF THE VARIOUS ASSOCIATION
SEASONS, WITH SPECIAL ARTICLES ON BASE
BALL TOPICS OF INTEREST.

TOGETHER WITH THE

*SEASON'S AVERAGES OF ALL PROFESSIONAL
ASSOCIATIONS FOR 1885,*

AND ALSO

The College Club Statistics for 1885.

ADDED TO WHICH IS THE

Complete Official League Record for 1885,

Including the Playing Rules in their Revised Form; Official Record
of all League Games and Players; and the Official
Schedule of League Games for 1886,

AS ADOPTED AT THE MEETINGS OF THE LEAGUE.

PUBLISHED BY

A. G. SPALDING & BROS.,

NEW YORK AND CHICAGO.

Entered according to Act of Congress, in the year 1886, by A. G. Spalding & Bros., in the
Office of the Librarian of Congress at Washington.

PUBLISHERS' NOTICE.

"Spalding's Base Ball Guide" again greets the base ball public with the official records of America's national game. First issued in 1877, it has grown in popularity, has been enlarged and improved from year to year, and is now the recognized authority upon base ball matters. The statistics contained in the "Guide" can be relied upon, nearly all of them having been compiled from official records.

The "Guide" has attained such a size—160 pages—as to preclude the possibility of publishing in the same issue the League Constitution in full, and other interesting League matter. We are therefore compelled, in addition, to publish the "Official League Book," which contains only official League matter as furnished by Secretary Young, including the League Constitution in full.

Copies of the "Guide" or "League Book," will be mailed to any address upon receipt of ten cents each. Trade orders supplied through the News Companies, or direct from the publishers.

A. G. SPALDING & BROS.,

108 Madison St., 241 Broadway,
CHICAGO. NEW YORK.

WASHINGTON, D. C., March 3, 1886.

By the authority vested in me, I do hereby certify that Messrs. A. G. Spalding & Bros., of Chicago, Ill., have been granted the *exclusive* right to publish the Official League Book for 1885. N. E. YOUNG,
Secretary National League of Professional Base Ball Clubs.

THE SPALDING TRADE MARK.

Experience has shown that in Sporting Goods, as in all other lines of business, unprincipled persons are always eager to prey on the reputation gained by honest dealing and good business management. We regret to state that we have not escaped the attention of such parties, who have appropriated our original designs, styles and names, and by using similar illustrations and descriptions, deceive the public into believing that the articles were manufactured by us, and that we are responsible for their inferior quality. A wide acquaintance with sportsmen, and an extended experience with the various sports, has enabled us to anticipate the wants of our patrons in securing outfits, and to offer only such articles as were perfectly satisfactory for our own use, knowing by practical tests that they would serve the purpose properly, and be unfailing to the purchaser.

In order to protect our customers, and to preserve our reputation, we have found it necessary to place our "Trade Mark" on the higher grades of goods that we manufacture and introduce. The care and discrimination exercised in selecting only articles of the highest quality as being worthy of bearing our trade mark, has resulted in giving them a reputation as being practically the best of their kind that could be produced.

In our opinion a satisfied customer is the best advertisement that we can have, and dealers and individuals will please bear in mind that on whatever article our TRADE MARK appears, we guarantee it to be exactly as represented, and wherever just cause for complaint exists, we will thank the purchaser for returning the article to us, and receiving a perfect one in return, or the refunding of the purchase money.

A. G. SPALDING & BROS.,

108 Madison St., CHICAGO.   241 Broadway, NEW YORK.

OUR PUBLICATIONS.

The popular encouragement given to the pursuit of Athletic Sports, Recreative Amusements, Gymnastic Exercises, etc., and the comparative scarcity of mediums of instruction on these subjects, suggested the publication of our *Library of Athletic Sports*. The benefits of Athletic and other manly exercises, from an educational as well as from a moral and recreative point of view, are now so generally recognized that the right method of promoting man's physical welfare should be readily accessible.

No.	1.	Spalding's Official Base Ball Guide	Price each,	10c.
"	2.	Spalding's " League Book	"	10c.
"	3.	Spalding's Illustrated Hand Book of Pitching and Fielding	"	25c.
"	4.	Spalding's Illustrated Hand Book of Batting and Base Running	"	25c.
"	7.	Spalding's Illustrated Foot Ball Rules and Referees' Book	"	10c.
"	8.	Spalding's Lawn Tennis Manual	"	10c.
"	9.	Spalding's Manual of Roller Skating	"	25c.
"	10.	Spalding's Official Croquet Manual	"	10c.
"	11.	Spalding's Manual of Boxing, Indian Club Swinging and Manly Sports	"	25c.
"	13.	Spalding's Hand Book of Sporting Rules and Training	"	25c.
"	14.	Practical Gymnastics without a Teacher	"	50c.

Any of the above books mailed upon receipt of price.

OUR COMPLETE CATALOGUE.

We have just issued the largest and most complete Sporting Goods Catalogue ever published, containing over 1,000 separate illustrations of various articles used in sport, together with a carefully prepared price list and description of each article. We have endeavored to make the illustration and description so plain that customers from a distance can select an article quite as intelligently as if they had called at our Chicago or New York Stores in person. In addition to its value as a catalogue, it contains a complete and valuable set of Sporting Rules, embracing Athletic Sports, Archery, Badminton, Bagatelle, Bicycling, Billiards, Pool, Boating, Boxing, Bowling, Caledonian Games, Club Swinging, Cricket, Croquet, Curling, Fly Casting, Foot Ball, Fencing, Gymnastics, Hand Ball, Lawn Tennis, Lacrosse, Polo, Quoits, Racquet, Running, Shooting, Skating, Walking, Wrestling Rules.

With each Catalogue purchased of us a certificate is inclosed entitling the holder to use it as 25 cents toward payment of goods where the amount equals or exceeds $1.00. Mailed to any address upon receipt of 25 cents.

A. G. SPALDING & BROS.,
108 Madison St., CHICAGO.   241 Broadway, NEW YORK.

CORRECT DIAGRAM OF A BALL GROUND.

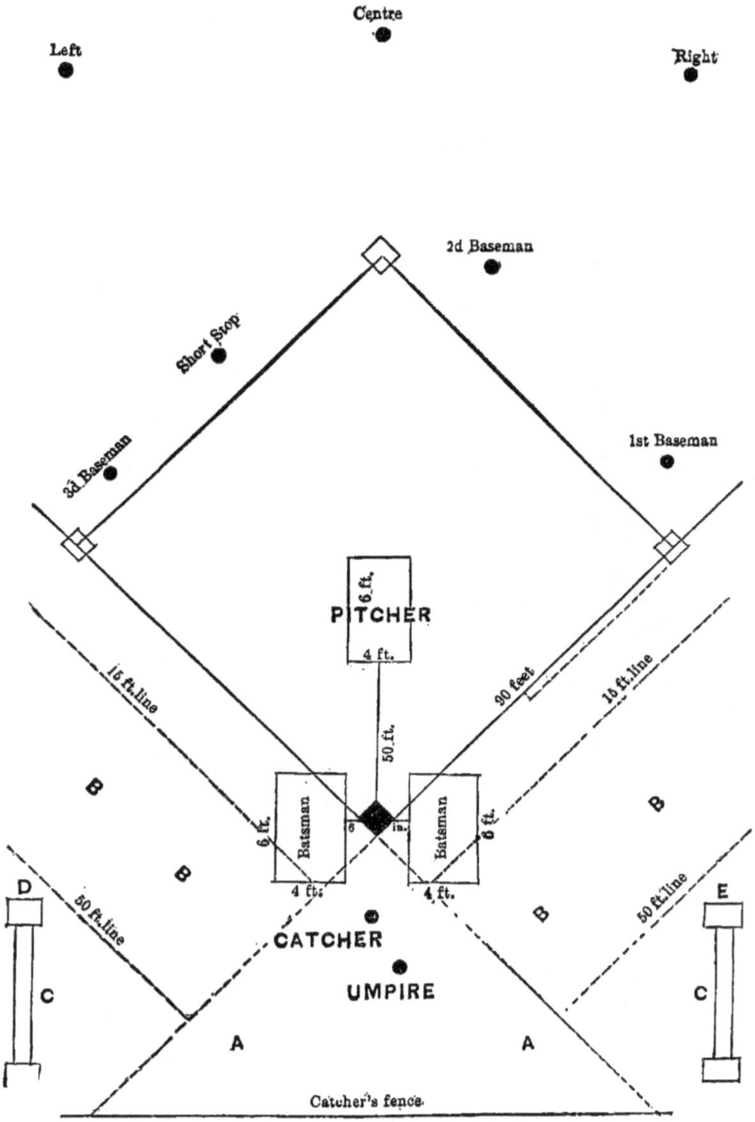

A. A. A.—Ground reserved for Umpire, Batsman and Catcher.
B. B. B.—Ground reserved for Captain and Assistant.
C.—Players' Bench.   D.—Visiting Players' Bat Rack.
E.—Home Players' Bat Rack.

INTRODUCTION.

It is now over a quarter of a century since the game of base ball became popularized as the game of games for American youth; and within that period it has so extended itself in its sphere of operations that it is now the permanently established national field game of America. Unlike many sports taken up by our people, which have ridden into general favor on the wave of a public furore, base ball has come to stay. Not even the great war of the rebellion could check its progress to any great extent; in fact, in one way—through the national army—it led to its being planted in a Southern clime, and now base ball can be said to "know no North, no South, no East, no West." It has even crossed the border into Canada, and in addition, like cricket, has found its way at times to foreign shores. Within the past fifteen years, too, the national game has burst its youthful bonds, and from the amateur period of its early growth it has entered upon the more advanced condition of its career under the professional system, which system has developed its innate attractions within a single decade to an extent it otherwise could not have reached in thrice the amount of time. In 1871 the first professional association was established, and now, in 1885, we find the professional fraternity, after their passage through the Red Sea of gambling abuses so thoroughly controlled in the interests of honest play, by the existing professional organizations, that the evils which attach themselves to professionalism, in sports generally, no longer find space for existence within the arena of professional base ball playing. In fact, our national game now stands alone as a field sport in the one important fact that it is the only public sport in which professional exemplars take part which possesses the power to attract its thousands of spectators without the extrinsic aid of gambling. It is very questionable whether there is any public sport in the civilized portion of the world so eminently fitted for the people it was made for as the American national game of base ball. In every respect is it an outdoor sport admirably adapted for our mercurial population. It is full of excitement, is quickly played, and it not only requires vigor of constitution and a healthy physique, but manly courage, steady nerve, plenty of pluck, and considerable powers of judgment to excel in it.

What can present a more attractive picture to the lover of outdoor sports than the scene presented at a base ball match between two trained professional teams competing for championship honors, in which every point of play is so well looked after in the field, that it is only by some extra display of skill at the bat, or a lucky act of base-running at an opportune moment, that a single run is obtained in a full nine innings game? To watch the progress of a contest in which only one run is required to secure an important lead, and, while the game is in such a position, to see hit after hit made to the field, either in the form of high fly balls splendidly caught on the run by some active out-fielder, or a sharp ground hit beautifully picked up in the in-field, and swiftly and accurately thrown to the right baseman in time, is to see the perfection of base ball fielding, and that surpasses the fielding of every other known game of ball. Then there is the intense excitement incident to a contest in which one side is endeavoring to escape a "whitewash," while the other side as eagerly strives to retain their lead of a single run; and with the game in such position, a three base hit sends the runner to third base before a single hand is out, only to see the hit left unrewarded by the expected run, owing to the telling effect of the strategic pitching, and the splendid field support given it. Add to this the other excitement of a high hit over the out-fielder's head, made while two or three of the bases are occupied with the result of a tie score, or the securing of a lead at a critical point of the game, and a culmination of attractive features is reached, incidental to no other field game in vogue. If it is considered, too, that the pursuit of base ball is that of a healthy, recreative exercise, alike for the mind and body, suitable to all classes of our people, and to the adult as well as the mere boy, there can be no longer room for surprise that such a game should reach the unprecedented popularity that the American game of base ball has attained.

THE NATIONAL LEAGUE AND ITS HISTORY.
From 1876 to 1886.

The completion of the first decade in the history of the National League, makes it imperative to occupy the pages of the GUIDE for 1886 with a reference history of the career of the organization from its inaugural season in 1876 to the completion of the first ten years of its existence in 1886. In transcribing this historical record from the annual publications of the League books, we propose only to make this chapter of the *Guide* a matter of reference for needed information in regard to the annual progress of the League, from its early period of existence to its first entrance upon its teens in life. To give the detail of its history would be to go entirely beyond the scope of the annual book of the League. As this information is timely and necessary we present it at once without any apology for using valuable space for a purpose, which, in a measure, may be said to be outside of our usual course in editing the *Guide*.

THE SEASON OF 1876.

The close of the professional base ball season in 1876 left anything but a desirable condition of things prevailing in the then existing National Professional Association. That bane of all sports, pool gambling, had found an opening for its poisonous influence in the ranks of the fraternity, and the old National Association found itself powerless to drive it out of the base ball body politic. In fact, the time was ripe for needed reformatory measures, and the best men in the legislative councils of the fraternity deemed it proper to take the initiative in a strenuous effort to improve the morale of the professional ranks, and to raise the stock company club business up to the plane of honorable work, alike in the clubs as on the fields. With this object in view, a preliminary meeting of Western base ball men was held at Louisville, Ky., in January, 1876, at which time the first steps were taken towards the organization of the National League. There were present at this meeting Messrs. W. A. Hulbert, A. G. Spalding, and Louis Meacham, of Chicago; Chas. A. Fowle, of St. Louis; Chas. E. Chase, of Louisville; and John A. Joyce, of Cincinnati. The outcome of this preliminary meeting at Louisville was the appointment of a special committee, who was given the power to confer with representatives of all the clubs desirous of taking part in the reform work. What the objects in view were are succinctly expressed in the circular letter of the committee sent to the clubs in question, which we append.

CHICAGO, Jan. 23, 1876.

The undersigned have been appointed by the Chicago, Cincinnati,

Louisville and St. Louis Clubs a committee to confer with you on matters of interest to the game at large, with special reference to the reformation of existing abuses, and the formation of a new association, and we are clothed with full authority in writing from the above named clubs to bind them to any arrangement we may make with you. We therefore invite your club to send a representative, clothed with like authority, to meet us at the Grand Central Hotel, in the city of New York, on Wednesday the 2d day of February next, at 12 M. After careful consideration of the needs of the professional clubs, the organizations we represent are of the firm belief that existing circumstances demand prompt and vigorous action by those who are the natural sponsors of the game. It is the earnest recommendation of our constituents that all past troubles and differences be ignored and forgotten, and that the conference we propose shall be a calm, friendly and deliberate discussion, looking solely to the general good of the clubs who are calculated to give character and permanency to the game. We are confident that the propositions we have to submit will meet with your approval and support, and we shall be pleased to meet you at the time and place above mentioned.

Yours respectfully,
W. A. HULBERT.
CHAS. A. FOWLE.

This circular letter was sent to the Bostons, Hartfords, Athletics of Philadelphia, and Mutuals of New York.

The effect of the above circular was a gathering of duly accredited representatives of the Chicago, Cincinnati, St. Louis and Louisville clubs of the West, for which Messrs. W. A. Hulbert and Chas. A. Fowle were empowered to act; and of the Athletic, Boston, Mutual, and Hartford clubs of the East, respectively represented by G. W. Thompson, N. T. Apollonio, W. H. Cammeyer, and M. G. Bulkeley; the meeting in question being held at the Grand Central Hotel in New York, on Feb. 2, 1876. Mr. Bulkeley acted as Chairman, and Harry Wright, of the Boston Club, as Secretary. The Western Committee, who had inaugurated the reform movement, came prepared with a constitution and by-laws, which were adopted with but slight alterations. Under this new constitution important changes were introduced in the government of the new association, the first of which made it a league of clubs, instead, as before, an association of players. Then, too, the entrance fee for membership was changed from ten dollars to one hundred. In addition, no club could be admitted to membership from any city less than 75,000 inhabitants, nor from any town within less than five miles from the *locale* of a League club, this latter clause giving for the first time proprietary rights over the city the club represented. The new League was governed by a board of five directors, who had charge of all the affairs of the organization. Special rules governing the engagement of regular players were adopted for the first time, the same being in the form of written contracts. This at once put a stop to the "revolving" which had previously been indulged in with impunity. The expulsion of a player from a club cut him off from employment in any League club until he was reinstated. All players expelled for proved dishonesty were forever debarred from future employment in any League club. Thus was the needed reform in the business of running stock company professional clubs, duly inaugurated. The first president of the League was M. G. Bulkeley, who, together with Messrs. Apollonio, Cammeyer, Fowle, and Chase comprised the first Board of Directors, they representing the Hartford, Boston, Mutual, St. Louis, and Louisville clubs. N. E. Young was elected Secretary at a salary of $400 a year. All the clubs of the newly formed League formally resigned from the "National Association of Professional Base Ball players," and that Association then became a defunct institution. The playing rules of the League for 1876 admitted of a substitute entering a game prior to the fourth innings. A special rule rendered any player interested in a bet on the game, or who had purchased a pool ticket on the contest, subject to prompt expulsion. The pitcher occupied a position six feet square, and he was required to deliver the ball "with the arm swinging nearly perpendicular at the side of the body," and the arm, in being swung forward, had to pass below the line of his hip. This was designed to prevent the underhand throw, but it failed of its object. Virtually nine unfair balls were allowed to be delivered before the batsman was given his base on called balls. There was no rule in the code that year prohibiting the fair foul hit. There was then no special staff of umpires, and the result was continued disputes about selecting umpires for match games, five names having to be submitted, from which list a choice was to be made. Altogether, though the new code was an improvement over the old one, the amended rules were lacking in many essential points.

The official list of League Club players for 1876, as published in the League Guide of that year was as follows:—

Athletic (of Philadelphia).—A. J. Reach, A. Knight, W. R. Coon, W. D. Fisler, W. Fouser, D. W. Force, E. B. Sutton, G. W. Hall, D. Eggler, and J. Meyerle.

Boston.—H. Wright, J. E. Borden, T. McGinley, T. Murnan, T. I. Beals, H. C. Schafer, A. J. Leonard, J. O'Rourke, J. F. Manning, F. T. Whitney, W. R. Parks, and Geo. Wright. Manager, H. Wright.

Chicago.—A. G. Spalding, J. White, C. A. McVey, R. C. Barnes, A. C. Anson, J. P. Peters, P. A. Hines, O. Bielaski, J. W. Glenn, J. F. Cone, R. Addy, and F. H. Andrus. Manager and Captain, A. G. Spalding.

Cincinnati.—C. H. Gould, S. J. Fields, W. C. Fisher, C. J. Sweasy, H. Kessler, E. Snyder, C. W. Jones, R. Clack, D. P. Pierson and A. S. Booth. Manager, C. H. Gould.

Hartford.—Robt. Ferguson, D. Allison, W. A. Cummings, Thos. Bond, E. Mills, J. J. Burdock, T. Carey, T. York, J. J. Remsen, Cassidy, R. Higham, and W. H. Harbidge. Manager and Captain, Robt. Ferguson.

Louisville.—J. C. Chapman, *J. A. Devlin*, W. Scott Hastings, C. Snyder, W. L. Hague, J. Gerhardt, C. Fulmer, A. A. Allison, J. C. Carbine, G. Bechtel, and J. J. Ryan. Manager, J. C. Chapman.

Mutual—(of New York).—Robt. Mathews, N. W. Hicks, J. Start, *Jas. Hallman*, A. H. "Nichols," E. Booth, J. J. Shandley, W. J. Boyd, and W. H. Craver. Manager, W. H. Cammeyer.

St. Louis.—G. W. Bradley, L. Pike, E. E. Cuthbert, J. V. Battin, R. J. Peake, J. W. Blong, D. McGee (Mack). Thos. P. Miller, *H. T. Dehlman*, M. H. McLeary and John E. Clapp. Manager, S. M. Graffen.

The names in italics are those of players since dead.

The officers of the above clubs were as follows:

Athletic.—Th s. J. Smith, President; A. H. Wright, Secretary.
Boston.—N. J. Apollonio, President; Harry Wright, Secretary.
Chicago.—W. A. Hulbert, President; A. G. Spalding, Secretary.
Cincinnati.—J. L. Keck, President; G. H. Van Vorhees, Secretary.
Hartford.—M. G. Bulkeley, President; W. F. Hilton, Secretary.
Louisville.—W. N. Haldeman, President; G. K. Speed, Secretary.
Mutual.—W. H. Cammeyer, President and Secretary.
St. Louis.—J. R. C. Lucas, President; Chas. A. Fowle, Secretary.

Of the above list of players, those in active service in the field ten years afterward, were: Knight, Force, Sutton, Eggler, O'Rourke, Manning, White, Anson, Hines, Jones, Burdock, York, Remsen, Harbidge, Snyder, Gerhardt, Matthews, Start and Battin.

Of the delegates who were present at the first meetings in Louisville and New York, only Harry Wright and A. G. Spalding are still identified with the game.

The championship of 1876 was won by the Chicago club, the Hartfords being second and the St. Louis club third. At the close of the season the Athletic and Mutual clubs were expelled for not fulfilling their engagements to other League clubs in playing return games. Each club was required to play ten games with every other League club. Barnes led the League average at the bat in 1876 with an average of per cent of base hits to times at the bat of .403, thirteen other players having an average of over .300—Anson's figures being .342; Clinton's, .338; Jas. White, .335; Hines, .330; and O'Rourke, .312. Fisler, of the Athletic club, led the first base men in the fielding averages with a percentage of .978; Gerhardt, of the Louisville club, leading the second base men with .950; Battin, of the St. Louis, the third base men with .867; Peters, of Chicago, the short-stops with .932; and Cassidy, Hines and Leonard, respectively of the Hartford, Chicago and Boston clubs, at right, center and left fields, with .998, .917 and .913. Allison led the catchers with an average of .844, and Bradley the pitchers with an average of runs earned off his pitching of but 1-12 to a game.

THE SEASON OF 1877.

The first annual convention of the League was held at the Kennard House, Cleveland, on Dec. 7, 1876. At this meeting seven of the eight clubs were represented by Messrs. Apollonio and H. Wright, of Boston; Chase and Johnstone, of Louisville; Hulbert, Spalding and Mills, of Chicago; R. Ferguson, of Hartford; Fowle, of St. Louis; Keck, of Cincinnati; and Thompson, of the Athletic. The most important business transacted was the adoption of the report of the Board of Directors by a unanimous vote, declaring that the Mutual and Athletic clubs had forfeited their membership and were thereby expelled. A resolution was adopted to the effect that after March 15, 1877, "No League club shall employ, or play in its nine, any player to whose services any other club of good standing, either in or out of the League, is entitled by legal contract." The election of officers resulted in the choice of W. A. Hulbert for President, N. E. Young as Secretary, and Messrs. Soden, Chase, Bulkeley, Hulbert and Fowle as the Board of Directors. Secretary Young's salary was increased to $500. The special rule for the clubs which governed the League in 1877 provided for the payment to the visiting club, out of the gate receipts at each championship match, of the sum of fifteen cents for each person admitted to the grounds. For the purpose of this special rule it was decided that the playing of one complete inning should constitute a game requiring a division of the gate receipts. The home club was required to pay the Umpire five dollars for his services in each match. Players were required to pay thirty dollars for their uniform and half a dollar each day for their board while on a club tour.

The change in the playing rules introduced in 1877 included the following amendments: No substitute could be introduced in a nine after the first innings had been ended. The exceptions to the previous definition of foul balls, which put a stop to fair foul hitting, went into force this year. A special code of scoring rules also went into effect for the first time in 1877.

The published official list of the club teams for 1877 included the following additional players to those of the list of 1876:

Boston.—J. Morrill, L. Brown, W. E. White, Jas. White, Thos. Bond and E. B. Sutton. The retiring players were Manning, Borden, McGinley, Beals, Parks and Frank Whitney.

Chicago.—C. C. Wait, G. W. Bradley and H. W. Smith. The retired players were White, Bielaski, Cone and Addy.

Cincinnati.—Hicks, Mathews, W. B. Foley, Hallinan and Pike. The retired players were Gould, Fields, Fisher, Sweasy, E. Snyder, Jones, Clark and Pierson.

Hartford.—Start, Holdsworth and Cassidy. The retired players were Cummings, Bond, E. Mills, Remsen and Higham.

St. Louis.—F. C. Nichols, pitcher; Force, M. C. Dorgan, Remsen and A. Croft. The retired players were Bradley, Pike, Miller, Pearce, McGee and Cuthbert.

Louisville.—Crowley, Hall, Schaffer, Craver and Latham. The retired players being Hastings, Bechtel, Fulmer, Carbine and Arthur Allison.

Nineteen professional clubs belonged to the League Alliance in 1877, the Red Caps, of St. Paul, winning the championship of that class over the Indianapolis, Minneapolis, Milwaukee, Janesville and Memphis clubs of the Western section, and Stars, of Syracuse, over the Crickets of Binghamton, Lowell and Fall River of the Eastern section.

Jas. White, of the Boston team, led the batting average of 1877 with a percentage of .385. In fielding, Croft, of St. Louis, led the first base men with a percentage of .965; Burdock, of the Hartfords, the second base men with .905; McGeary, of the St. Louis, the third base men with .907; Force, of the St. Louis, the short-stops with .903; Glenn, of the Chicago, the left fielders with .941; Remsen, of the St. Louis, the center fielders with .902, and White, of the Boston, the right fielders with .954; Snyder of the Louisvilles, led the catchers with a percentage of .913; and Larkin, of the Hartfords, had the best average of base hits against his pitching, the earned runs figures not being counted this year.

THE SEASON OF 1878.

The second annual convention of the National League was held at the Kennard House, Cleveland, on Dec. 5, 1877, when the business appertaining to the ensuing season of 1878 was transacted. At this meeting the report of the Board of Directors stated that the Cincinnati club, having failed to pay its annual dues, and thereby forfeited its membership, was not entitled to have its games counted, and consequently their games were thrown out. The convention declared that the Boston club had won the championship, Louisville being second, Hartford third, St. Louis fourth, and Chicago fifth and last. The board also approved of the action of the Louisville club in expelling Jas. A. Devlin, W. H. Craver, A. H. "Nichols" and G. W. Hall "for conduct in contravention of the objects of the League," as set forth in Article 2 of its constitution. Also that of the Red Cap club, of St. Paul, in expelling Oscar Walker for breach of contract.

The convention readmitted the Cincinnati club as a member of the League for 1878, as also the Indianapolis, Milwaukee and Providence clubs, and accepted the resignation of the St. Louis club; they also indorsed the action of the Board of Directors in regard to the vacation of membership of Hartford club. The delegates who took part in the proceedings were as follows: Messrs. Hulbert, Mills and Spalding, of the Chicago; Soden and Harry Wright, of the Boston; C. E. Chase and C. W. Johnstone, of the Louisville; J. M. W. Neff, of the Cincinnati; W. P. Rogers, of the Milwaukee; W. B. Pettit, of the Indianapolis; and H. B. Winship, of the Providence. The turnstile counting machines were first introduced by the League in 1878.

President Hulbert and Secretary Young were both re-elected, and the following Board of Directors was chosen, viz.: Messrs. Soden, Neff, Pettit and Rogers. E. Nolan was expelled from the Indianapolis club in 1878 for breach of club rules.

The official list of players for 1878 recorded in the Guide of that year, was as follows:—

Boston.—Geo. Wright, O'Rourke, Morrill, Manning, Burdock, Leonard, Harry Schafer, Sutton, Bond, and Snyder. Manager, Harry Wright.

Chicago.—Ferguson, Frank Larkin, Harbidge, Hallinan, Remsen, Hankinson, Cassidy, Start, Anson, McClellan, and I. P. Ries. Captain of team, Ferguson.

Cincinnati.—McVey, Gerhardt, Jones, Will White, Mitchell, J. F. Sullivan, Geer, Pike, M. J. Kelly, and James White.

Providence.—D. Allison, Fred Nichols, L. Brown, Sweasy, Hague, York, Hines, Murnan, Higham, and Fred Corey.

Indianapolis.—E. S. Nolan, Jos. L. Quest, F. J. Warner, E. N. Williamson, Geo. Schafer, F. S. Flint, R. E. McKelvey, Jas. McCormick, John Nelson, Clapp, and Croft.

Milwaukee.—S. H. Weaver, J. Goodman, W. B. Foley, W. Holbert, W. T. Redmond, G. Creamer, A. Dalrymple, J. J. Ellick, C. W. Bennett, Peters, and Andrus.

No players were entered from the Louisville club, that club disbanding at the close of the year.

The League averages of 1878 placed Dalrymple, of the Milwaukee club, at the head of the list with a percentage at the bat of .356. Sullivan, of the Cincinnati club, led the first base man with a percentage of .974. Burdock, of the Boston, was second base man with .917. Hague, of the Providence, the third base man with .918. George Wright, of the Boston, the short stops with .947. Jones, of the Cincinnati, the left fielders with .893. Remsen, of the Chicago, the center fielders with .934. Geo. Schafer, of the Indianapolis, the right fielders with .844. Snyder, of the Boston, leading the catchers with .841; Ward, of the Providence club, led the pitchers in best average of base hits off his pitching, his percentage being .233. No special changes of importance were made in the rules for 1878. The rule adopted to govern the numbers of championship games to be played each season was to the following effect:—

If six or seven clubs enter the list twelve games each; if eight or nine, ten games; if ten clubs, eight games. The League clubs were prohibited from playing with non-League clubs before the championship season, except with their own local clubs; and from playing non-League clubs on League grounds during the championship season.

THE SEASON OF 1879.

The third annual meeting of the National League was held at the Kennard House, Cleveland, on Dec. 4, 1878, when the preliminary business for 1879 was transacted. The delegates at the Convention were as follows: Messrs. Hulbert and Spalding of Chicago; Soden and H. Wright of Boston; Neff and E. M. Johnson of Cincinnati; H. T. Root and Geo. Wright of Providence; W. B. Pettit of Indianapolis; E. B. Smith and John B. Sage of Buffalo; R. Townsend and H. G. White of Syracuse; and J. F. Evans and Chas. T. Wesley of Cleveland. The three latter clubs were admitted to membership at the convention, the Indianapolis club resigning. The Troy club also entered the League this year, Gardner Earl being their President and delegate. A special staff of umpires were chosen at this convention, from whom clubs were to take the umpire for each match. The staff in 1879 included C. Daniels, W. McLean, M. Walsh, Jas. Sumner, W. E. Furlong, C. E. Wilbur, A. D. Hodges, Geo. Seward, J. A. Williams, W. H. Geer, J. Dunn, J. A. Cross, R. Wheeler, G. W. Bredburg, C. G. Stamburgh, T. H. Brunton, T. Gilliam, F. W. Faber, J. Young, and E. G. Fountain. Messrs. Hulbert and N. E. Young were again re-elected, and the Board of Directors chosen were Messrs. Neff, Evans, Root, and White. The changes in the playing rules were as follows: The pitcher was required to face the batsman when in the act of delivering the ball to the bat, and nine called balls were introduced instead of the calling of every third unfair ball as "one ball."

In the batting averages of 1879 Anson, of the Chicago, headed the list with a percentage of .407, thereby leading Barnes' previously unequaled record of 1876 of .403. Anson also led the first baseman in the fielding averages, his percentage of chances accepted being .974; Quest of the Chicago, led the second baseman with .926; McLeary, of Providence, the third baseman with .916; George Wright of the same club the short stops with .926; Jones, of the Boston, the left fielders with .933; Eggler, of the Buffalo, the center fielders with .918; and Evans, of the Troy, the right fielders with .885; Flint, of the Chicago, led the catchers with .830; Ward of Providence, leading the pitchers with a percentage of base hits off his pitching of .241.

The official list of players published in the Guide of 1879 included the following:

Boston.—Snyder, Bond, Morrill, Burdock, Sutton, Houck, Jones, John O'Rourke, Haines, and Foley, with Harry Wright as manager.

Chicago.—Flint, Larkin, Anson, Quest, Hankinson, Peters, Dalrymple, Geo. F. Gore, Geo. Schaffer, and E. N. Williamson.
Cincinnati.—W. H. White, McVey, Jas. White, Barnes, Gerhardt, M. J. Kelly, P. J. Hotaling, L. C. Dickinson, M. E. Burke, and W. B. Foley.
Providence—J. M. Ward, Robt. Mathews, I. J. Brown, F. Start, M. H. McGeary, W. L. Hague, Geo. Wright, James O'Rourke, P. A. Hines, Thos. York. Manager, George Wright.
Buffalo.—Jas. F. Galvin, Wm. McGunnigle, Clapp, S. Libby, H. Richardson, C. Fulmer, D. W. Force, J. Hornung, D. Eggler, and W. Crowley.
Cleveland.—Jas. McCormick, R. M. Mitchell, M. J. Kennedy, W. B. Phillip, G. A. Strief, F. J. Warner, J. W. Glasscock, W. C. Riley, Thos. J. Carey, and C. M. Eden.
Syracuse.—H. McCormick, M. Dorgan, W. W. Carpenter, J. Farrell, C. A. Allen, J. Richmond, M. R. Mansell, W. Purcell, and J. Macullar.
Troy.—G. W. Bradley, C. Riley, H. Clapp, T. P. Howkes, H. Doesher, E. Caskins, Thos. Mansell, A. Hall, J. Evans, P. McManus, and J. Shupe.

McKinnon was expelled in 1879 for alleged breach of contract. The championship was awarded to the Providence club this year.

THE SEASON OF 1880.

The fourth annual convention of the National League was held at Pierce's Hotel, Buffalo, on Dec. 3, 1879, on which occasion the following club delegates were present: Chicago, Messrs. Hulbert and Spalding; Boston, Soden and H. Wright; Buffalo, Smith and Sage; Cleveland, Evans; Providence, Root; Cincinnati, Justus Thorner and O. P. Caylor; Troy, Earl and C. R. De Freest. The report of the Board of Directors declared that the Star Club of Syracuse had forfeited its membership. Messrs. Hulbert and Young were again elected President and Secretary of the League, and the Board of Directors elected were Messrs. Soden, Sage, Evans, and Thorner.

On Feb. 26, 1880, a special meeting of the League was held at the Osborne House, Rochester, N. Y., the most important item of the business transacted being the issuing of the appended address to players by President Hulbert.

Address to the Players of League Clubs, drafted and formally adopted by the League, at a special meeting held in the city of Rochester, N. Y., on the 26th day of February, 1880:

DISCIPLINE AND PENALTIES.

In view of the various new and important features introduced into League legislation, touching the relation of players to their clubs, it seems eminently wise and proper that a statement be made concerning the intention and effect of the alterations and amendments in question, in order that there shall be a distinct understanding as to the rights, responsibilties and duties of both players and clubs. The purpose actuating the members of the League in thus drawing more tightly the reins of discipline has been simply and solely the carrying out, in letter and spirit, of that clause in the League Constitution wherein it is declared that the objects of the League are, among other things, "to protect and promote the mutual interests of professional base-ball clubs and professional base-ball players." That the amended code of the League for 1880 is directly in the line of this object, will indisputably appear after a careful survey of the situation in its altered aspects. The effect of the new penalties and system of discipline, prescribed by the League, will be, primarily, to hold to a stricter accountability than heretofore that class of players who are in need of some powerful restraining influence to help them guard against a tendency toward intemperance and excess. It is best to be plain and unequivocal in this matter, and to waste no words in coming to the point—which is, that **hereafter** it is not proposed to permit or tolerate drunkenness or bummerism in the playing members of League Clubs. It is not designed to interfere with the personal liberty of any player, by the imposition of foolish and impracticable restrictions upon his conduct while off the ball field, further than to require that he shall not disgrace his club and his avocation by scandalous and disreputable practices. A player's habits amd deportment when not before the public in his professional capacity are matters which himself alone can regulate by the light of his interests and his conscience. Every ball player is competent to see for himself that intemperance is a two-edged sword in the hands of an adversary—cutting one way in the loss of the money he spends in the gratification of his appetite for liquor; cutting the other way in the loss of standing in his profession. Who does not know that the ball players in America receiving the highest compensation for their services are they who are scrupulously temperate and well-governed in their habits? There are players of the other class of a higher degree of skill, but who are handicapped in the matter of compensation and standing by s reputation for objectionable habits. The players receiving the highest salaries, by reason of their exemplary habits and consequent greater uniformity of skill and efficiency on the ball field, gain another advantage, the great value of which it is not easy to estimate. This is in respect to their reputation and standing before the whole world of base-ball patrons. A player's reputation is not confined to any one city; it is well known and correctly gauged all over the country, and sobriety and gentlemanly conduct make firm friends who will, some day, be of value and benefit to a player after he has, voluntarily, or by reason of some disabling injury, retired permanently from base ball. Instances of the value and advantage to a player of friendship and good will thus acquired could be multiplied indefinitely. There can be no two opinions on the subject of the importance to players of gaining for themselves such a reputation as will not only yield them present profit, but will insure them the respect and good will of the great public by which the game of base ball is supported, and thus put them in the way of future benefits and advantages, which the brilliant but unreliable player can never hope to realize.

As before stated, the direction of the latest League legislation is toward stricter discipline and more effectual pains and penalties for misconduct. Beginning with Section 1 of Article V of the League Constitution, the power to *suspend* is additionally conferred upon each club for any act or deed of omission or commission by which a player's services to his club are impaired in their efficiency and value. The player *must render a full equivalent for his salary ;* he *must* live up to his contract, or suffer the consequences of an infraction of such contract. Each player should not fail to read carefully, again and again, the language of his contract, which has been devised by the League to meet every known or imaginable exigency in the case, and the use of which contract is, by League law, made compulsory upon every club in the engagement of every player. The contract is printed in clear type, so that every player may read for himself, and understand fully, the obligation he is taking upon himself. The contract speaks for itself; its provisions are known to every player now under engagement in the clubs belonging to the League. It is with the new powers created for the enforcement of the contract that we now have to deal, and which we desire to bring to the notice of the players of the League, hoping thereby to bring about a fair understanding as to their rights and duties, and to secure their co-operation in the measures devised for the benefit alike of the honorable player, the honorable club management, and the honorable game of base ball.

In Section 5, Article V, the words "or of any dishonorable or disreputable conduct" no longer appear; this cause is no longer sufficient to warrant expulsion, but is provided for an entirely new section (Sec. 6), by which a club is not only empowered to punish or discipline a player for so much as remains of the season during which the offense was committed, but can go beyond that, beyond the life of its contract with that player, and suspend or disqualify him for *the whole of the ensuing season*, during which he is as absolutely shelved, disabled, annihilated, so far as playing in or against any League club is concerned, as though he had lost an arm or a leg. All this time he is not under salary, and is practically debarred from earning a living at base ball. The causes for which this penalty of suspension may be imposed are, "*drunkenness, insubordination, or any dishonorable or disreputable conduct;*" and while the punishment may at first seem excessive, it will be recognized as a wholesome and reasonable restraint when its purpose and application are considered. Section 6 is designed to prevent that condition of demoralization into which players of the intemperate or insubordinate class relapse toward the close of the playing season, when their club has no longer any prospect of winning the championship, when their own bad conduct and bad play have rendered it certain that they will not be re-engaged in that club for the next year, and they have accordingly become reckless, defiant, and altogether unendurable to the club management. Very likely the player in question has overdrawn his salary, and for that reason is indifferent to the threat of suspension for the rest of the season, for he has drawn nearly all the money coming to him anyhow, and suspension has no terrors. But the extension of the penalty over into the next following playing season puts a different phase upon the case. He *must* render satisfactory service to his club during the whole time he is under contract, or, failing therein, he may be disqualified from play for the entire season succeeding. There need be no fear that a penalty so severe will be inflicted without just and ample cause. It is earnestly to be hoped it may never be inflicted, but its presence among the penalties authorized by the League Constitution cannot fail to prove a wholesome and beneficial restraint upon that class of ball players to meet whose case the law was devised.

Suitable provision has been made for the enforcement of all disciplinary or restrictive legislation, whether relating to clubs or players. Section 7, Article V of the Constitution imposes the penalty of forfeiture of membership in the League upon any club taking part in any game of ball on Sunday, or which shall fail to immediately expel any man under contract with it, who shall take part in any such game, either as player, umpire, or scorer; while in Section 10, Article V, every League club is prohibited from playing in its nine a player who has been expelled or suspended from the League, and the League clubs are moreover forbidden to play any club employing or presenting in its nine a player under the ban of expulsion or suspension. And it is important to notice that the disciplining of a player for misconduct rests not alone with the club by which he is employed; on the contrary, such player may be expelled by the board of directors of the League, upon the complaint of another club (Sec. 1, Art. VII), for a repetition of misconduct, even though his own club should decline to prosecute and impose the penalty. Further than this, the terms of the League contract constitute in themselves a direct and effectual means of holding the player to the same degree of accountability for the satisfactory character of the service rendered that is exacted by every business man at the hands of the person in his employ. To this end, it is expressly stipulated in the League contract that the player may be suspended from play, *and from pay*, at any time when he shall be deemed by the club management to be disqualified from playing with the requisite skill, by reason of illness, injury, insubordination, or misconduct of any kind; or, whenever he shall, by the captain or manager of the nine, be considered as lacking in the zeal, willingness, or physical condition necessary to the rendering of satisfactory service as a ball player. As an inducement to every player to so regulate his habits and actions as to keep at all times in a sound and healthy condition, the League contract provides that there shall be no wages paid where no services are rendered; that for the period during which a player is suspended or excused from play, for any of the above mentioned reasons, he shall forfeit such a ratable proportion of his wages, for the season, as the number of games not played in by him bears to the total number of games scheduled for the season. It cannot be denied that the placing of this power in the hands of club managers is a measure of necessary protection against habits of intemperance and their attendant evils of unsound physical condition, moral recklessness, loose play, and general demoralization. Experience has amply demonstrated the necessity for some plan of discipline that will reach the pocket as well as the pride of a player who deliberately and systematically falls short of the honorable discharge of his obligations toward the club and the patrons of base ball. The compensation paid to players in League clubs is so liberal as to entitle the clubs to the highest degree of skill and the best service a player can render, and it is the intention of the League to exact precisely this, and nothing less. There is not a condition or penalty prescribed in the League contract, constitution, or playing rules, that will work a hardship to any conscientious, earnest, deserving player. It is only players of the opposite character who will suffer, and it is their turn to suffer. The clubs have had more than their share of the pecuniary loss, the aggravation, annoyance and mortification caused by the state of affairs which these conditions and penalties have been devised to correct. Justice to the players is a demand and obligation at all times recognized; justice to the club managers and stockholders, who have made good the deficiencies in the club treasuries, season after season; justice to the public, upon whose respect and patronage the clubs must depend for an existence; justice to the noble game of base ball, which it has been the constant aim of the League to elevate, perfect and popularize—these, and these alone, are the considerations which have influenced end brought about the League's latest legislation on the subject of discipline and penalties.

At this special meeting an agreement was entered into by the eight clubs of the League (the Worcester club having been admitted since the annual meeting in 1879), as follows:

The undersigned Associations, members of the National League of Professional B. B. Clubs, do hereby agree each with the others, that neither they nor any officer, member or agent of their respective organizations shall contract with, employ, engage, or negotiate with any player for services during the season of 1881, or subsequent seasons, prior to Oct. 23, 1880.

In testimony whereof the parties hereto have hereunto set their names in the city of Rochester, this 26th day of February, 1880.

  THE BOSTON B. B. ASSOCIATION,
    By A. H. Soden, President.
  THE PROVIDENCE B. B. ASSOCIATION,
    By Henry T. Root, President.
  THE BUFFALO B. B. CLUB,
    By Jno. B. Sage, President.
  THE WORCESTER B. B. CLUB,
    By Freeman Brown, Delegate.
  THE CINCINNATI B. B. CLUB,
    By Justus Thorner, President.
  THE CLEVELAND B. B. ASSOCIATION,
    By J. F. Evans, President.
  THE CHICAGO BALL CLUB,
    By W. A. Hulbert, President.
  THE TROY CITY B. B. ASSOCIATION,
    By Gardner Earle, President,
    Per Robt. Ferguson.

This put a stop to the demoralizing effect of the negotiating for players before the regular close of each season.

The players engaged for 1880, as published in the League Guide for that year, were as follows:

Boston.—Brown, Bond, Morrill, Burdock, Sutton, Houck, Jones, Jno. O'Rourke, Jas. O'Rourke, Foley and Powers.

Buffalo.—J. C. Rowe, Thos. Poorman, McGunnigle, Walker, S. N. Crane, H. Richardson, Force, Hornung, Crowley and C. Radbourn.

Chicago.—Flint, Corcoran, Anson, Quest, Williamson, Burns, Dalrymple, Gore, Kelly, E. E. Goldsmith and Thos. L. Beal.

Cincinnati.—W. H. White, Clapp, Manning, C. M. Smith, Carpenter, Sam Wright, Leonard, Purcell and M. Mansell.

Cleveland.—McCormick, Kennedy, Phillips, F. Dunlap, Hankinson, Glasscock, E. Hanlon, Hotaling, Schaffer, A. Hall and Gilligan.

Providence.—Bradley, Ward, E. M. Gross, Start, Farrell, McGeary, York, Hines and Dorgan.

Troy.—Holbert, Welch, Larkin, Coggswell, Ferguson, Dickinson, Caskins, Gillespie, Conner, Cassidy, Evans and Harbidge.

Worcester.—J. L. Richmond, A. J. Bushong, J. F. Sullivan, G. Creamer, A. W. Whitney, A. A. Irwin, G. A. Wood, A. Knight, H. D. Stovey, F. C. Nichols and Chas. W. Bennett.

Gore, of Chicago, led the batting averages of the League in 1880, with a percentage of base hits of .365. In the fielding averages, Sullivan, of Worcester, led the first base men with a percentage of chances accepted of .982; Burdock, of Boston, the second base men with .922; Williamson, of Chicago, the third base men with .893; Force, of Buffalo, the short stops with .924; York, of Providence, the left fielders with .932; Hines, of the same club, the center fielders with .925; Evans, of Troy, the right fielders with .906; and Bushong, of Worcester, the catchers with .845. In pitching, Corcoran, of the Chicago team, had the best average in percentage of base hits off his pitching.

A special meeting of the League was held at the Cataract House, Niagara Falls, N. Y., on May 25, 1880, at which a complaint made by the Providence Club against the Troy Club was acted upon, and a pledge was made to add a forfeiture of membership for selling malt or spirituous liquors on League grounds, or in any building owned or occupied by a League club. This was aimed at the Cincinnati club, and it led to that club's vacating its membership in the League at the close of the season of 1880.

The only important changes made in the rules were those changing the number of called balls from nine to eight, and the making it necessary for the ball to be caught on the fly by the catcher to put the batsman out on strikes. The base runners were also to be declared out whenever they allowed a batted ball to strike them.

THE SEASON OF 1881.

The fifth annual convention of the League was held on Dec. 8, 1880, at the St. James hotel, New York, where the preliminary business of the ensuing season was duly transacted. The delegates present included— Messrs. Hulbert, Spalding and Mills, of Chicago; Jas. Moffatt and Truth, of Buffalo; F. Brown, of Worcester; Soden and H. Wright, of Boston; and Root, of Providence. Afterward the Detroit club was admitted to membership, and W. G. Thompson acted as its delegate. The report of the Board of Directors declared the Cincinnati club had vacated its membership, having failed to comply with the constitutional rules as regards the sale of liquors on its grounds. The Chicago club was declared the champion club for the season of 1880. The convention adopted the following resolution:

WHEREAS, Repeated applications have been made by or on behalf of James A. Devlin, Geo. Hall, W. H. Craver, and A. H. "Nichols," to this Board, or members thereof, for the removal of their disabilities resulting from their expulsion from the League, for dishonest ball playing,

Resolved, That notice is hereby served on the persons named, and on

their friends, defenders and apologists, that the Board of Directors of this League will never remit the penalties inflicted on such persons, nor will they hereafter entertain any appeal from them or in their behalf.
    (Signed)   W. A. HULBERT, Chairman.
                             J. F. EVANS,
                             A. H. SODEN,   } Directors.
                             JNO. B. SAGE,

    Messrs. Hulbert and Young were again elected President and Secretary of the League for 1881. The Board of Directors chosen were Messrs. J. Jewett, F. Brown, W. G. Thompson and A. L. Hotchkiss.

    The official list of players in the Guide for 1881 was as follows:

    Boston.—Jas. E. Whitney, C. N. Snyder, Morrill, Burdock, Sutton, Geo. Wright, Hornung, Richmond, Crawley, Thos. Deasley and Bond.

    Buffalo.—Galvin, Lynch, T. J. Sullivan, Rowe, Jas. White, H. Richardson, J. H. Morrissey, Force, Jas. O'Rourke, Foley and Peters. Manager, Jas. O. Rourke.

    Chicago.—Corcoran, Goldsmith, Flint, Anson, Quest, Williamson, Burns, Dalrymple, Gore, Kelley and Piercy. Manager, Adrian C. Anson.

    Cleveland.—McCormick, Kennedy, Phillips, Dunlap, McGeary, Glasscock, Purcell, J. J. Smith, Schaffer and John Clapp.

    Detroit.—G. H. Denby, Bennett, W. G. Sweeny, J. J. Gerhardt, C. Reilley, Bradley, Wood, Hanlon, Knight and L. J. Brown. Manager, Frank Bancroft.

    Troy.—Wm. Ewing, M. Welch, R. Connor, Ferguson, Hankinson, Caskins, Gillespie, Cassidy, Evans and Holbert.

    Providence.—Ward, Gross, Radbourn, Gilligan, Start, Farrell, J. Denny, Hauck, W. H. McClellan, Hines and Matthews.

    Worcester.—Richmond, Bushong, Sullivan, Creamer, Carpenter, Irwin, Stovey, Hotaling, Corey.

    Anson, of the Chicago club, led the batting average of 1881 with a percentage of base hits of .399. In the following averages Anson led the first base men with a percentage of chances accepted of .975; Quest, of Chicago, the second base men with .929; Williamson, of Chicago, the third base men with .909; Force, of Buffalo, the short-stops with .945; Hornung, of Boston, the left fielders with .947; Hanlon, of Detroit, the center fielders with .896; and Dorgan, of the Worcester, the right fielders with .907. Bennett, of the Detroit, led the catchers with .896; Radbourn, of the Providence, led the pitchers with a percentage of base hits off his pitching of .227.

    The changes in the rules involved the placing of the pitcher's position distant fifty feet from the home base instead of forty-five feet, as before, and the narrowing the pitcher's lines from six feet square to six feet by four. Club managers, too, were prohibited from going on the field during a match game. This was directed against Harry Wright. The number of players constituting a side in a match were also designated in the rules for the first time this year. Substitutes were also prohibited from taking a place in a nine unless to replace an injured player. The number of unfair balls allowed to be pitched were reduced from eight to seven. The base runner was to be declared out if after three strikes he failed to run to the base. This rule put a stop to the chance to make a double or triple play from the catcher's failure to take the ball on the fly after three strikes had been called, for the purpose of forcing runners off when all the bases were occupied when the third strike was called. The pitcher, too, was amenable to a fine for intentionally hitting the bat man with a pitched ball.

THE SEASON OF 1882.

    The sixth annual meeting of the National League was held on Dec. 7, 1881, at the Tremont House, Chicago, on which occasion the following delegates were present: Messrs. Hulbert, Mills and Spalding, of Chicago;

Soden and H. Wright, of Boston; Evans, of Cleveland; Winship, of Providence; Hotchkiss, of Troy; Smith, of Buffalo; and Brown, of Worcester. Messrs. Hulbert and Young were again elected President and Secretary of the League for 1882, and the following Board of Directors were chosen, viz.: Messrs. Jewett, Thompson, Brown and Hotchkiss. The Chicago club was awarded the championship for 1881. The convention decided to have special uniforms for League nines, the colors for the clubs being as follows: Chicago, white; Boston, red; Providence, light blue; Cleveland, navy blue; Troy, green; Buffalo, grey; Worcester, brown; and Detroit, old gold.

The official list of club players in the League Guide for 1882 was as follows:

Boston.—Whitney, Deasley, Matthews, Remsen, Morrill, Burdock, Sutton, S. W. Wise, Hornung, Hotaling and H. M. McClure.

Buffalo.—Galvin, Rowe, D. Brouthers, H. Richardson, Morrissey, Force, Purcell, J. O'Rourke, Foley and Hugh Daily.

Chicago.—Corcoran, Flint, Anson, Quest, Williamson, Dalrymple, Gore, Kelley, Goldsmith and Hugh Nicol.

Cleveland.—McCormick, Kennedy, Phillips, Dunlap, M. Muldoon, Glasscock, T. J. Esterbrook, Richmond, Schaffer, J. Kelly and Bradley.

Detroit.—Geo. E. Weidman, S. W. Tratt, M. J. Powell, J. Troy, Jos. F. Farrell, Gerhardt, Wood, Hanlon, Knight, Darby and Bennett.

Providence.—Radbourn, Gilligan, Start, Farrell, Denny, Ward, York, Hines, Tim Manning and Jos. Start.

Worcester.—Richmond, Bushong, Coggswell, Creamer, F. I. Mann, Irwin, Stovey, L. J. McP. Rundlett, Evans, Bond and John J. Hayes.

Troy.—Welch, Ewing, Connor, Ferguson, J. J. Smith, F. Pfeffer, Gillespie, Jas. Raseman, Cassidy, T. J. Keefe and Holbert.

Brouthers, of the Buffalo club, led the batting averages for 1882 with a percentage of base hits of .367. In the fielding averages Brouthers also led the first base men with a percentage of chances accepted of .974; Burdock, of Boston, leading the second base men with .929; Ewing, of Troy, the third base men with .889; McGeary, of Detroit, the short-stops with .935; Hornung, of Boston, the left fielders with .930; Esterbrook, of Cleveland, the center fielders with .893; and Evans, of Worcester, the right fielders with .910; Bennett, of Detroit, led the catchers with a percentage of .874; while Corcoran, of Chicago, led the pitchers with a percentage of base hits off his pitching of .208.

The changes in the rules did not include any radical amendments this year.

At a special meeting of the League held at the Russell House, Detroit, on June 24, 1882, at which Jas. A. Mugridge acted as chairman and F. Brown as secretary, charges were preferred against Richard Higham by the Detroit club for "crooked" work as umpire in collusion with certain pool gamblers, and he was expelled from the League.

It was during this year that the League suffered its greatest loss in the death of its president and founder, Mr. W. A. Hulbert, who died in April, at his residence in Chicago.

THE SEASON OF 1883.

The seventh annual convention of the National League was held at the Hotel Dorrance, Providence, on Dec. 6, 1882, on which occasion the following club delegates were present: Soden and A. S. Chase, of Boston; Geo. H. Hughson, of Buffalo; Mills and Spalding, of Chicago; C. H. Bulkeley and G. W. Howe, of Cleveland; Thompson, of Detroit; Winship and H. Wright, of Providence; Hotchkiss, of Troy, and Brown, of Worcester. A resolution in reference to the death of President Hulbert was the first thing attended to at this convention. The Troy and Worcester clubs then resigned their membership, and they were both elected honorary members of the League. The New York and Philadelphia clubs were then elected members of the League in place of the clubs which had resigned, and John B. Day and C. T. Dillingham were admitted as the New York club delegates, and A. J. Reach as that of Philadelphia. The following list of players who had been disqualified for various reasons, not involving "crooked" play, however, were reinstated, viz: S. P. Houck, L. Pike, L. P. Dickerson, M. J. Dorgan, J. J. Fox, E. Nolan, W. Crowley, E. M. Gross, L. J. Brown, E. J. Caskins and John E. Clapp. The election for President for 1883 resulted in the choice of A. G. Mills, of the Chicago club, N. E. Young being again elected Secretary. A. H. Soden acted as President from the time of the death of President Hulbert up to the date of the convention of 1882. Messrs. Soden, Reach, Spalding and Thompson were chosen as the Board of Directors for 1883.

The Chicago club was awarded the championship for 1882, having won it for three consecutive seasons. The League had an appropriate memorial stone placed on the grave of their late President. The report of the Board of Directors contained the expulsion of Herman Doescher for dishonest conduct and a provision for the playing of an extra number of schedule games in the case of there being a tie in the championship record at the close of the season. At a special meeting of the League—it being, in fact, a continuation of the adjourned annual meeting of December, 1882,—the Conference Committee, comprising Messrs. Mills, Day and Soden, made their report, which embodied the recognition of the contracts made by clubs of the American Association and Northwestern League. An arbitration committee was also appointed to take cognizance of matters of importance occurring during the period between the annual meetings of the League, the committee comprising Messrs. Mills, Soden and Day. At this meeting the disabilties affecting the status of the following players of the League clubs were removed, viz: Alex. McKinnon, Philip Baker, C. W. Jones and J. J. Gerhardt, their offences having been of a rather trivial nature. A regular staff of umpires for 1883, having regular salaries and positions, independent of club influences, were appointed at this meeting, the staff in question including S. M. Decker, of Bradford, Pa.; Frank Law, of Norwalk, O.; W. E. Furlong, of Kansas City, Mo., and A. F. Odlin, of Lancaster, N. H.

The official list of players contained in the League Guide of 1883 were as follows:

Boston.—Whitney, Deasley, Buffinton, M. M. Hackett, M. Hines, Morrill, Burdock, Sutton, Wise, Hornung, Dickerson and P. R. Radford.

Buffalo.—Galvin, Kennedy, Brouthers, Richardson, Derby, Rowe, Foley, Jas. O'Rourke and Schaffer. Manager, Jas. O'Rourke.

Chicago.—Corcoran, Flint, Anson, Pfeffer, Williamson, Burns Dalrymple, Gore, Kelly, Goldsmith and L. C. Stockwell. Manager, Adrian C. Anson.

Cleveland.—McCormick, Chas. Briody, Phillips, Dunlap, Muldoon, Glasscock, York, Hotaling, Evans, Daily, Bushong, Bradley and C. C. Broughton, with Bancroft as manager.

Detroit.—Weidman, Bennett, Powell, Quest, Farrell, Hauck, Wood, Hanlon, T. Mansell, R. S. Burns, Trett, with Chapman as manager.

Providence.—Radbourn, Gilligan, Start, Farrell, Denny, Irwin, Cliff, Carroll, Hines and Nava, with Harry Wright as manager.

New York.—Welch, Clapp, Ward, Ewing, John G. Reilly, Troy, Hankinson, Caskins, Gillespie, Connor, Dorgan and Jas. E. O'Neill.

Philadelphia.—John F. Coleman, F. C. Ringo, John Manning, C. T. Roberts, Chas. W. Gaunt, W. H. McClellan, Purcell, John Neagle, E. M. Gross, H. Henderson and F. Lewis. Robt. Ferguson, manager.

In 1883 Brouthers, of the Buffalo club, again led the batting averages, his percentage of base hits being .371. In the fielding averages Morrill, of the Boston club, led the first basemen with a percentage of chances accepted of .974; Farrell, of Providence, leading the second basemen with .925; Denny, of Providence, the third basemen with .875; Glasscock, of

Cleveland, the short stops with .918; Hornung, of Boston, the left fielders with .936; Hines, of Providence, the center fielders with .913; Evans, of Cleveland, the right fielders with .902; Bennett, of Detroit, the catchers with .859, and McCormick, of Cleveland, the pitchers with an average of earned runs off his pitching of 1-35 to a game, this criterion of pitching being first introduced in the League records this year. He also led in having the smallest per cent. of base hits off his pitching, viz: .209.

The changes in the rules for 1883 involved the legal introduction of the throwing of the ball to the bat provided the arm was not raised above the shoulder. The foul bound catch was also abolished.

A noteworthy feature of the legislation of 1883 was the organization of a Board of Arbitration.

Previous to 1883 there had existed among clubs and associations a regular system of "piracy"—a sort of selfish ruinous policy which actuated every club manager to make inroads upon and injure other clubs whenever he could. This evil existed especially in the coaxing away of favorite players from one club by the manager of another club with the temptation of excessive salaries, all of which had a depressing effect upon the patronage of the base-ball public. There was a recognized need of some central power in base ball to govern all associations by an equitable code of general laws to put the game on a prosperous and lasting basis. It was such a recognized need which led to the formation of the celebrated Arbitration Committee which met at the Fifth Avenue Hotel, New York City, Feb. 17, 1883. It consisted of A. G. Mills, A. S. Soden and John B. Day, of the National League; Lewis Simmons, William Barnie and O. P. Caylor, of the American Association, and Elias Matter, of the Northwestern League. The committee organized with the election of A. G. Mills, Chairman; O. P. Caylor, Secretary and Custodian, and Elias Matter, Treasurer. They then drew up the famous Triparte Agreement, which was the supreme central law of the three above named professional associations in 1883.

So great was the success of the Triparte Agreement that when the committee met for the second time in New York, in October, 1883, they changed the name of the instrument to the NATIONAL AGREEMENT, so as to open it to all other associations who were willing to subscribe to and live up to its requirements. The result was the immediate addition of a fourth member—the Eastern League of eight clubs, and the qualified admission of half a dozen State and minor associations.

THE SEASON OF 1884.

The eighth annual meeting of the National League was held at the Riggs House, Washington, D. C., on Nov. 21, 1883, on which occasion the following club delegates were present: Messrs. Soden and Chase, of Boston; Jewett and Hughson, of Buffalo; Spalding and John A. Brown, of Chicago; Bulkeley and Howe, of Cleveland; Thompson, of Detroit; Day and Dillingham, of New York; Reach and John T. Rogers, of Philadelphia, and J. E. Allen and H. T. Root, of Providence. The report of the Board of Directors awarded the championship of 1883 to the Boston club. Messrs. Mills and Young were re-elected President and Secretary of the League, and Messrs. Spalding, Thompson, Reach and Allen as the Board of Directors. The system of reserving twelve players of a club team was introduced at this convention.

On March 4, 1884, a special meeting of the League was held at the Genessee House, Buffalo, at which action was taken completing the compact with the American Association known as the "National Agreement," which did more to harmonize the two associations than anything previously done in the legislation of the two organizations.

The official list of players contained in the League Guide for 1884 were as follows:

Boston.—Whitney, Buffinton, Hackett, Hines, Gunning, Morrill, Burdock, Sutton, Wise, Hornung. Jas. H. Manning, Crowley, E. Moriarty, M. Barrett and W. P. Annis.

Buffalo.—Galvin, W. T. Serad, Rowe, Brouthers, Richardson, Jas. White, G. D. Myers, Force, Chas. Collins, Jas. O'Rourke and Eggler. Manager, Jas. O'Rourke.

Chicago.—Corcoran, Goldsmith, Flint, Anson, Pfeffer, Williamson, Burns, Dalrymple, Gore, Kelly, Wm. Sunday, M. Deponghter, H. W. Graham, Thos. F. Lee, G. W. Crosby, G. Whiteley and W. H. Kinzie.

Cleveland.—McCormick, Briody, Phillips, Muldoon, Glasscock, Hotaling, Evans, J. J. Haskins, Jas. McGuire, L. R. Moffitt, J. R. Hoyle, H. W. Smith, L. D. Drake, H. Arundel, C. H. Evensen, D. W. Mulholland and J. H. Ardner.

Detroit.—Weidman, F. L. Shaw, Bennett, M. P. Scott, W. Geiss, Farrell, F. W. Meinke, Wood, Hanlon, Geo. A. Wood, A. L. Richardson, W. F. Prince, W. S. Walker and C. S. Maxwell. Manager, John C. Chapman.

New York.—Ewing, Welch, Clapp, McKinnon, Troy, Connor, Caskins, Gillespie, D. Richardson, Dorgan, D. Creeden, C. F. Jones, D. N. Tarbox and M. J. Kennedy.

Philadelphia.—C. J. Ferguson, Coleman, W. M. Vinton, Ringo, J. F. Cahill, S. D. Farrar, G. E. Andrews, J. H. Mulvey. W. H. McClellan, W. H. Purcell, J. J. Remsen, Jas. Fogarty, John E. Manning, L. Daniels, Jas. Donaghue, C. Ingraham, G. Patrick, E. L. Ford, H. Allen, W. N. Chatfeld, J. W. Knight, J. F. Waring, and F. Reilly. Manager, Harry Wright.

Providence.—Radbourn, Chas. Sweeny, Gilligan, Nava, Start, Farrell, Denny, Irwin, Carroll, Hines, Radford, M. J. Murray, and J. A. Jones. Manager, Frank Bancroft.

In the batting averages for 1884 Jas. O'Rourke, of the Buffalo club, took the lead, his percentage of base hits being .350. In the fielding averages Start, of Providence, led the first base men with a percentage of chances accepted of .974; Burdock, of Boston, led the second basemen with .925; Sutton of Boston, the third basemen with .906; Smith, of Cleveland, the short stops with .904; Hornung, of Boston, the left fielders with .913; Fogarty, of Philadelphia, the center fielders with .915; and Evans, of Cleveland, the right fielders with .911; Hackett, of Boston, led the catchers with .879; and Radbourn, of Providence, the pitchers, with an average of runs earned off his pitching of but 1-15 to a game. In this year Dunlap, McCormick, and Glasscock, of the Clevelands, broke their contracts and left their club in the lurch: as also Fred Shaw of the Detroits, Chas. Sweeny of the Providence, and others of less note. All of the League players were justly expelled for their conduct. The changes made in the playing rules for 1884 admitted of the legal delivery of the ball to the bat by an overhand throw. The legal number of unfair balls allowed to be delivered was changed from seven to six. The rule requiring the batsman to be declared out for failing to run to a base after three strokes, was thrown out.

THE NATIONAL AGREEMENT.

Our history of the League would be incomplete without the text of the famous "National Agreement," and accordingly we append it in full, prefacing it with the able address of Messrs. Mills and Caylor of the committees of the League and American Association through whose efforts it was brought about.

{ FIFTH AVENUE HOTEL, New York, Oct. 27, 1883.

TO THE NATIONAL LEAGUE, AMERICAN ASSOCIATION, AND NORTHWESTERN LEAGUE.

Your joint Committee on Arbitration beg to congratulate you, and all patrons of the National Game, upon the conclusion of the most brilliant, and in all respects satisfactory playing season in the annals of the game; and we especially congratulate you upon the fact that during the entire season no dispute nor complaint has been submitted for our decision; that the relations of the different Associations toward each other have been harmonious and satisfactory; that every game of ball played by the clubs of the three Associations has been decided solely upon its merits under the playing rules, and that there has not been in the ranks of any club of the three Associations a single case of dishonest play, or breach of contract. These credentials and satisfactory achievements are, we think, in some degree due to the joint agreement entered into by you, prior to the beginning of the season just ended, and we confidently believe that a faithful adherence to the principles upon which that is based, will serve not only to place the exhibition of the game upon an enduring business basis, assuring players the certainty of receiving, and clubs the means of paying them just compensation for their services, but also will insure the patrons of the game a larger percentage of close and honest contest than any other system could afford them.

Your Committee believe that it would be well for the cause of professional base ball, and highly beneficial alike to clubs and players, if the provisions of this agreement could be made to extend to all respectable clubs, and accordingly advise that any association or professional base ball clubs now existing, or that may hereafter be organized upon the basis of honest play and financial responsibility, and not located in cities or towns already occupied by your clubs, should be admitted on equal terms with yourselves to this agreement, but if any such association should decide not to avail itself of such privilege, but, on the contrary, should disregard the obligations assumed by your respective bodies, you should prohibit your clubs from intercourse with the clubs of any such association, in the manner indicated in one of the amendments herewith submitted.

Your Committee deem it wise to discourage making players ineligible for causes other than dishonest play, breach of contract, or other conduct in itself disreputable; and adcordingly, in preparing the amendments herewith submitted, have attempted to clearly define and limit the duration of the reservation of players, so as to take from the reserving club the temptation to find some pretext for expelling, or suspending, the reserved player under the terms of his unexpired contract, in case such reserved player should refuse to enter into a contract for the ensuing year, on or immediately after the tenth day of October; and, also, to take from associations the temptation to make the refusal of a reserved player to contract with the reserving club a cause of permament disqualification, as in the case of failure to perform a contract. Other amendments suggested by us are intended to define more clearly than the existing agreement does, the release of players from contract, or reservation: the possible relation of umpires and club managers to matters affected by the joint agreement, and a fuller definition of the term and jurisdiction of the Arbitration Committee, all of which we trust will be found self explanatory.

A copy of the joint agreement, in the form in which we think it should be as amended, is transmitted herewith, and we unanimously recommend its adoption by your respective bodies.

Respectfully submitted,
By order of the Committee,
{ A. G. MILLS, *Chairman*.
{ O. P. CAYLOR, *Secretary*.

The text of the "National Agreement," which went into force in 1884, is as follows:

THE NATIONAL AGREEMENT OF PROFESSIONAL BASE BALL ASSOCIATIONS.

The parties hereto, in consideration of the mutual advantages to be derived therefrom, agree each with the other, as follows:

FIRST.—When a player under contract by any club, member of any party hereto, is expelled, black-listed, or suspended, in accordance with its rules, by such party hereto, notice of such disqualification shall be served upon the secretaries of the other associations, parties hereto, by the secretary of the association from whose club such player shall have been thus disqualified; and the secretaries of such other association shall forthwith serve notice of such disqualification upon the club members of such other associations, and from the receipt of such notice, all club members of all the parties hereto, shall be debarred from employing, or playing with, or against such disqualified player, until the period of disqualification shall have terminated, or the disqualification be revoked by the association from which such player was disqualified, and due notice of such revocation served upon the secretaries of the other associations, and by them upon their respective clubs; provided, that if such disqualification terminates, or is revoked on or after the expiration of the player's contract, such player shall not be eligible to contract with any club until the expiration of ten days from the date of mailing of written notice of such termination or revocation by the association secretary, to the secretaries of the other parties hereto, and such date of mailing shall be specified in such secretary's notice to the other secretaries, and by all the secretaries in their notices to the clubs of their respective associations.

SECOND.—No contract shall be made for the services of any player by any club, member of either of the parties hereto, for a longer period than seven months, beginning April 1, and terminating October 31, and no such contract for services to be rendered after the expiration of the current year shall be made prior to the tenth day of October of such year, nor shall any negotiation be entered into by or between any club or agent thereof and any player, for services to be rendered in an ensuing year, prior to the said tenth day of October.

THIRD.—On the twenty-fifth day of September of each year, each club member of the parties hereto shall transmit to the secretary of its association a list of names of any players, not exceeding eleven in number, on that date under contract with such club which such club desires to reserve for the ensuing year, accompanied by a statement over the signature of the secretary of such club, that such club is willing to pay not less than one thousand dollars, (except a North Western League Club, whose minimum shall be seven hundred and fifty dollars) as the compensation of each player so reserved, in the contract to be made with him for the ensuing season; and the secretary of each association shall, on the first day of October transmit to the secretaries of the other associations, parties hereto, a full list of players thus reserved. The secretary of each association shall thereupon, on the fifth day of October, transmit to each club member of such association a full list of all players so reserved by all clubs then composing the associations parties hereto, and no club member of either of the parties hereto shall contract, negotiate with, or employ any player while so reserved by any other club member of either of the parties hereto. Such reservation shall terminate when the reserving club enters into contract with the reserved player, or releases him from such reservation, or disbands, or is expelled by or resigns from its association, party hereto, without entering into such contract, or releasing such player from such reservation.

FOURTH.—Any contract between a club, member of any of the parties hereto, and a player, made in accordance with the provisions of this agreement, shall be deemed valid and binding, and all other clubs shall be debarred from employing or negotiating with such player during the continuance of such contract; unless it remains in force on October 10th, when such player may be negotiated or contracted with for the ensuing year, if not reserved as provided by this agreement; provided that such contract shall be considered to take effect upon receipt of written notice thereof by the club members of the parties hereto, and the transmission of such notice by the respective secretaries of the parties hereto, each to the other, and to their respective clubs, is hereby made mandatory upon said secretaries; and such notice must follow immediately upon receipt of the contracting club's notice, in any form complying with its association's rules, to the secretary of the association to which such contracting club belongs.

FIFTH.—In case any club, member of any party hereto, holding a player under reservation or by contract, shall release such player from such reservation or such contract, or shall disband or resign from, or be expelled by its association, the secretary of such association shall at once notify by mail in writing the secretaries of the other associations, parties hereto, of such release of the player or disbandment, resignation or expulsion of the club, as the case may be, and such player shall not be eligible to contract with any other club until the expiration of ten days from the date of mailing of such written notice by the secretary of the association of which such releasing or retired club is or was a member, and such date of mailing shall be specified in such secretary's notice to the other secretaries, and by all the secretaries in their notices to the clubs of their respective associations.

SIXTH.—No umpire or club manager under contract in any association, party hereto, shall be employed in or by any other association, party hereto, for service as umpire, manager or player, for the term of such contract or any part thereof, unless duly released from such contract, and the secretary of each association shall notify the secretaries of all other associations, parties hereto, of all contracts with, and releases of umpires and club managers.

SEVENTH.—No club that was not a member of any party hereto on the tenth day of October, 1883, shall be entitled to membership in any party hereto, or be admitted to membership by any party hereto, from any city or town in which, on that date, any club, member of any party hereto, was located, and any club, member of any party hereto, shall forfeit all rights and privileges conferred by this agreement in the event of its removal from the city or town where located when admitted to membership by any party hereto; provided, that nothing herein contained shall be construed to prohibit any club, member of any party hereto, from resigning its membership in any party hereto, and being admitted to membership in any other party hereto, with all rights and privileges conferred by this agreement.

EIGHTH.—No game of ball shall be played between any club member of any party hereto, and any other club that employs, or presents in its nine, any player held by reservation or contract by any club, member of any party hereto, under the terms of this agreement, or disqualified by any party hereto, nor shall any club, member of any party hereto, play against any club that shall have, at any time during the same playing season, played a game of ball with any other club employing or presenting in its nine any player ineligible, as specified in this section. Provided, that in case the club employing such ineligible player shall discharge him from its service, club members of the parties hereto, may thereafter play against such club, and against other clubs that may have played such club while employing such player.

NINTH.—Any disputes or complaints arising out of the performance of the stipulation of this agreement, and any alleged violations of this agreement; also, any question of interpretation of any stipulation of this agree. ment shall be referred to an arbitration committee to consist of three representatives of each party hereto, to be appointed prior to the thirty-first day of March, in each year, by the parties hereto; notice of such appointment to be served upon the secretaries of each association; and the decisions of such arbitration committee upon such matters, or any of them, shall be final and binding upon the parties hereto.

TENTH.—The term of service of each member of the arbitration committee shall be one year, ending March thirty-first, and any vacancy arising in said committee shall be filled by the party hereto in whose delegation such vacancy occurs. Any party hereto shall, also, have the right to change its representation in such committee at any time.

ELEVENTH.—The arbitration committee shall have power to inflict upon any club, member of any party hereto, the penalty of forfeiture of all rights and privileges derived by such club from this agreement, for the violation by such club of any of the stipulations or requirements of this agreement, and such forfeiture shall take effect upon the receipt by the secretaries of the parties hereto of a certificate of the findings and verdict of the arbitration committee.

In witness whereof, the said parties have, by president of each of the parties hereto, thereunto duly authorized, signed this agreement on the dates set opposite their respective signatures.

         A. G. MILLS, *President.*
National League of Professional B. B. C.   Nov. 22, 1883.
        H. D. MCKNIGHT, *President.*
American Association of B. B. C.   Dec. 13, 1383.
        ELIAS MATTER, *President.*
Northwestern League of Professional B. B. C.   Jan. 10, 1884.
        WM. C. SEDDEN, *President.*
Eastern League of Professional B. B. C.   Feb. 19, 1884.

THE SEASON OF 1885.

The ninth annual meeting of the National League was held at the Fifth Avenue Hotel, in New York, on Nov. 19, 1884, and it was a beginning of a series of the most exciting meetings ever held by the League. The delegates present on the occasion were as follows: Messrs. Soden and H. W. Conant, of Boston; Jewett and S. Clinton, of Buffalo; Spalding and Brown, of Chicago; Howe, of Cleveland; Thompson, of Detroit; Day and W. S. Appleton, of New York; Reach and Rogers, of Philadelphia; and Root and Allen, of Providence. At this meeting Mr. A. G. Mills, who, like the dead President of the League, had done so much to conserve the best interests of the National League, positively declined a re-election as President, and he was made an honorary member of the League, the vote being accompanied by a highly complimentary resolution. N. E. Young was then elected President as well as Secretary and Treasurer—a well earned act of promotion for ten years of faithful services as Secretary. The Board of Directors chosen were: Messrs. Reach, Day, Clinton and Mahoney. The report of the Board of Directors awarded the championship to the Providence club.

At a special meeting Mr. Rogers was elected a member of the Arbitration Committee, in the place of ex-President Mills.

At the special meeting of the League held at the Fifth Avenue Hotel, New York, on March 5, 1885, the action of the special committee appointed to consider the question of the application of H. V. Lucas, the President of the defunct Union Association, for membership of the League, was voted upon, and the St. Louis club, with Messrs. Lucas and N. Crane as delegates, was admitted to membership. A Board of Conference was also appointed to confer with a like board of the American Association, this board consisting of Messrs. Soden, Spalding and Day.

At a special meeting of the League held on Jan. 10, 1885, at the Fifth Avenue Hotel, resolutions of condolence on the death of J. Ford Evans, of the Cleveland club, were adopted, and the meeting accepted the resignation of the Cleveland club as a member of the League.

Another special meeting of the League was held at the Fifth Avenue Hotel, New York, on Jan. 21, at which the principal business was the discussion of the question of the reinstatement of the contract breakers.

The last special meeting of the League for 1885 was held at the same hotel on April 13, 1885, and at this meeting the contract breakers, McCormick, Briody and Glasscock, were reinstated, as well as those who broke the reserve rule, viz.: Dunlap, Schaffer and Sweeny; the former being fined $1,000 each and the latter $500.

The official list of League clubs published in the Guide for 1885 was as follows:

Boston.—Whitney, Buffinton, Morrell, Burdock, Sutton, Wise, Hornung, Manning, J. A. Davis, Gunning and Hines.

Buffalo.—Galvin, Serad, Rowe, J. A. McCauley, Brouthers, Richardson, White, Myers, Force, Wm. Crowley, J. J. Lillie, E. J. Hengle, R. Blakeston and J. Connor.

Chicago.—Corcoran, J. G. Clarkson, Flint, Anson, Pfeffer, Williamson, Burns, Dalrymple, Gore, Kelly, Sunday, O. P. Beard, C. Marr, E. E. Sutcliffe and Joe Brown.

Detroit.—Weidman, Bennett, Chas. Getzein, Scott, Mienke, Farrell, Wood, Hanlon, J. F. Dorgan, C. H. Morton and Marr Phillips.

New York.—Welch, Hope, Ewing, Connor, Gerhardt, D. Richardson, Gillespie, Jas. O'Rourke and McKinnon.

Philadelphia.—Ferguson, Vinton, E. M. Daily, A. Cusick, Andrews, Mulvey, C. J. Bastian, Purcell, Fogerty, E. E. Foster, A. Myers, C. W. Ganzell, Thos. J. Lynch, J. Clements and E. Nolan.

Providence.—Radbourn, Gilligan, Start, Farrell, Denny, Irwin, Carroll, E. N. Crane, C. F. Daily, Radford, C. E. Bassett and U. T. Murray.

St. Louis.—H. T. Boyle, G. F. Baker, F. W. Bandle, W. O. Donnell, F. P. Sullivan, J. F. Staples, F. Lewis, T. Quinn and W. H. Colgan.

THE PROFESSIONAL SEASON OF 1885.

The professional base ball clubs of the country had a very successful season in 1885, considering the rather depressed condition of business affairs; and as regards the leading clubs of the principal professional associations, they nearly all enjoyed a profitable season last year. One fact prominently connected with the chapter of base ball history made by the events of 1885, was the rapid extension of professional base ball playing in the Southern States, while the American national game greatly prospered in Canada, at least in the Province of Ontario, where the British element of the population of the Dominion largely prevails. In the French Canadian district manly sports of the field, like base ball and cricket, do not flourish as they do in Upper Canada. A year or two more will see base ball as popular throughout the whole of the Southern States as it is in the Northern; and as for Canada, base ball is rapidly obtaining an equal foothold with both cricket and lacrosse, the latter being the Canadian's national field game, as base ball is ours, and cricket that of England.

The record of the championship contests in the professional arena in 1885 presents the figures of a very close contest for the pennant between the two leading National League Clubs of Chicago and New York; while in the American Association pennant race the St. Louis club took a winning lead from the start, and had the race well in hand before the season was half over. In the Eastern League the contest was rendered comparatively uninteresting from the fact that the race lay entirely between the Nationals of Washington and Virginias of Richmond for the early part of the season, and then the Nationals had it all their own way. In the new Southern League the inaugural season of the Association proved to be a very creditable one. In this Association pennant race the Atlanta club bore off the honors, with the Augusta a close second.

Another feature of the season of 1885 was the starting of several State Leagues, prominent among which was the New York League. In the latter's pennant race the Syracuse Stars bore off the championship honors.

Two New England Leagues were enrolled among the professional associations of 1885, the Eastern New England League proving to be the most flourishing, and its championship honors were borne off by the Lawrence club. On the Pacific coast the Haverly Club of San Francisco won the championship, and the Colorado League's championship was won by the Denver club. A number of Interstate and State Leagues started on the wave of the spring enthusiasm of the season, but they all played themselves out before the Fourth of July. The championship of the Canadian League was won by the Hamilton club. This League, by the way, will eventually be a noteworthy institution. Already strong clubs exist in Toronto, Hamilton, London, and Guelph, and others will be added as the game extends in popularity. Looking beyond the American continent it is a noticeable fact that base ball games were played in 1885 in Havana, Honolulu, Melbourne, Australia, and the Sandwich Islands, and even in the American colony in China.

In the amateur arena the championship of the American College Association was won by the Harvard nine, for the first for several years past, their championship record for 1885 being made specially noteworthy by the fact that they won every game of the championship series. In the State College Associations, the Bowdoin nine won the Maine championship, and the Cornell nine that of New York.

Another year's experience of the working of the Arbitration Committee, and the "national agreement" system proved even more than before, the great benefits accruing from both the control of the committee and the rules of the "agreement." In fact, the national agreement has been shown to be the very bulwark of honest play in the ranks, and the only foundation on which professional stock companies can be built up with any hope of pecuniary success.

We regret to have to chronicle the fact that the season's championship contests were again marked by discreditable disturbances on several professional club ball-fields, all of which were entirely due to the neglect on the part of the home clubs to strictly enforce their club association rules, which require each club "to furnish sufficient police force upon its own grounds to preserve order." It goes without saying that the game cannot be played without an umpire; nor can it be successfully played without the Umpire is one suited for the position; and such a man, if found, will not be likely to accept the position, unless fully insured against the insults of a partisan crowd, and against the "kicking" propensities of badly managed teams. It is a conceded fact, too, that integrity of character, sound judgment, and thorough impartiality as essentials in Umpires and umpiring, are vital necessities of the game, and the basis of its very existence. But how are these essentials to be made available unless the position of umpire is itself properly protected and guarded from the assaults of "club heelers" and betting roughs? These facts have been forcibly presented to the officials of the several professional associations by each season's experience, and yet but little advance had been made toward an improved condition of things up to 1886.

THE LEAGUE SEASON OF 1885.

The League season of 1885 was inaugurated on the 1st of April by the Philadelphia and New York clubs, the former by a match game with the Brown University nine from Providence, the professionals winning by a score of 9 to 1. The same day the New York team played their opening game at the polo grounds in a practice match with the Jasper nine of Manhattan College, which the professionals won by 16 to 2. The same day, too, the Providence team began play at Norfolk, Va., with the Eastern League team of that city, which the veterans won by a score of 5 to 4 only. On April 2 the Chicago team took the field for the first time in 1885, they playing at Louisville with the American club of that city, which they defeated by 11 to 9 only. The same day the Boston team opened play on their own grounds at Boston, on which occasion they had a close contest with a strong picked nine, the regular team winning by 3 to 1 only. On April 3 the Buffalo team began play for the season in an exhibition game at Baltimore with the American team of that city, and after a ten innings contest the best they could do was to draw the game, leaving the score at 3 to 3. On April 6 the Detroit club opened their season in an exhibition game at Pittsburg with the American team of that city, and after a ten innings game the visitors won by 1 to 0 only. On April 11 the new League club of St. Louis had their first match of the season, and in an exhibition game with the American club of St. Louis, the League team were "Chicagoed" by a score of 7 to 0. Thus was the exhibition portion of the League season opened in April of 1885.

The championship season of the League began on April 30 at St. Louis, on which occasion the new St. Louis team defeated the Chicago team by 3 to 2. On May 1 the Detroit and Buffalo clubs opened their championship season in a match together at Detroit, which the Detroits won by 8 to 3. The New York and Boston clubs opened their championship season on the polo grounds, New York, when the Bostons were defeated by 2 to 1; while at Philadelphia the same day the Providence and Philadelphia clubs played their opening match together, and Providence won by 8 to 2.

The progress of the championship campaign can best be seen by studying the monthly records which we present below.

THE MONTHLY RECORDS.

The most interesting chapter of the championship campaigns of each year, is that relating to the progress made each month by each competing team, toward the goal of the season's championship. The monthly record shows when each team "spurted" in the race, or fell off in the running, and when they showed the most strength or displayed their weakness most. A great deal of important information, too, can be derived from a careful comparison of the monthly record; especially in regard to the strength a team possesses in rallying for the lead toward the close of the season.

THE MAY RECORD.

The end of the first week in May saw the Detroit club in the van, with the Chicagos second, and the New Yorks third. After this the Detroit team lost ground considerably, and by the end of the month Detroit stood at the foot of the class, New York being in the van with Chicago second and Philadelphia third, New York having won seventeen out of twenty-one games during the May campaign, while Chicago only won fourteen out of twenty, the latter losing three out of their four games played at the Polo grounds this month. The Detroit club's record was almost the very reverse of that of New York, the former losing sixteen out of twenty. The full record for May shows the clubs occupying the following relative positions for the month's work:

MAY RECORD.

	New York.	Chicago.	Philadelphia.	Providence.	Boston.	St. Louis.	Buffalo.	Detroit.	Games Won.
New York.......................	....	3	0	2	2	3	3	4	17
Chicago........................	1	....	4	3	2	3	1	0	14
Philadelphia...................	0	0	....	1	2	4	3	4	14
Providence....................	1	1	1	....	0	2	4	4	13
Boston.........................	0	1	2	0	....	1	1	3	8
St. Louis.......................	1	*1	0	1	3	....	0	1	7
Buffalo........................	1	0	1	0	2	0	....	0	4
Detroit.........................	0	0	0	0	1	0	3	....	4
Games Lost....................	4	6	8	7	12	13	15	16	81

*The game of April 30 is added to the May record, the St. Louis nine then defeating Chicago at St. Louis.

THE JUNE RECORD.

In June Chicago made the best month's record of the season, that club winning no less than twenty-one games out of twenty-three games played in June. New York was next with fifteen victories out of twenty games, Providence being third, as Philadelphia fell off badly this month, they losing fourteen out of twenty-one games. Boston did not do as well this month as in May, while Detroit lost more ground than in May. It was beginning to be plainly evident even at this period of the season that the struggle for the pennant would be between Chicago and New York. By the end of June New York had won eighteen out of the twenty-four games they had thus far played with the Western teams, and had won fourteen out of the nineteen they had played with the three Eastern teams, while Chicago had won twenty out of twenty games thus far played with the three Western teams, and had won fourteen out of twenty-one with the four Eastern teams, the two clubs thus plainly showing their superior strength to all except each other. The record for June left the eight clubs standing as follows in victories and defeats scored during June:

JUNE RECORD.

	Chicago.	New York.	Providence.	St. Louis.	Buffalo.	Philadelphia.	Boston.	Detroit.	Games Won.
Chicago........................	....	0	0	4	4	2	3	8	21
New York......................	0	....	2	0	4	4	4	1	15
Providence.....................	0	2	....	0	2	3	5	2	14
St. Louis.......................	0	0	0	....	3	3	0	3	9
Buffalo........................	0	0	1	4	....	0	0	3	8
Philadelphia....................	2	2	1	0	0	....	2	0	7
Boston........................	0	0	1	4	0	2	....	0	7
Detroit........................	0	1	1	1	1	0	0	....	4
Games Lost...................	2	5	6	13	14	14	14	17	85

THE JULY RECORD.

During July the contest for supremacy between Chicago and New York was a "nip and tuck" battle, each winning eighteen games during that month, while Chicago sustained but six defeats to New York's seven. Detroit made a rally this month, that club winning fifteen games out of the twenty-four they played this month, it being their best record of the season. All the other clubs lost more games in July than they won, Boston and Buffalo playing very poorly in July, each losing seventeen games out of twenty-four played. The record in full for the month is appended:

JULY RECORD.

	Chicago.	New York.	Detroit.	Providence.	Philadelphia.	St. Louis.	Boston.	Buffalo.	Games Won.
Chicago.........................	....	1	0	4	2	0	6	5	18
New York.......................	3	....	4	2	0	6	1	2	18
Detroit..........................	0	2	....	0	4	4	5	0	15
Providence.....................	3	1	0	....	2	3	0	3	12
Philadelphia...................	0	0	4	0	....	2	1	2	9
St. Louis.......................	0	2	0	3	3	....	0	0	8
Boston..........................	0	1	1	0	1	0	....	5	8
Buffalo.........................	0	0	0	2	2	0	4	....	8
Games Lost..................	6	7	9	11	14	15	17	17	96

THE AUGUST RECORD.

New York had the best of the August campaign, that club winning eighteen out of the twenty-one games played that month, while Chicago only won fifteen out of nineteen. Buffalo took a turn in the rallying business, they winning thirteen out of the twenty games they played that month. Philadelphia and Boston lost as many as they won, while Providence fell off badly, Detroit and St. Louis tying for lost place, each winning but three games out of nineteen played in August. The full record is appended:

AUGUST RECORD.

	New York.	Chicago.	Buffalo.	Philadelphia.	Boston.	Providence.	Detroit.	St. Louis.	Games Won.
New York.......................	....	3	1	6	4	4	0	0	18
Chicago.........................	1	....	1	2	0	0	7	4	15
Buffalo.........................	0	0	....	1	0	0	4	8	13
Philadelphia...................	1	0	3	....	2	5	0	0	11
Boston..........................	1	0	0	2	....	3	2	2	10
Providence.....................	0	0	0	0	2	....	3	2	7
Detroit..........................	0	1	1	0	0	1	....	0	3
St. Louis.......................	0	0	1	0	2	0	0	....	3
Games Lost..................	3	4	7	11	10	13	16	16	80

THE SEPTEMBER RECORD.

In September Chicago won seventeen games out of twenty, while New York had to be content with thirteen victories out of nineteen games played this month. Detroit materially strengthened their nine this month, that club winning eleven out of nineteen games. Philadelphia also gained ground, and Boston pulled up a little. But Providence completely collapsed, that club only winning three games out of twenty-two which they played in September, it being the worst month's record of the season. By this time all the interest in the pennant race had been monopolized by the Chicago and New York clubs. In fact, no other clubs had a chance for the pennant after the end of July. The full record for September is as follows:

SEPTEMBER RECORD.

	Chicago.	New York.	Detroit.	Philadelphia.	Boston.	St. Louis.	Buffalo.	Providence.	Games Won.
Chicago	....	2	0	0	3	3	5	4	17
New York	0	....	3	1	2	0	5	2	13
Detroit	0	1	....	3	0	4	0	3	11
Philadelphia	0	2	1	....	2	1	3	1	10
Boston	1	1	0	0	....	1	2	5	10
St. Louis	1	0	0	0	3	....	0	4	8
Buffalo	0	0	4	1	0	1	....	0	5
Providence	1	0	0	1	0	1	0	....	3
Games Lost	3	6	8	6	10	10	15	19	77

Before the expiration of the month the Chicago club had virtually won the championship, they defeating the New York club at Chicago in three straight games the last of September and first of October. But for the weakening of the Buffalo club by the withdrawal of their four leading players, New York would have added two more defeats to their September record.

THE OCTOBER RECORD.

In October Philadelphia made a successful rally for third place, and won it, Chicago falling off in its play in October after winning the pennant, while Detroit pulled up. The record of the month was as follows:

OCTOBER RECORD.

	Philadelphia.	Detroit.	Providence.	New York.	Boston.	Chicago.	St. Louis.	Buffalo.	Won.
Philadelphia	....	0	0	0	0	3	2	0	5
Detroit	0	....	1	0	3	0	0	0	4
Providence	0	0	....	0	0	0	0	4	4
New York	0	0	0	....	0	1	3	0	4
Boston	0	1	0	0	....	0	0	2	3
Chicago	1	0	0	1	0	....	0	0	2
St. Louis	0	0	0	0	0	0	....	0	1
Buffalo	0	0	0	0	0	0	0	....	0
Lost	1	1	1	2	3	4	5	6	23

SUMMARY OF VICTORIES.

	May.	June.	July.	Aug.	Sept.	Oct.	Total.
Chicago	14	21	18	15	17	2	87
New York	17	15	18	18	13	4	85
Philadelphia	14	7	9	11	10	5	56
Providence	13	14	12	7	3	4	53
Boston	8	7	8	10	10	3	46
Detroit	4	4	15	3	11	4	41
Buffalo	4	8	8	13	5	0	38
St. Louis	7	9	8	3	8	1	36
Totals	81	85	96	80	77	23	442

SUMMARY OF DEFEATS.

	May.	June.	July.	Aug.	Sept.	Oct.	Total.
Chicago	6	2	6	4	3	4	25
New York	4	5	7	3	6	2	27
Philadelphia	8	14	14	11	6	1	54
Providence	7	6	11	13	19	1	57
Boston	12	14	17	10	10	3	66
Detroit	16	17	9	16	8	1	67
Buffalo	15	14	17	7	15	6	74
St. Louis	13	13	15	16	10	5	72
Totals	81	85	96	80	77	23	442

THE CHAMPIONSHIP RECORDS.

THE OLD NATIONAL ASSOCIATION RECORD.

Up to 1870 but one National Association existed in the entire country and the last convention held by that organization occurred in that year. In 1871 Mr. Chadwick divided the clubs into two classes, and he organized the first regular professional association in that year, the convention which he called, assembling at Collier's Saloon—the well known actor—on the corner of Broadway and Thirteenth Street, New York, on the night of March 17, 1871. At that convention the first special code of championship rules ever put in operation were adopted, and in that year the first officially recognized championship contests known in the history of the game were played. The season began in May with the Athletic, Boston, Chicago, Cleveland, Forest City Club, Haymakers of Troy, Mutual, Olympic, of Washington, Kekionga and Rockford, Forest City Clubs, in the arena. The Eckfords entered in August, but their games were not counted. The Kekionga games were thrown out owing to illegal games after July. The record which decided the championship of 1871 was as follows:

BASE BALL GUIDE.

RECORD FOR 1871.

CLUB.	Athletic.	Boston.	Chicago.	Mutual.	Olympic.	Haymaker.	Cleveland.	Kekionga.	Rockford.	Games Won.
Athletic...............	....	1	3	3	3	3	3	3	3	22
Boston................	3	....	1	3	3	3	3	3	3	22
Chicago...............	2	3	....	3	3	1	2	3	3	20
Mutual................	2	2	1	....	1	1	2	3	3	17
Olympic...............	0	1	2	1	....	3	3	3	3	16
Haymaker.............	0	2	1	3	2	....	2	3	2	15
Cleveland.............	0	1	1	3	0	2	....	0	3	10
Kekionga..............	0	0	0	1	1	1	3	....	1	7
Rockford..............	0	0	0	1	0	1	1	3	....	6
Games Lost...........	7	10	9	18	15	15	19	21	21	135

In 1872 the Baltimores entered the list, as also the Atlantics of Brooklyn, and the Troy Club, and Washington sent two clubs, both of which failed, however; the brunt of the battle that year lying between the five clubs of Boston, Baltimore, New York, Philadelphia and Troy. The result of the pennant race of 1872 was as follows:

RECORD FOR 1872.

CLUB.	Boston.	Baltimore.	Mutual.	Athletic.	Troy.	Atlantic.	Cleveland.	Mansfield.	Eckford.	Olympic.	National.	Games Won.
Boston............	....	7	7	4	2	7	4	3	3	1	1	39
Baltimore........	0	....	5	4	3	4	4	4	5	2	3	34
Mutual...........	2	4	....	3	3	6	2	4	5	1	1	34
Athletic..........	4	5	3	....	2	4	3	2	5	1	1	30
Troy..............	1	0	2	0	....	2	1	4	3	1	1	15
Atlantic..........	1	1	2	0	0	....	0	2	2	0	0	8
Cleveland........	0	1	1	0	0	1	....	0	1	1	1	6
Mansfield........	0	0	0	0	0	1	1	....	2	0	1	5
Eckford..........	0	1	0	0	0	2	0	0	....	0	0	3
Olympic..........	0	0	0	0	0	0	0	0	0	....	2	2
National.........	0	0	0	0	0	0	0	0	0	0	....	0
Games Lost......	8	19	20	14	10	27	15	19	26	7	11	176

In 1873 the Athletics had a local rival team to meet in the championship arena, in the new Philadelphia Club, which, but for crookedness in its ranks, would have won the championship that year. Baltimore also sent two clubs, and Elizabeth, N. J. entered the lists. The record for 1873 was as follows:

RECORD FOR 1873.

CLUB.	Boston.	Philadelphia.	Baltimore.	Mutual.	Athletic.	Atlantic.	Washington.	Resolute.	Maryland.	Games Won.
Boston................		5	7	6	4	8	9	4	0	43
Philadelphia.........	4	...	6	6	4	7	3	4	0	36
Baltimore............	2	3	....	6	3	7	6	3	3	33
Mutual...............	3	4	3	...	4	7	4	4	0	29
Athletic..............	5	1	4	5	...	5	6		0	28
Atlantic..............	1	2	2	2	4	...	3	3	0	17
Washington.........	0	2	0	1	0	2	....	1	2	8
Resolute..............	1	0	0	0	0	1	0	....	0	2
Maryland............	0	0	0	0	0	0	0	0	...	0
Games Lost	16	17	22	24	23	37	31	21	5	196

In 1874 Hartford sent a club to compete for the pennant. The Olympic, Kekionga, Rockford, Eckford, Mansfield, Maryland, and Haymakers having retired since 1871 and up to 1873 Inclusive. The Chicago Club which had been broken up by the great fire of October, 1871, and had been out of the race in 1872 and 1873, again entered the lists. At the end of the season the record stood as follows:

RECORD FOR 1874.

CLUB.	Boston.	Mutual.	Athletic.	Philadelphia.	Chicago.	Atlantic.	Hartford.	Baltimore.	Games Won.
Boston................	....	5	8	8	7	6	9	9	52
Mutual................	5	....	4	1	9	7	8	8	42
Athletic...............	2	6	...	9	3	6	5	2	33
Philadelphia.........	2	5	1	...	7	6	4	4	29
Chicago	3	1	4	3	...	4	4	9	27
Atlantic...............	4	3	1	3	3	...	5	3	23
Hartford.............	1	2	3	1	1	3	...	3	17
Baltimore............	1	1	2	1	1	1	2	.	9
Games Lost.........	18	23	23	29	31	33	37	38	232

The season of 1875 saw the last of the old National professional Association, it being superseded by the League in 1876. In 1875 St. Louis entered the lists and before the season expired there were thirteen competitors in the arena, and things became decidedly mixed, and demoralization set in. The outcome of the contest however, was the success of the Boston

BASE BALL GUIDE. 39

Club, which had won the championship each successive season since 1871.

The record of the last season's campaign of the old National Association which closed its season in 1875, was as follows.

RECORD FOR 1875.

CLUB.	Boston.	Athletic.	Hartford.	St. Louis.	Philadelphia.	Chicago.	Mutual.	New Haven.	Red Stock'gs.	Washington.	Centennial.	Atlantic.	Western.	Games Won.
Boston...............	...	8	9	7	6	5	10	5	1	5	5	6	1	71
Athletic...............	2	...	3	6	8	7	6	5	0	5	2	7	2	53
Hartford	1	4	...	5	4	6	8	5	3	4	1	10	0	54
St. Louis..............	2	1	5	...	5	5	8	2	2	3	0	2	4	39
Philadelphia.........	0	2	4	5	...	7	2	4	1	2	3	7	0	37
Chicago...............	2	1	4	5	3	...	3	2	4	0	0	2	4	30
Mutual................	0	3	2	0	5	3	...	4	2	0	2	7	1	29
New Haven...........	1	0	1	1	0	1	1	...	0	1	0	1	0	7
Red Stockings........	0	0	0	0	0	0	0	0	...	2	0	0	2	4
Washington	0	0	0	0	0	0	0	4	0	...	0	0	0	4
Centennial...........	0	1	0	0	0	0	0	1	0	0	...	0	0	2
Atlantic..............	0	0	0	0	0	0	0	2	0	0	0	...	0	2
Western..............	0	0	0	0	0	0	0	0	1	0	0	0	...	1
Games Lost..........	8	20	28	29	31	37	38	39	14	22	13	42	13	333

THE LEAGUE CHAMPIONSHIP RECORD.

FROM 1876 TO 1884 INCLUSIVE.

The record of the League championship contest each season from 1876—the year the League was organized—to 1884 inclusive, presents a very interesting array of statistics showing the varying features of the several clubs which have entered the League arena within the past nine years. This year completes the first decade in the history of the League organization, and the record of the full period will make up an exceedingly interesting history of professional ball playing in the palmiest days of its history.

In the inaugural year of the League eight clubs entered the lists for championship, the clubs represented being Boston, Hartford, New York, and Philadelphia in the East, and Chicago, Cincinnati, Louisville and St. Louis in the West. The record for that year gave the championship to the Chicago Club, as will be seen by the appended table.

THE CHAMPIONSHIP RECORD FOR 1876.

	Chicago.	Hartford.	St. Louis.	Boston.	Louisville.	Mutual.	Athletic.	Cincinnati.	Games Played.	Games Lost.	Games Won.
Chicago................	....	6	4	9	9	7	7	10	66	14	52
Hartford...............	4	....	4	8	9	4	9	9	68	21	47
St. Louis..............	6	6	....	6	6	6	8	7	64	19	45
Boston................	1	2	4	....	5	8	9	10	70	31	39
Louisville.............	1	1	4	5	....	5	6	8	66	36	30
Mutual................	1	4	1	2	3	....	3	7	56	35	21
Athletic...............	1	1	0	1	2	4	....	5	59	45	14
Cincinnati.............	0	1	2	0	2	1	3	....	65	56	9
Games Lost............	14	21	19	31	36	35	45	56	514	257	257

In 1877 the Mutual Club of New York and the Athletic of Philadelphia were not among the contestants, owing to their failure to fulfill their scheduled engagements of the previous season; and consequently only five clubs of the eight which entered the lists in 1876 took part in the championship campaign of 1877. This year Boston went to the front again while Chicago had to be content with the rear rank position, as will be seen fron the appended record:

THE RECORD FOR 1877.

	Boston.	Louisville.	Hartford.	St. Louis.	Chicago.	Games Played.	Games Lost.	Games Won.
Boston................	....	8	7	6	10	48	17	31
Louisville.............	4	....	6	10	8	48	20	28
Hartford..............	5	6	....	5	8	48	24	24
St. Louis.............	6	2	4	....	4	48	29	19
Chicago...............	2	4	7	8	....	48	30	18
Games Lost...........	17	20	24	29	30		120	120

In 1878 only six clubs took part in the season's campaign as in 1877; but Providence took the place of Hartford, Indianapolis filled Louisville's place, and Milwaukee that of St. Louis. Once more the championship honors were held by Boston, while Chicago pulled up to a better position than they held in 1877, as the appended record shows:

THE RECORD FOR 1878.

	Boston.	Cincinnati.	Providence.	Chicago.	Indianapolis.	Milwaukee.	Games Played.	Games Lost.	Games Won.
Boston	....	6	6	8	10	11	60	19	41
Cincinnati	6	....	9	10	4	8	60	23	37
Providence	6	3	....	6	10	8	60	27	33
Chicago	4	2	6	....	8	10	60	30	30
Indianapolis	2	8	2	4	....	8	60	36	24
Milwaukee	1	4	4	2	4	....	60	45	15
Games Lost	19	23	27	30	36	45	360	180	180

In 1879 eight clubs once more entered the lists for the League championship, and this number was finally fixed upon as the maximum of membership of the National League. In the place of Indianapolis and Milwaukee Buffalo and Cleveland entered the race, while two new members were taken in from Syracuse and Troy. It was in this year that George Wright left the Boston Club and became the manager of the rival club of that city from Providence, and he signalized the event by winning the pennant from Boston for the Providence Club, the Stars of Syracuse being distanced in the pennant race, while Troy made a very poor show, as the record below proves.

THE RECORD FOR 1879.

	Providence.	Boston.	Chicago.	Buffalo.	Cincinnati.	Cleveland.	Troy City.	Syracuse.	Games Played.	Games Lost.	Games Won.
Providence	....	8	7	6	10	8	10	6	78	23	55
Boston	4	....	4	9	7	10	11	4	78	29	49
Chicago	5	8	....	6	3	8	8	6	76	32	44
Buffalo	6	3	6	....	7	8	11	3	76	32	44
Cincinnati	2	5	8	3	....	8	9	3	74	36	38
Cleveland	4	2	4	4	4	....	5	1	77	53	24
Troy City	2	1	3	1	2	6	....	4	75	56	19
Syracuse	0	2	0	3	3	5	2	....	42	27	15
Games Lost	23	29	32	32	36	53	56	27		288	288

In 1880 eight clubs again entered the arena, Worcester taking the place of the disbanded Syracuse Stars, which club found their League adversaries altogether too strong for them. This year Chicago went to the front again, Cincinnati falling off so badly in the race that at the finish they were found to be badly distanced, as the record below shows:

THE RECORD FOR 1880.

	Chicago.	Providence.	Cleveland.	Troy City.	Worcester.	Boston.	Buffalo.	Cincinnati.	Games Played.	Games Lost.	Games Won.
Chicago...........	....	9	8	10	10	9	11	10	84	17	67
Providence........	3	....	9	7	6	7	10	10	84	32	52
Cleveland.........	4	3	....	9	6	7	9	9	84	37	47
Troy City.........	2	5	3	....	5	2	11	10	83	42	41
Worcester.........	2	6	6	7	....	8	3	8	83	43	40
Boston............	3	5	5	7	4	....	9	7	84	44	40
Buffalo............	1	2	3	1	9	3	....	5	82	58	24
Cincinnati.........	2	2	3	1	3	5	5	....	80	59	21
Games Lost........	17	32	37	42	43	44	58	59		332	332

In 1881 no change was made in the League ranks, and the same cities were represented in the pennant race of that year as in 1880. Once more the Chicago Club bore off the season's honors, that club having learned the value of team-work as a potent factor in winning the League championship honors. This year Worcester, which club made so good a fight in 1880, fell off to last place, and Boston also occupied an inferior position in the year's campaign, their falling off during 1880 and 1881 being a feature of the year's events. Then, too, Cincinnati was forced to tender its resignation and Detroit was given that club's place, and the new club made a very good showing in the campaign of '81, as will be seen by the appended record:

RECORD OF 1881.

	Chicago.	Providence.	Buffalo.	Detroit.	Troy City.	Boston.	Cleveland.	Worcester.	Games Played.	Games Lost.	Games Won.
Chicago...........	....	9	7	7	8	10	6	9	84	28	56
Providence........	3	....	5	8	6	7	9	9	84	37	47
Buffalo...........	5	7	....	9	3	8	7	6	83	38	45
Detroit...........	5	4	3	....	7	8	7	7	84	43	41
Troy City.........	4	6	9	5	....	5	6	4	84	45	39
Boston............	2	5	4	4	7	....	8	8	83	45	38
Cleveland.........	6	3	5	5	6	4	....	7	84	48	36
Worcester.........	3	3	5	5	5	8	3	....	82	50	32
Games Lost........	28	37	38	43	45	45	48	50		334	334

In 1884 the same eight clubs again entered the lists, and for the third time in succession Chicago carried off the championship, with Providence a close second again as they were in '81 and '80. Worcester was again badly distanced, and as a penalty the club was retired at the close of the season. The Troy Club, too, did not show up well this year, and they, too, shared the fate of the Worcesters. The record at the close stood as follows:

RECORD OF 1882.

	Chicago.	Providence.	Buffalo.	Boston.	Cleveland.	Detroit.	Troy City.	Worcester.	Games Played.	Games Lost.	Games Won.
Chicago..........	....	8	6	6	9	8	9	9	84	29	55
Providence.......	4	....	6	6	8	9	9	10	84	32	52
Buffalo..........	6	6	....	5	6	5	6	11	84	39	45
Boston...........	6	6	7	....	7	8	4	7	84	39	45
Cleveland........	3	4	6	5	....	4	9	11	82	40	42
Detroit..........	4	3	7	4	7	....	8	9	83	41	42
Troy City........	3	3	6	8	2	4	....	9	83	48	35
Worcester........	3	2	1	5	1	3	3	....	84	66	18
Games Lost.......	29	32	39	39	40	41	48	66		334	334

In 1883 New York and Philadelphia were elected as League cities in the place of Troy and Worcester, and this time the Boston Club, by a plucky rally toward the close of the season, managed to get in front of Chicago, the latter club being obliged to be content with second place. Neither New York or Philadelphia made much of a show in the campaign, both of them occupying rear positions, as will be seen by the appended record:

RECORD OF 1883.

	Boston.	Chicago.	Providence.	Cleveland.	Buffalo.	New York.	Detroit.	Philadelphia.	Games Played.	Games Lost.	Games Won.
Boston...........	....	7	8	10	7	7	10	14	98	35	63
Chicago..........	7	....	7	6	9	9	9	12	98	39	59
Providence.......	6	7	....	6	7	9	12	11	98	40	58
Cleveland........	4	8	8	....	7	8	9	12	97	42	55
Buffalo..........	7	5	7	7	....	8	9	9	97	45	52
New York.........	7	5	5	6	5	....	6	12	96	50	46
Detroit..........	4	5	2	5	5	8	....	11	98	58	40
Philadelphia.....	0	2	3	2	5	2	3	....	98	81	17
Games Lost.......	35	39	40	42	45	50	58	81		390	390

In 1884 the same eight clubs again entered the lists, and this time the Providence Club took the lead of both Boston and Chicago, and came in victors after the most brilliant campaign known in the history of the club, the team toward the close working together as a whole in model style. New York and Philadelphia improved upon their previous season's record, but failed to reach the position in the race they had expected. Cleveland fell off badly in the race, and finally resigned its membership early in the ensuing year. The record for 1884 is as follows:

RECORD OF 1884.

	Providence.	Boston.	Buffalo.	Chicago.	New York.	Philadelphia.	Cleveland.	Detroit.	Games Played.	Games Lost.	Games Won.
Providence............	....	9	10	11	13	13	13	15	112	28	84
Boston................	7	....	9	10	8	13	14	12	111	38	73
Buffalo...............	6	6	....	10	5	11	14	12	111	47	64
Chicago...............	5	6	6	....	12	14	8	11	112	50	62
New York..............	3	8	11	4	....	11	11	14	112	50	62
Philadelphia...........	3	3	5	2	5	....	10	11	112	73	39
Cleveland.............	3	2	2	8	5	6	....	9	112	77	35
Detroit................	1	4	4	5	3	5	7	....	112	84	28
Games Lost...........	28	38	47	50	50	73	77	84		447	447

In 1885 Cleveland retired from the League, and St. Louis was elected to fill the vacancy, and again eight clubs entered the lists. In the pennant race both New York and Philadelphia improved upon their work in 1884, the former team giving the Chicago team a very close push for the goal, Philadelphia coming in a good third. The full record of the season in the championship arena is as follows:

RECORD OF 1885.

	Chicago.	New York.	Philadelphia.	Providence.	Boston.	Detroit.	Buffalo.	St. Louis.	Total Played.	Games Lost.	Won.
Chicago...............	..	6	11	11	14	15	16	14	112	25	87
New York.............	10	..	11	12	13	12	15	12	112	27	85
Philadelphia..........	5	5	..	8	9	9	11	9	110	54	56
Providence...........	5	4	7	..	9	7	13	8	110	57	53
Boston...............	2	3	7	9	..	7	10	8	112	66	46
Detroit...............	1	4	7	6	9	..	5	9	108	67	41
Buffalo...............	0	1	5	3	6	11	..	12	112	74	38
St. Louis..............	2	4	6	8	8	4	4	..	108	72	36
Lost.................	25	27	54	57	66	67	74	72		442	442

BASE BALL GUIDE.

The record showing how each series of games was won in the League championship arena in 1885, is as follows. The names are given in the order of series won and lost:

	New York.	Chicago.	Philadelphia.	Providence.	Boston.	Detroit.	Buffalo.	St. Louis.	Won.	Tied.	Unfinished.
New York..........	....	10-6	11-5	12-4	13-3	12-4	15-1	12-4	7	0	0
Chicago............	6-10	....	11-5	11-5	14-2	15-1	16-0	14-2	6	0	0
Philadelphia.......	5-11	5-11	....	8-7	9-7	9-7	11-5	9-6	4	0	2
Providence........	4-12	5-11	7-8	....	7-9	9-6	13-3	8-8	3	..	2
Boston.............	3-13	2-14	7-9	9-7	....	7-9	10-6	8-8	2	1	0
Detroit.............	4-12	1-15	7-9	6-9	9-7	....	5-11	9-4	2	0	2
Buffalo.............	1-15	0-16	5-11	3-13	6-10	11-5	....	12-4	2	0	0
St. Louis..........	4-12	2-14	6-9	8-8	8-8	4-9	4-12	....	0	3	2
Lost..............	0	1	2	3	4	5	5	5	25	4	8

"CHICAGO" GAMES.

The following is the record of "Chicago" games played in the League championship arena in 1885. The table gives the Chicago victories and defeats of each club:

	New York.	Chicago.	Philadelphia.	Boston.	Providence.	Detroit.	Buffalo.	St. Louis.	Won.
New York..........	....	2	1	1	3	2	4	3	16
Chicago............	0	....	4	1	4	2	2	1	14
Philadelphia.......	0	1	....	1	4	0	1	3	10
Boston.............	1	0	3	....	2	0	2	1	9
Providence........	0	0	1	1	....	1	4	1	8
Detroit.............	1	1	0	0	1	....	0	3	6
Buffalo.............	0	0	0	0	0	0	....	4	4
St. Louis..........	0	0	0	0	2	0	0	....	3
Lost..............	2	4	9	4	16	6	13	16	70

The summary of the play of the eight clubs in the championship arena for 1885 is as follows:

	Won.	Lost.	Played.	To Play.	Drawn.	Series Won.	Series Lost.	Series Tied.	Series Unfinishd	Per Cent. Victories.
Chicago...........	87	25	112	0	1	6	1	0	0	.776
New York.........	85	27	112	0	0	7	0	0	0	.758
Philadelphia......	56	54	110	2	1	4	2	0	2	.509
Providence.......	53	57	110	2	0	2	3	1	2	.481
Boston	46	66	112	0	1	2	4	1	0	.410
Detroit............	41	67	108	4	0	2	5	0	2	.379
Buffalo............	38	74	112	0	0	2	5	0	0	.339
St. Louis.........	36	72	108	4	3	0	5	2	2	.333
Totals.........	442	442								

EXTRA INNINGS GAMES.

The extra innings games played in the League championship arena in 1885 were as follows:

July 29, Chicago vs. Providence, at Providence (14 innings).........	3—2
Sept. 5, Detroit and St. Louis, at Detroit (13 innings).............	2—0
June 20, Providence vs. Boston, at Boston (13 innings).............	9—8
Sept. 17, New York vs. Detroit, at Detroit (13 innings).............	1—0
Sept. 8, Chicago vs. St. Louis, at St. Louis (11 innings)...........	1—1
Sept. 2, Boston vs. Providence, at Boston (11 innings).............	4—3
May 21, Buffalo vs. New York, at New York (11 innings)..........	4—3
July 6, St. Louis vs. Providence, at St. Louis (11 innings).........	5—4
June 3, New York vs. Philadelphia, at Philadelphia (11 innings)..	8—7
May 4, Detroit vs. Buffalo, at Detroit (11 innings)................	10—4
June 20, Philadelphia vs. New York, at New York (11 innings)....	11—8
July 1, Philadelphia vs. St. Louis, at St. Louis (10 innings).......	1—0
Aug. 6, New York vs. Chicago, at New York (10 innings).........	1—0
June 2, Providence vs. Boston, at Providence (10 innings)........	1—1
July 1, New York vs. Detroit, at Detroit (10 innings).............	2—1
Aug. 2, New York vs. Boston, at New York (10 innings).........	2—1
July 17, New York vs. Boston, at New York (10 innings).........	3—2
July 18, New York vs. St. Louis, at New York (10 innings).......	3—2
June 26, Philadelphia vs. Chicago, at Chicago (10 innings)........	4—3
July 6, St. Louis vs. Providence, at St. Louis (10 innings)........	5—4
July 18, Providence vs. Buffalo, at Providence (10 innings).......	5—4
July 15, New York vs. Providence, at New York (10 innings).....	7—6
Oct. 8, Detroit vs. Boston, at Detroit (10 innings)................	7—6
May 16, Philadelphia vs. Detroit, at Philadelphia (10 innings).....	8—7
July 21, New York vs. Detroit, at New York (10 innings).........	8—7
Oct. 9, Philadelphia vs. Chicago, at Chicago (10 innings)........	12—11

A FIFTEEN YEARS' RECORD.

As a matter of interesting reference we append the record of the total games played by the three leading clubs in the old National Association championship matches, and the National League, pennant races, from 1871 to 1885 inclusive:

OLD NATIONAL ASSOCIATION.

Year.	Clubs.	Won.	Lost	Year.	Clubs.	Won.	Lost.
1871.	Athletic.........	22	7	1873.	Boston.........	43	16
1871.	Boston..........	22	10	1873.	Philadelphia ..	36	17
1871.	Chicago.........	20	9	1873.	Baltimore.......	33	22
1872.	Boston..........	39	8	1874.	Boston.........	52	18
1872.	Baltimore.......	34	19	1874.	Mutual.........	42	23
1872.	Mutual..........	34	20	1874.	Athletic........	33	23

1875—Boston, 71—8; Athletic, 53—20; Hartford, 54—28.

NATIONAL LEAGUE GAMES.

Year.	Clubs.	Won.	Lost.	Year.	Clubs.	Won.	Lost.
1876.	Chicago.........	52	14	1881.	Chicago.........	56	28
1876.	Hartford........	47	21	1881.	Providence......	47	37
1876.	St. Louis	45	19	1881.	Buffalo.........	45	38

NATIONAL LEAGUE GAMES—CONTINUED.

Year.	Clubs.	Won	Lost.	Year.	Clubs.	Won.	Lost.
1877.	Boston	31	17	1882.	Chicago	55	29
1877.	Louisville	28	20	1882.	Providence	52	32
1877.	Hartford	24	24	1882.	Buffalo	45	39
1878.	Boston	41	19	1883.	Boston	63	35
1878.	Cincinnati	37	23	1883.	Chicago	59	39
1878.	Providence	33	27	1883.	Providence	58	40
1879.	Providence	55	23	1884.	Providence	84	28
1879.	Boston	49	29	1884.	Boston	73	28
1879.	Chicago	44	33	1884.	Buffalo	64	47
1880.	Chicago	67	17	1885.	Chicago	87	25
1880.	Providence	52	32	1885.	New York	85	27
1880.	Cleveland	47	37	1885.	Philadelphia	56	54

EAST VS. WEST.

THE LEAGUE RECORDS.

One of the most interesting of the records of the professional club arena during the past decade is that of the contests between the clubs of the two sections of the League, West vs. East, and a review of the contests for supremacy shows that the Eastern clubs won the honors. A correct record of the figures in these games dates only from the organization of the League, and this record began in 1876. In the ten years of playing, ending at the close of the season of 1885, the Eastern clubs took the lead in 1877, 1878, 1879, 1880, 1884 and 1885, six seasons; while the Western clubs held the lead in 1876, 1881, 1882 and 1883, four seasons. From the beginning of the season of 1876, to the ending of that of 1885 the Eastern clubs won 926 games to 853 games by the Western clubs. The record in full for the ten years is as follows:

Year.	Clubs.	Score of Victories.
1876.	West vs. East	77 to 66
1877.	East vs. West	43 to 29
1878.	East vs. West	62 to 34
1879.	East vs. West	84 to 81
1880.	East vs. West	101 to 89
1881.	West vs. East	106 to 85
1882.	West vs. East	113 to 78
1883.	West vs. East	122 to 100
1884.	East vs. West	162 to 93
1885.	East vs. West	145 to 109

The summary of the above record is as follows:

EASTERN VICTORIES.

1877	43 to 29	1880	101 to 89
1878	62 to 34	1884	162 to 93
1879	84 to 81	1885	145 to 109

Total, 597 victories for the East to 435 for the West.

WESTERN VICTORIES.

1876............................... 77 to 66		1882........................... 113 to 78
1881............................. 106 to 85		1883........................... 122 to 32

Total, 418 victories for the West to 329 for the East.

From the above record it will be seen that the Eastern clubs scored their greatest success in 1884, and the Western clubs theirs in 1882. It was a close fight in 1879 only. In regard to the season's record, the Eastern teams took the lead in six years out of ten, and the Western in four years.

THE CONTESTS EACH YEAR.

THE RECORD OF 1876.

Eight clubs entered the lists in 1876, and the West won by the score of 77 victories to the East's 66, as follows:

1876.

	Hartford	Mutual	Boston	Athletic	Won		Chicago	St. Louis	Louisville	Cincinnati	Won
Chicago...........	6	7	9	7	29	Hartford...........	4	4	9	9	26
St. Louis...........	6	6	6	8	26	Boston.............	1	4	5	10	20
Louisville.........	1	5	5	6	17	Mutual.............	1	1	3	7	12
Cincinnati.........	1	1	0	3	5	Athletic............	1	0	2	5	8
Lost..............	14	19	20	24	77	Lost...............	7	9	19	31	66

THE RECORD OF 1877.

In 1877 six clubs entered the pennant race, but only four completed their schedule of games, the Cincinnati club's games being thrown out of the count. The full record gave the East 61 victories to the West's 33, but the legal count lessened these figures to 43 for the East against 29 for the West, as will be seen by the appended table. As two Eastern clubs played against four Western teams, the victory was quite noteworthy. The record is as follows:

1877.

	St. Louis	Louisv'le	Chicago	Won		Boston	Hartford	Won
Boston............	6	8	10	24	St. Louis..........	6	4	10
Hartford..........	5	6	8	19	Louisville.........	4	6	10
					Chicago...........	2	7	9
Lost.............	11	14	18	43	Lost..............	12	17	29

BASE BALL GUIDE.

THE RECORD OF 1878.

In 1878 six clubs again entered the race and the two from the East again defeated the four from the West by 62 victories to 34, another signal mark of superiority for the Eastern teams. The record is as follows:

1878.

	Cincinnati	Chicago	Milwaukee	Indianapolis	Won		Boston	Providence	Won
Boston	6	8	11	10	35	Cincinnati	6	9	15
Providence	3	6	8	10	27	Chicago	4	6	10
						Milwaukee	1	4	5
						Indianapolis	2	2	4
Lost	9	14	19	20	62	Lost	13	21	34

THE RECORD OF 1879.

By 1879 eight clubs began to be the regular number of contestants in the League arena, and they have been kept at that number ever since. In this year the East once more went to the front, but the contest proved to be a close one, as the Eastern clubs only won the lead by 84 victories to 81, as will be seen by the appended record:

1879.

	Chicago	Buffalo	Cincinnati	Cleveland	Won		Syracuse	Providence	Boston	Troy	Won
Providence	7	6	10	8	31	Chicago	6	5	8	8	27
Boston	4	9	7	10	30	Buffalo	3	6	3	11	23
Troy	3	1	2	6	12	Cincinnati	3	2	5	9	19
Syracuse	0	3	3	5	11	Cleveland	1	4	3	5	12
Lost	14	19	22	29	84	Lost	13	17	18	33	81

THE RECORD OF 1880.

In 1880 the East for the fourth successive season bore off the palm by a record of 101 victories to 89, as follows:

1880.

	Chicago	Cleveland	Buffalo	Cincinnati	Won		Providence	Troy	Boston	Worcester	Won
Providence	3	9	10	10	32	Chicago	9	10	9	10	38
Troy	2	3	11	10	26	Cleveland	3	9	7	6	25
Boston	3	5	9	7	24	Buffalo	2	1	3	9	15
Worcester	2	6	3	8	19	Cincinnati	2	1	5	3	11
Lost	10	23	33	35	101	Lost	16	21	24	28	98

THE RECORD OF 1881.

In 1881 the West began to take the lead, they winning this year by a record of 106 victories to 85, as follows:

1881.

	Providence	Troy	Worcester	Boston	Won		Chicago	Detroit	Buffalo	Cleveland	Won
Chicago	9	8	9	10	36	Providence	3	8	5	9	25
Detroit	4	7	7	8	26	Troy	4	5	9	6	24
Buffalo	7	3	6	8	24	Worcester	3	5	5	5	18
Cleveland	3	6	7	4	20	Boston	2	4	4	8	18
Lost	23	24	29	30	106	Lost	12	22	23	28	85

THE RECORD OF 1882.

In 1882 the Western clubs made their best record of the ten years, they winning by 113 victories to 78, as follows:

	Boston	Providence	Troy	Worcester	Won		Chicago	Cleveland	Buffalo	Detroit	Won
Chicago	6	8	9	9	32	Boston	6	7	7	8	28
Cleveland	5	4	9	11	29	Providence	4	8	6	9	27
Buffalo	5	6	6	11	28	Troy	3	2	6	4	15
Detroit	4	3	8	9	24	Worcester	3	1	1	3	8
Lost	20	21	32	40	113	Lost	16	18	20	24	78

THE RECORD OF 1883.

In 1883 the West went to the front for the last time in the first decade of the League's history when they took the lead by 122 victories to 100, as follows:

BASE BALL GUIDE. 51

	Boston.	Providence.	New York.	Philadelphia.	Won.		Chicago.	Cleveland.	Buffalo.	Detroit.	Won.
Chicago...........	7	7	9	12	35	Boston............	7	10	7	10	34
Cleveland..........	4	8	7	12	31	Providence........	7	6	7	12	32
Buffalo............	7	7	8	9	31	New York.........	5	6	5	6	22
Detroit............	4	2	8	11	25	Philadelphia.......	2	2	5	3	12
Lost..............	22	24	32	44	122	Lost.............	21	24	24	31	100

THE RECORD OF 1884.

In 1884 the Eastern Clubs again resumed their old time lead, and they claim that they went to the front to stay. In this year the East won by 162 victories to 93, then the best record, as follows:

	Chicago.	Buffalo.	Cleveland.	Detroit.	Won.		Providence.	Boston.	New York.	Philadelphia.	Won.
Providence........	11	10	13	15	49	Chicago...........	5	5	13	14	37
Boston............	10	9	14	12	45	Buffalo...........	6	6	5	11	28
New York.........	4	11	11	14	40	Cleveland.........	3	2	5	6	16
Philadelphia.......	2	5	10	11	28	Detroit...........	1	4	2	5	12
Lost..............	27	35	48	52	162	Lost.............	15	18	24	36	93

THE RECORD OF 1885.

In 1885 the East again took the lead, this time by 145 victories to 109, as follows:

	Chicago.	Detroit.	St. Louis.	Buffalo.	Won.		New York.	Providence.	Philadelphia.	Boston.	Won.
New York.........	10	12	12	15	49	Chicago...........	6	11	11	14	42
Providence........	5	9	8	13	35	Detroit...........	4	6	7	9	26
Philadelphia.......	5	9	9	11	34	St. Louis..........	4	8	6	8	26
Boston............	2	7	8	10	27	Buffalo...........	1	3	5	6	15
Lost..............	22	37	37	49	145	Lost.............	15	28	29	37	109

The clubs which led in their respective sections each season were as follows: Chicago and Hartford in 1876; Boston and

St. Louis in 1877; Boston and Cincinnati in 1878; Providence and Chicago in 1879 and also in 1880 and 1881; Chicago and Boston in 1882 and 1883; Providence and Chicago in 1884; and New York and Chicago in 1885. By the above it will be seen that Chicago has occupied first or second place in the League race eight times during the ten years' existence of the League, while she has won the League pennant five times, Boston three times and Providence twice.

HOME AND HOME RECORD OF 1885.

The record of the home and home games played by the Eastern and Western clubs in the League championship arena in 1885 is as follows:

	New York.	Philadelphia.	Boston.	Providence.	Won.		Chicago.	Buffalo.	Detroit.	St. Louis.	Won.
New York..........		11	13	12	36	Chicago...........		16	15	14	45
Philadelphia.......	5		8	9	22	Buffalo...........	0		11	12	23
Boston.............	3	7		9	19	Detroit...........	1	5		9	15
Providence........	4	7	7		18	St. Louis.........	2	4	4		6
Lost..............	12	25	29	29	95	Lost.............	3	25	30	35	93

It will be seen that the Chicagos and New Yorks lead in their respective sections.

THE AMERICAN CAMPAIGN OF 1885.

The American Association clubs began play for the season early in March, they wisely beginning practice down South with Southern clubs, thereby insuring better weather for the sport at an earlier period of the season than is possible in the North or West. The Louisville club was the first to get to work in the field, they opening play in a series of matches at Atlanta, which began on March 12, when the Southern nine troubled the visitors to beat them by 10 to 9. The first game of the regular Spring exhibition series was played on April 1, at Washington, when the new Brooklyn nine encountered the Nationals and could only make a drawn game at 3 to 3. The Metropolitans opened at the polo grounds on April 2 in a game with the Yale College nine, which the professionals won by 5 to 2 only. The same day the Baltimores opened play in a game at Baltimore with the Brown University nine, which the professionals won by 10 to 3. On April 4 the Athletics took the field for the first time in a game with the Yale nine at Philadelphia, the collegians being defeated by 8 to 6 only. The same day the St. Louis team began play for the season in a game with the visiting Milwaukee team, the home club winning by 4 to 2. On April 5 the Pittsburg and Cincinnati teams foolishly played an exhibition game together at Cincinnati, and the latter were deservedly beaten by 9 to 8 for their pains.

The championship season opened on April 18, when the Metropolitans visited Philadelphia and the St. Louis team went to Pittsburg, the Athletics taking the "champions" into camp by 13 to 2, and Pittsburg "Chicagoing" the St. Louis team by 7 to 0. On the 19th of April the Louisville team visited Cincinnati where they were whipped by 4 to 1. On April 20 the Brooklyn team opened their championship season at Baltimore, they defeating the home team by 7 to 3. Thus was the season of 1885 inaugurated in the championship arena. Below we give the

MONTHLY RECORDS

of the championship campaign which were last year a specialty of the GUIDE.

The first week's play in the championship arena saw the Cincinnati club in the van, with the Baltimore and St. Louis clubs second and third. By the close of the month the St. Louis club had secured a lead in the pennant race, Brooklyn standing second and Cincinnati third, while the champions were a tie with Louisville for last place. The record for April shows the eight clubs occupying the following relative positions at the end of the opening month's play:

APRIL RECORD.

	St. Louis.	Brooklyn.	Cincinnati.	Athletic.	Baltimore.	Pittsburg.	Louisville.	Metropolitan.	Won.
St. Louis	....	0	3	0	0	2	1	0	6
Brooklyn	0	....	0	2	3	0	0	0	5
Cincinnati	1	0	....	0	0	1	3	0	5
Athletic	0	1	0	....	0	0	0	4	5
Baltimore	0	2	0	0	....	0	0	2	4
Pittsburg	1	0	1	0	0	....	2	0	4
Louisville	1	0	0	0	0	2	....	0	3
Metropolitan	0	0	0	2	1	0	0	....	3
Lost	3	3	4	4	4	5	6	6	35

In May the Western teams began to show themselves stronger than the Eastern, and the St. Louis team already began to occupy a prominent position as the leading club of the Association. Of the four Eastern teams Baltimore held the most advantageous position at the end of the month, the Brooklyn team, from which so much had been expected, doing but little effective team work together, while the champion

Metropolitans were quite weak, as also were the Athletics. At the end of the month the St. Louis club had secured a capital lead, their team losing but two games out of the eighteen won and lost in May, Pittsburg standing second, and Cincinnati third, while the Athletics were the last on the month's record, the figures for the games played in May showing the eight clubs occupying the following relative positions:

MAY RECORD.

	St. Louis.	Pittsburg.	Cincinnati.	Louisville.	Baltimore.	Brooklyn.	Metropolitan.	Athletic.	Won.
St. Louis...........	....	0	0	1	4	3	4	4	16
Pittsburg...........	1	....	1	0	4	3	3	3	15
Cincinnati..........	0	2	....	0	2	4	3	3	14
Louisville..........	1	0	1	....	2	2	3	4	13
Baltimore..........	0	0	2	2	....	0	2	1	7
Brooklyn...........	0	1	0	4	0	....	0	1	6
Metropolitan.......	0	3	1	1	0	1	....	0	6
Athletic............	0	1	3	0	0	1	0	....	5
Lost...............	2	7	8	8	12	14	15	16	82

During June the visit of the Western clubs to the East enabled the Eastern clubs to rally a little, and accordingly we find the Athletics prominent in recovering from their poor campaign work in May, they winning fourteen of their twenty-one games of June, the St. Louis team for the first time having to be content with second place in the month's record, Baltimore holding third, while the champion Metropolitans were forced down to last position. The record at the end of June left the eight clubs occupying the following relative positions in the month's record:

JUNE RECORD.

	Athletic.	St. Louis.	Baltimore.	Cincinnati.	Pittsburg.	Brooklyn.	Louisville.	Metropolitan.	Won.
Athletic...........	....	2	3	2	3	0	3	1	14
St. Louis..........	2	....	2	2	3	2	0	2	13
Baltimore.........	1	1	....	2	2	1	3	1	11
Cincinnati.........	0	1	2	....	0	2	1	4	10
Pittsburg..........	1	1	2	1	....	3	2	0	10
Brooklyn..........	2	2	0	2	1	....	1	2	10
Louisville.........	1	1	1	2	1	1	....	2	9
Metropolitan......	0	2	1	0	1	2	2	....	8
Lost..............	7	10	11	11	11	11	12	12	85

BASE BALL GUIDE.

In July the Western clubs resumed their leading positions, they winning sixty of the month's games to twenty-seven by the four Eastern clubs, the Metropolitans this month losing fifteen out of twenty games played, while the Brooklyn record was nearly as bad. At the end of the month St. Louis led the month's record, with Louisville a close second, and Pittsburg third, the Mets. again being at the tail end. The full record of the July games is appended:

JULY RECORD.

	St. Louis.	Louisville.	Pittsburg.	Cincinnati.	Athletic.	Baltimore.	Brooklyn.	Metropolitan.	Won.
St. Louis	....	0	1	0	3	5	4	3	16
Louisville	2	....	0	3	2	4	2	3	16
Pittsburg	1	1	....	2	1	3	4	2	14
Cincinnati	0	0	0	....	4	2	3	3	12
Athletic	1	2	3	0	....	2	1	0	9
Baltimore	0	0	1	2	1	....	1	2	7
Brooklyn	0	2	0	1	1	0	....	2	6
Metropolitan	1	1	1	1	1	0	0	....	5
Lost	5	6	6	9	13	16	15	15	85

In August the Brooklyn club took a turn in the rallying business, and after a partial re-organization of the club team they won fourteen out of nineteen games, it being their best month's record of the season. In this month's work St. Louis had to stand second to Brooklyn, while the Cincinnatis held third position, Baltimore having fallen back to last place, the August figures leaving the eight clubs occupying the appended relative positions:

AUGUST RECORD.

	Brooklyn.	St. Louis.	Cincinnati.	Athletic.	Pittsburg.	Metropolitan.	Louisville.	Baltimore.	Won.
Brooklyn	....	0	0	5	0	3	0	6	14
St. Louis	0	....	5	0	4	0	4	0	13
Cincinnati	0	4	....	0	4	0	4	0	12
Athletic	1	0	0	....	0	6	0	2	9
Pittsburg	0	2	1	0	....	0	5	0	8
Metropolitan	1	0	0	0	2	....	0	4	7
Louisville	0	2	2	0	3	0	....	0	7
Baltimore	3	0	0	2	0	0	0	....	5
Lost	5	8	8	9	11	9	13	12	75

September saw the Metropolitans make an effective rally to escape the rear position which they had occupied nearly every month of the season thus far. Out of twenty-one games in September they won fourteen, this being their best month's record. For the month they stood second to St. Louis, while the Athletics occupied third place, they, too, having pulled up well in the race in September, three of the Western teams falling off badly this month, notably the Pittsburg team, which lost fourteen out of nineteen games this month. The record at the end of the month left the eight clubs standing as follows;

SEPTEMBER RECORD.

	St. Louis	Metropolitan	Athletic	Brooklyn	Cincinnati	Baltimore	Louisville	Pittsburg.	Won.
St. Louis....................		3	3	3	0	3	3	0	15
Metropolitan................	1		0	4	3	0	3	3	14
Athletic......................	1	0		0	2	3	3	2	11
Brooklyn.....................	1	1	0		2	0	3	4	11
Cincinnati...................	0	0	2	2		4	0	2	10
Baltimore....................	1	0	1	0	0		1	3	6
Louisville....................	0	2	1	0	1	1		0	5
Pittsburg.....................	0	1	1	1	0	2	0		5
Lost.........................	4	7	8	10	8	13	13	14	77

Only six games were played in October, of these the Athletics won two, they defeating the Pittsburg and Brooklyn teams, the Baltimores winning one from Louisville, the Brooklyns one from St. Louis, and the Metropolitans one from Cincinnati.

The summary of each month's victories by the eight clubs is appended, the totals showing the number of games played each month of the championship campaign, as also the whole number of victories scored by each club.

FULL MONTHLY RECORD.
SUMMARY OF VICTORIES.

	Apr.	May.	June.	July.	Aug.	Sept.	Oct.	Total.
St. Louis.....................	6	16	13	16	13	15	0	79
Cincinnati....................	5	14	10	12	12	10	0	63
Pittsburg.....................	4	15	10	14	8	5	0	56
Athletic......................	5	5	14	9	9	11	2	55
Brooklyn.....................	5	6	10	6	14	11	1	53
Louisville....................	3	13	9	16	7	5	0	53
Metropolitan.................	3	6	8	5	7	14	1	44
Baltimore....................	4	7	11	7	5	6	1	41
Totals.....................	35	82	85	85	75	77	5	444

SUMMARY OF DEFEATS.

	April.	May.	June.	July.	August.	September.	October.	Total.
St. Louis	3	2	10	5	8	4	1	33
Cincinnati	4	8	11	9	8	8	1	49
Pittsburg	5	7	11	6	11	14	1	55
Athletic	4	16	7	13	9	8	0	57
Brooklyn	3	14	11	15	5	10	1	59
Louisville	6	8	12	6	13	13	1	59
Metropolitan	6	15	12	15	9	7	0	64
Baltimore	4	12	11	16	12	13	0	68
Totals	35	82	85	85	75	77	5	444

EAST AND WEST.

The annual contests between the Eastern and Western clubs of the American Association have only been in progress four years and in that time the Western teams have borne off the palm each season.

In the inaugural season of the American Association in 1882, the Western clubs took the lead over those of the Eastern section by a record of eighty-six victories for the West to fifty-eight for the East. This was with six clubs in the campaign of that year. In 1883 the West improved upon this record by scoring 186 victories to only 96 by the East. Then they had eight clubs in the arena. In 1884 with twelve clubs the West took the lead by a record of 200 victories to 150 by the Eastern clubs. In 1885, with eight clubs, the West led the East by 155 victories to 100 by the Eastern clubs. This gives a total of 627 victories for the West against 404 for the East in four campaigns from 1882 to 1885 inclusive. The records for the four years are appended:

RECORD OF 1882.

WESTERN CLUB VICTORIES.	Athletic.	Allegheny.	Baltimore.	Games Won.	EASTERN CLUB VICTORIES.	Cincinnati.	Louisville.	St. Louis.	Games Won.
Cincinnati	10	10	14	34	Athletic	6	11	11	28
Louisville	5	10	13	28	Allegheny	6	6	10	22
St. Louis	5	6	13	24	Baltimore	2	3	3	8
Games Lost	20	26	40	86	Games Lost	14	20	24	58

RECORD OF 1883.

WESTERN CLUB VICTORIES	Athletic.	Metropolitan.	Baltimore.	Allegheny.	Games won.	EASTERN CLUB VICTORIES	St. Louis.	Louisville.	Cincinnati.	Columbus.	Games won.
St. Louis....	5	11	12	12	40	Athletic....	9	7	5	13	34
Louisville....	9	4	11	8	33	Metropolitan.	3	6	10	11	30
Cincinnati....	7	7	8	11	32	Baltimore....	2	6	3	6	17
Columbus....	1	3	7	10	21	Allegheny...	2	3	6	4	15
Games lost...	22	25	38	41	186	Games lost...	16	22	24	34	96

RECORD OF 1884.

	Metropolitan.	Baltimore.	Athletic.	Brooklyn.	Allegheny.	Virginia.	Games won.		St. Louis.	Cincinnati.	Columbus.	Louisville.	Toledo.	Indianapolis.	Games Won.
St. Louis.....	4	5	7	7	9	8	40	Metropolitan.	5	6	5	7	5	8	36
Cincinnati...	4	6	4	8	8	10	40	Baltimore....	5	6	6	6	5	9	35
Columbus....	4	4	5	7	9	7	36	Athletic......	3	6	5	3	6	6	29
Louisville....	3	4	6	6	7	8	34	Brooklyn.....	3	2	3	3	4	7	22
Toledo......	4	5	3	5	5	9	31	Allegheny·..	1	1	1	2	5	6	16
Indianapolis..	2	1	4	3	4	5	19	Virginia.....	2	0	3	2	1	4	12
Games Lost	21	25	29	36	42	47	200	Games Lost..	19	19	23	23	26	40	150

RECORD OF 1885.

	Athletic.	Metropolitan.	Brooklyn.	Baltimore.	Won.		St. Louis.	Cincinnati.	Pittsburg.	Louisville.	Won.
St. Louis..............	12	12	12	14	50	Athletic...............	4	7	10	8	29
Cincinnati............	9	10	11	10	40	Metropolitan.........	4	6	8	7	25
Pittsburg............	6	7	10	10	33	Brooklyn...........	4	5	6	10	25
Louisville	8	9	6	9	32	Baltimore.............	2	6	6	7	21
Lost	35	38	39	43	155	Lost..............	14	24	30	32	100

THE HOME AND HOME GAMES.

The record of the games played—victories and defeats—between the clubs of the West together, and those in the East on each others' grounds, for the season of 1885 is as follows:

BASE BALL GUIDE.

	St. Louis.	Cincinnati.	Pittsburg.	Louisville.	Won.		Brooklyn.	Athletic.	Baltimore.	Metropolitan.	Won.
St. Louis........	..	10	10	9	29	Brooklyn........	..	11	9	8	28
Cincinnati.......	6	..	9	8	23	Athletic	5	..	10	11	26
Pittsburg........	6	7	..	10	23	Baltimore........	7	6	..	7	20
Louisville.......	7	8	6	..	21	Metropolitan....	8	5	6	..	19
Lost...........	19	25	25	27	96	Lost...........	20	22	25	26	93

It will be seen that St. Louis leads in the West, and Brooklyn in the East.

The American championship records for the past four years of the history of the organization are appended as a matter of necessary reference:

RECORD OF 1882.

	Cincinnati.	Athletic.	Eclipse.	Allegheny.	St. Louis.	Baltimore.	Won.	Lost.	Played.	Per Cent. of Victories.
Cincinnati.......	..	10	11	10	10	14	55	25	80	.68
Athletic.........	6	..	11	6	11	7	41	34	75	.54
Eclipse	5	5	..	10	9	13	42	38	80	.52
Allegheny.......	6	10	6	..	10	7	39	39	79	.50
St. Louis........	6	5	7	6	..	13	37	43	80	.46
Baltimore.......	2	4	3	7	3	..	19	54	74	.26

RECORD OF 1883.

	Athletic.	St. Louis.	Cincinnati.	Metropolitan.	Louisville.	Columbus.	Allegheny.	Baltimore.	Games Won.	Games Lost.	Games Play'd	Per cent. of Victories.
Athletic.........	..	9	5	9	7	13	12	11	66	32	98	.67
St. Louis........	5	..	6	11	8	11	12	12	65	33	98	.66
Cincinnati.......	9	8	..	4	10	11	9	11	62	36	98	.64
Metropolitan....	5	3	10	..	6	11	9	10	54	42	98	.56
Louisville.......	7	6	4	7	..	9	11	8	52	45	97	.53
Columbus.......	1	3	3	3	5	..	10	7	32	65	97	.33
Allegheny.......	2	2	5	5	3	4	..	9	30	68	98	.30
Baltimore.......	3	2	3	3	0	6	5	..	28	68	96	.29

RECORD OF 1884.

	Metropolitan	Columbus	Louisville	St. Louis	Cincinnati	Baltimore	Athletic	Toledo	Brooklyn	Virginia	Pittsburg	Indianapolis	Washington	Games Won	Games Lost	Games Played	Per cent of Victories
Metropolitan		5	7	5	6	5	8	8	9	2	9	8	6	75	32	107	.700
Columbus	4		5	5	7	4	5	5	7	2	9	8	5	69	39	108	.638
Louisville	3	5		5	5	4	6	9	6	4	8	9	4	68	40	108	.629
St. Louis	4	5	5		6	6	5	7	5	7	3	9	6	67	40	107	.626
Cincinnati	4	3	5	4			4	7	8	4	8	9	6	68	41	109	.623
Baltimore	5	6	6	5	4		3	5	5	5	9	9	2	63	43	106	.594
Athletic	2	5	3	3	6	7		6	6	2	8	6	7	61	47	108	.564
Toledo	4	1	1	5	3	5	3		4	4	5	6	5	46	58	104	.442
Brooklyn	1	3	3	2	5	3	3	4			3	4	7	3	40	64	104	.384
Virginia	0	2	1	1	0	0	0	0	2		4	2	0	12	30	42	.285
Pittsburg	1	1	2	1	1	0	2	5	6	1		6	4	30	78	108	.277
Indianapolis	2	2	1	3	1	1	4	3	3	1	4		4	29	78	107	.271
Washington	2	1	1	1	0	1	1	1	1	0	1	2		12	51	63	.190

RECORD OF 1885.

	St. Louis	Cincinnati	Pittsburg	Athletic	Brooklyn	Louisville	Metropolitan	Baltimore	Games Won	Games Lost	Games Played	Per cent of Victories
St. Louis		10	10	12	12	9	12	14	79	33	112	.705
Cincinnati	6		9	9	11	8	10	10	63	49	112	.562
Pittsburg	6	7		6	10	10	7	10	56	55	111	.504
Athletic	4	7	10		5	8	11	10	55	57	112	.491
Brooklyn	4	5	6	11		10	8	9	53	59	112	.473
Louisville	7	8	6	8	6		9	9	53	59	112	.473
Metropolitan	4	6	8	5	8	7		6	44	64	108	.407
Baltimore	2	6	6	6	7	7	7		41	68	109	.376

THE LEADING BATSMEN OF 1885.

Selecting nine players from the list contained in the official averages of the four professional associations which were most prominent in 1885, and choosing those only who played in more than twenty-five games in each association, we give them in their order of precedence, according to average, on the following pages.

BASE BALL GUIDE.

NATIONAL LEAGUE.

PLAYERS.	CLUBS.	No. Games.	Percentage.
O'Connor	New York	110	.371
Brouthers	Buffalo	98	.358
M. Dorgan	New York	88	.325
H. Richardson	New York	96	.319
Gore	Chicago	109	.312
Sutton	Boston	108	.312
Anson	Chicago	112	.310
Ferguson	Philadelphia	59	.306
Ewing	New York	81	.304

AMERICAN ASSOCIATION.

PLAYERS.	CLUBS.	No. Games.	Percentage.
Browning	Louisville	113	.367
Orr	Metropolitan	107	.366
Stovey	Athletic	112	.342
O'Neil	St. Louis	51	.342
Larkin	Athletic	108	.338
Jones	Cincinnati	112	.327
Coleman	Athletic	97	.309
Reilly	Cincinnati	106	.308
Brown	Pittsburg	108	.304

EASTERN LEAGUE.

PLAYERS.	CLUBS.	No. Games.	Percentage.
Casey	Newark	27	.391
Derby	Norfolk	48	.380
Johnston	Virginia	72	.340
Morrissey	National	31	.324
Henry	Norfolk	28	.323
Burch	National	56	.323
McTamany	Lancaster	67	.310
Jones	Newark	85	.306
Knowles	National	95	.303

SOUTHERN LEAGUE.

PLAYERS.	CLUBS.	No. Games.	Per centage.
Veach	Macon	44	.310
Sowders	Nashville	100	.309
Goldsby	Atlanta	93	.305
Beard	Nashville	66	.297
Cahill	Atlanta	90	.295
J. Dorgan	Columbus	28	.293
McVey	Atlanta	84	.290
Sullivan	Memphis	28	.286
H. Kappel	Augusta	39	.283

THE LEADING FIELDERS OF 1885.

Only those players' names are included who played in a majority of these club games.

NATIONAL LEAGUE.

POSITIONS.	PLAYERS.	CLUBS.	Games Played.	Per centage Accepted.
Catcher	Bennett	Detroit	63	.885
First base	McKinnon	St. Louis	100	.978
Second base	Dunlap	St. Louis	106	.933
Third base	Williamson	Chicago	111	.891
Short stop	Glasscock	St. Louis	109	.917
Left-field	Gillespie	New York	102	.941
Center-field	Lewis	St. Louis	45	.957
Right-field	Shaffer	St. Louis	69	.917

AMERICAN ASSOCIATION.

POSITIONS.	PLAYERS.	CLUBS.	Games Played.	Per centage Accepted.
Catcher	Milligan	Athletic	61	.936
First base	Scott	Pittsburg	55	.984
Second base	Barkley	St. Louis	97	.941
Third base	Hankinson	Metropolitan	95	.912
Short-stop	Whitney	Pittsburg	79	.943
Left-field	Sommer	Baltimore	107	.919
Center-field	Welch	St. Louis	112	.959
Right-field	Corkhill	Cincinnati	106	.935

EASTERN LEAGUE.

POSITIONS.	PLAYERS.	CLUBS.	Games Played.	Per centage Accepted.
Catcher	Cook	National	34	.927
First base	Baker	National	89	.970
Second base	Higgins	Virginia	85	.930
Third base	Nash	Virginia	73	.889
Short-stop	L. Smith	Newark	94	.893
Left-field	Burch	National	55	.927
Center field	McTamany	Lancaster	67	.904
Right-field	Brouthers	Trenton	45	.902

SOUTHERN LEAGUE.

POSITIONS.	PLAYERS.	CLUBS.	Games Played.	Per centage Accepted.
Catcher	Gillen	Macon	31	.972
First base	Andrews	Columbus	84	.960
Second base	Mack	Macon	89	.930
Third base	McSorley	Memphis	39	.894
Short-stop	Miller	Columbus	40	.917
Left-field	Zell	Macon	84	.927
Center-field	Deistel	National	60	.973
Right-field	Peltz	Macon	75	.884

LEAGUE VS. AMERICAN.

The American Association clubs of 1885 showed the marked improvement they had made in the strength of their teams by the increased number of victories they achieved over League clubs during the exhibition series of games in April and October, though it by no means shows the relative strength of the two associations, as the League players do not enter into their exhibition games with the same spirit and determination that characterizes their younger opponents, and furthermore nearly all these games are played on American Association grounds, with Association umpires.

LEAGUE CLUB VICTORIES.

April 2, Chicago vs. Louisville, at Louisville........................ 11—9
" 6, New York vs. Metropolitan, at New York .... 8—2
" 6, Detroit vs. Pittsburg, at Pittsburg (10 innings)........... 1—0

April	8, Chicago vs. Cincinnati, at Cincinnati	6—1
"	9, New York vs. Metropolitan, at New York	6—0
"	10, New York vs. Metropolitan, at New York	9—4
"	10, Buffalo vs. Baltimore, at Baltimore	8—3
"	13, Philadelphia vs. Athletic, at Philadelphia	3—2
"	13, Boston vs. Metropolitan, at New York	9—6
"	13, St. Louis vs. St. Louis, at St. Louis	6—4
"	14, Boston vs. Metropolitan, at New York	7—1
"	15, Philadelphia vs. Athletic, at Philadelphia	7—5
"	16, Buffalo vs. Pittsburg, at Pittsburg	1—0
"	18, Boston vs. Baltimore, at Baltimore	7—3
Oct.	15, Chicago vs. St. Louis, at St. Louis	5—4
"	15, Providence vs. Brooklyn, at Brooklyn	4—2
"	15, New York vs. Cincinnati, at Cincinnati	7—4
"	16, Boston vs. Brooklyn, at Brooklyn	5—3
"	16, Philadelphia vs. Athletic, at Philadelphia	17—2
"	16, Detroit vs. Cincinnati, at Cincinnati	8—4
"	17, " " " at "	2—1
"	19, Philadelphia vs. Athletic, at Philadelphia	6—3
"	19, New York vs. Metropolitan, at New York	5—3
"	20, New York vs. Brooklyn, at Brooklyn	4—2
"	20, Philadelphia vs. Athletic, at Philadelphia	9—4
"	22, Chicago vs. St. Louis, at Pittsburg	9—2
"	23, New York vs. Metropolitan, at New York	6—5
"	23, Chicago vs. St. Louis, at Cincinnati	9—2

AMERICAN CLUB VICTORIES.

April	6, Baltimore vs. Buffalo, at Baltimore	7—4
"	7, Athletic vs. Philadelphia, at Philadelphia	2—1
"	9, Cincinnati vs. Chicago, at Cincinnati	4—3
"	9, Baltimore vs. Philadelphia, at Baltimore	8—6
"	10, Athletic vs. Philadelphia, at Philadelphia	8—4
"	10, Louisville vs. Detroit, at Louisville	3—0
"	11, St. Louis vs. St. Louis, at St. Louis	7—0
"	11, Louisville vs. Detroit, at Louisville	8—5
"	13, Baltimore vs. Providence, at Baltimore	7—1
"	14, Pittsburg vs. Buffalo, at Pittsburg	4—2
"	15, Baltimore vs. Providence, at Baltimore	5—1
"	16, Athletic vs. Philadelphia, at Philadelphia	8—3
"	16, St. Louis vs. St. Louis, at St. Louis	8—0
"	16, Baltimore vs. Boston, at Baltimore	6—3
"	17, " " " at "	9—7
"	17, Athletic vs. Philadelphia, at Philadelphia	6—4
Oct.	14, Brooklyn vs. Boston, at Brooklyn	5—4
"	14, Cincinnati vs. New York, at Cincinnati	6—4
"	15, Metropolitan vs. Boston, at New York	5—0
"	15, Athletic vs. Philadelphia, at Philadelphia	7—2
"	16, St. Louis vs. Chicago, at St. Louis	7—4
"	17, " " " at "	3—2
"	17, Athletic vs. Philadelphia, at Philadelphia	7—1
"	17, Brooklyn vs. Providence, at Brooklyn	12—4
"	19, St. Louis vs. St. Louis, at St. Louis	5—2
"	20, Cincinnati vs. Chicago, at Cincinnati	6—5
"	24, St. Louis vs. Chicago, at Cincinnati	13—4
"	25, St. Louis vs. St. Louis, at St. Louis	6—0
Nov.	1, " " " at "	6—0

By the above record it will be seen that the American clubs scored 29 victories over League clubs, to the League's 28 over American clubs. The drawn games were as follows:

BASE BALL GUIDE.   65

DRAWN GAMES.

April 3, *Buffalo* vs. Baltimore, at Baltimore (10 innings)............ 3—3
 "   9, *Detroit* vs. Louisville, at Louisville....................... 3—3
Oct. 13, *St. Louis* vs. Louisville, at Louisville................... 1—1
 "   14, St. Louis vs. *Chicago*, at Chicago......................... 5—5
 "   24, *New York* vs. Brooklyn, at Brooklyn....................... —33

EASTERN LEAGUE VICTORIES.

The victories scored by Eastern League clubs in 1885 over clubs of the National League and the American Association were as follows:

VICTORIES OVER LEAGUE CLUBS.

April 4, Virginia vs. Providence, at Richmond.................... 4—0
 "   6,   "   "   "   at   "   .... 11—5
 "   16, National vs.   "   at Washington (14 innings)...... 3—2
 "   17,   "   vs. Buffalo, at Washington................... 5—3
 "   18,   "   vs.   "   at   "   .... 6—5
 "   20,   "   vs. Boston, at   "   .... 7—3
 "   22,   "   vs. Buffalo, at   "   .... 7—4
 "   23,   "   vs. New York, at "   .... 8—6
 "   27, Newark vs. Philadelphia, at Newark.................... 3—0
 "   30, Jersey City vs. Boston, at Jersey City................ 4—3
Oct. 16, Newark vs. Providence, at Newark..................... 1—0
 "   16, National vs. New York, at Washington................. 2—1
 "   17,   "   "   "   at   "   .... 2—1

VICTORIES OVER AMERICAN CLUBS.

April 3, National vs. Brooklyn, at Washington.................. 3—6
 "   4,   "   vs.   "   at   "   .... 15—0
 "   9, Virginia vs.   "   at Richmond................. 5—4
 "   21, National vs. Metropolitan, at Washington............. 12—1
 "   21, Newark vs. Athletic, at Newark....................... 12—8
May   6, National vs. Metropolitan, at Washington............. 7—3
 "   28,   "   vs. Baltimore, at   "   .... 3—2
Sept. 21, Trenton vs. Metropolitan, at Jersey City............. 8—6
 "   25, National vs. Louisville, at Washington............... 5—3
Oct.   2,   "   vs.   "   at   "   .... 10—4
 "   2, Newark vs. Baltimore, at Newark..................... 5—1
 "   3,   "   vs.   "   at   "   .... 4—0
 "   7,   "   vs. Athletic, at   "   .... 3—1
 "   9, National vs. Baltimore, at Washington............... 3—1
 "   10,   "   vs.   "   at   "   .... 2—0
 "   12,   "   vs.   "   at   "   .... 8—0
 "   14, Newark vs. Metropolitan, at Newark.................. 4—3
 "   15, National vs. Baltimore, at Washington............... 6—2
 "   17, Newark vs. Metropolitan, at New York................ 6—1
 "   22, National vs. Baltimore, at Norfolk.................. 15—10

DRAWN GAME.

April 27, New York vs. National, at Washington.................. 1—1

THE LEADING GAMES OF 1885.

The closing games of the championship series between the Chicago and New York clubs, which took place in Chicago on Sept. 29 and 30, and Oct. 1 and 3, proved to be exceptional contests in the excitement which characterized the meetings, the important issue of the games, and in the vast crowd of spectators which marked the series of games. The day before the first game the record of the two clubs in victories and defeats stood as follows: Chicago, victories 83, defeats 21; New York, victories 81, defeats 23, the latter club having to win three out of the last four games with their strongest adversaries, in order to tie the score in the pennant race. As Chicago had only won three out of twelve games played with the New York club up to the date of the first game of the last series, the New York club fully expected to tie their rival's score before the finish of the season. To their painful surprise, however, they lost the first three games of the series, and nearly lost the fourth, Chicago thereby winning the pennant. The score of those four games giving the aggregate figures, is appended:

CHICAGO.	Pos.	R.	1B.	P.O.	A.	E.	NEW YORK.	Pos.	R.	1B.	P.O.	A.	E.
Dalrymple	L F	3	7	12	0	0	O'Rourke	C F	5	5	3	0	1
Gore	C F	4	4	9	2	1	Connor	1 B	4	6	32	3	3
Kelly	C & R F	5	7	16	2	11	Ewing	C	2	3	24	5	6
							Gillespie	L F	1	3	7	1	0
Anson	1 B	1	1	33	3	4	Dorgan	R F	1	0	5	0	0
Pfeffer	2 B	4	4	12	16	3	Richardson	3 B	0	1	3	4	1
Williamson	3 B	2	1	4	2	3	Welch	P	1	2	2	7	8
Burns	S S	4	5	7	7	3	Gerhardt	2 B	2	2	11	12	5
McCormick	P	1	3	1	6	6	Ward	S S	1	1	11	7	1
Sunday	R F	1	1	1	0	0	Keefe	P	1	1	1	12	4
Clarkson	P	0	1	1	21	6	Esterbrook	3 B	0	0	0	0	0
Flint	C	0	0	6	2	7							
Totals		25	34	102	61	39	Totals		18	24	99	51	29

Chicago............ 6 6 2 3 2 0 1 0 5—25.
New York.......... 2 0 3 1 2 7 0 2 1—18.

Earned runs off McCormick, 2; off Clarkson, 4; off Keefe, 6; off Welch, 8. Struck out " " 3; " " 11; " " 10; " " 5. Bases on balls " " 6; " " 6; " " 4; " " 6. Passed balls by Kelly, 6; by Flint, 1; by Ewing, 6; Wild pitches by Welch, 1. Batting errors—Chicago, 16; New York, 17. Fielding errors—Chicago, 22; New York, 11.

THE UNITED STATES CHAMPIONSHIP.

The National League and the American Association both entitle their championship contests each season as those for the base ball championship of the United States. But no such championship can be settled until the championship clubs of each association enter the lists under a special code of rules adopted for the purpose, and with a schedule of regular games designed to settle the question permanently. A series of contests between the Providence champions of 1884 and the Metropolitan champions of that year took place in New York at the close of the regular season of 1884, in which the Providence team came off victors. A series of exhibition matches were played in 1885 between the National League champions of Chicago and the St. Louis champions of the American Association, but the result was very unsatisfactory to all parties concerned. The record of the Chicago and St. Louis games in 1885 is as follows:

Oct. 14, St. Louis vs. Chicago, at Chicago (8 innings)............... 5—5
" 15, Chicago vs. St. Louis, at St. Louis (6 innings) forfeited.... 5—4
" 16, St. Louis vs. Chicago, at St. Louis....................... 7—4
" 17, " vs. " at " .... 3—2
" 22, Chicago vs. St. Louis, at Pittsburg (7 innings)............. 9—2
" 23, " vs. " at Cincinnati...................... 9—2
" 24, St. Louis vs. Chicago, at " .... 13—4

Total victories for Chicago, 3; for St. Louis, 3, with one game drawn. Total runs scored by Chicago, 43; by St. Louis, 41.

In the contest of Oct. 15 at St. Louis, the umpire awarded the game to Chicago in the sixth innings by 9 to 0, and this award was concurred in by the St. Louis club. When the match was arranged Messrs. Spalding and Von der Ahe placed in the hands of the editor of *The Mirror of American Sports* a written document to the effect that the sum of $1,000 was to be paid to the club winning the series. As the record showed the contest to be a tie, by the written direction of Messrs. Spalding and Von der Ahe, the sums of $500 each were on the 28th day of last October paid to the Chicago and St. Louis clubs. Had the series stood three to two, St. Louis would have received $600 and Chicago $400 instead of $500 each. It may be well to add that there was not on either side the slightest dispute or difference of claim as to the equal division of the $1,000 on the basis of a tie. All bets go with the main stake, and every person whose money has been paid away on the basis of St. Louis winning the majority of the series, is entitled to demand the refunding of his money.

THE EASTERN LEAGUE.

The Eastern League began the season of 1885 with eight clubs, representing Washington, Richmond, Wilmington, Norfolk, Newark, Trenton, Lancaster and Jersey City. The Wilmington club retired in June, the Atlantic City team taking its place by transfer. Then the Jersey City team disbanded in July when the Trentons were transferred to that city, the Atlantic City team disbanding the same month. In August the Lancaster team retired, and the Bridgeports left their own league and entered in the place of the Lancasters. Then the Norfolk club retired and the Waterburys came in in September, and the latter part of that month the Virginias of Richmond left the arena. The five clubs remaining finished the season as follows, the Washington Nationals winning the championship:

	Washington.	Richmond.	Trenton.	Waterbury.	Newark.	Norfolk.	Lancaster.	Bridgeport.	Jersey City.	Atlantic City.	Won.	Per cent. of Victories.
Washington	..	10	12	1	11	13	8	6	3	6	70	.736
Richmond	8	..	16	0	9	11	10	2	1	10	67	.720
Trenton	6	1	..	2	11	7	4	4	6	2	43	.467
Waterbury	1	0	2	..	3	0	0	2	0	0	8	.470
Newark	6	6	7	2	..	3	6	3	6	2	41	.445
Norfolk	1	3	4	0	8	..	7	0	2	8	33	.445
Lancaster	3	2	5	0	3	5	..	0	8	2	28	.417
Bridgeport	0	3	1	4	4	0	0	..	0	0	12	.413
Jersey City	0	1	2	0	1	1	3	0	..	1	9	.250
Atlantic City	0	0	0	1	0	2	1	0	1	..	5	.139
Lost	25	26	49	9	51	12	39	17	27	31	316	

THE NEW ENGLAND LEAGUE.

Two Leagues, representing New England clubs, started in 1885, but only the Eastern New England League finished the season, the Southern New England League breaking up after a few months' play. When the season ended, Oct. 1, it was found that two clubs tied for the lead in the League pennant race. The Lawrence and Brockton clubs thereupon had to play off their tie record, and as the Lawrence won two games of the series, they were awarded the championship of the League. The complete record of the season's games is as follows:

	Lawrence.	Brockton.	Haverhill.	Portland.	Newburyport	Won.	Played.	Average Per cent.
Lawrence	..	13	8	12	17	50	81	.617
Brockton	8	..	13	13	14	48	81	.592
Haverhill	12	7	..	11	14	44	79	.557
Portland	8	7	8	..	10	33	79	.418
Newburyport	3	6	6	10	..	25	80	.313
Lost	31	33	35	46	55			

THE NEW YORK STATE LEAGUE.

The New York State League's inaugural season occurred in 1885, and it proved to be a very successful one for a new organization. The League started with six clubs, representing Syracuse, Rochester, Utica, Binghamton, Oswego and Albany, but the latter disbanded the last of July, leaving the other five clubs to complete the season. The record gave the championship to the Syracuse club, as will be seen by the appended table:

	Syracuse.	Rochester.	Utica.	Binghamton.	Oswego.	Games Won	Played	Per cent. won
Syracuse	..	9	11	11	14	45	77	.584
Rochester	9	..	11	10	10	40	76	.526
Utica	9	8	..	13	11	41	79	.518
Binghamton	9	9	7	..	11	36	78	.461
Oswego	5	10	9	8	..	32	78	.410
Games lost	32	36	38	42	46	194		

THE CANADIAN LEAGUE.

The Ontario League, the first regular organization of Canadian professional clubs to go through a season successfully, inaugurated its championship season in 1885, and the five clubs comprising the League presented an attractive series of contests from May to October, with the result of the success of the Clipper club of Hamilton as the champion Canadian club of the season. The appended table shows the standing of the League at the close of the season. None of the clubs completed the series, not being able to finish Oct. 1.

	Clipper.	London.	Toronto.	Maple Leaf.	Primrose.	Won.	Per cent.
Clipper, of Hamilton	..	4	10	10	10	34	.77
London	7	..	6	6	8	27	.69
Toronto	2	4	..	9	9	24	.54
Maple Leaf, of Guelph	1	0	3	..	4	8	.22
Primrose, of Hamilton	0	4	1	3	..	8	.20
Games Lost	10	12	20	28	31	101	

THE COLORADO LEAGUE.

Three clubs entered the lists for the championship of Colorado in 1885, and the pennant was won by the Denver club, as the appended record shows:

	Denver.	Pueblo.	Leadville.	Won.	Played.	Per cent. of Victories.
Denver....	..	6	6	12	20	.600
Pueblo....	4	..	7	11	20	.550
Leadville..	4	3	..	7	20	.350
Lost....	8	9	13			

THE PROFESSIONAL CHAMPIONSHIP NINES FROM 1871 TO 1884 INCLUSIVE.

LEAGUE CHAMPIONS.

Before the organization of the first Professional National Association, there was no recognized code of rules governing any championship contest in the base ball arena, only a nominal title existing prior to 1871, and even that was frequently disputed. The original champions of the old amateur class of clubs, which existed at the home of base ball, in New York and its suburbs, was the Atlantic Club, of Brooklyn, the champion team of that club, when it was in its palmiest amateur days, being M. O'Brien, pitcher; Boerum, catcher; Price, John Oliver and Charlie Smith on the bases; Dick Pearce, shortstop, and P. O'Brien, Archy McMahon and Tice Hamilton in the out-field. This was in 1860, when they won the championship from the Excelsiors. When they defeated the Mutuals and Eckfords, in 1864, their champion team was Pratt, pitcher; Ferguson, catcher; Start, Crane and Smith on the bases; Pearce, at short-field, and Chapman, Joe Oliver and Sid Smith in the out-field. The Eckfords held the nominal title in 1862 and '63, and in 1869 the Cincinnati Red Stockings were indisputably the champions of the United States. Their team in that year included Asa Brainard, as pitcher; D. Allison, as catcher; Gould, Sweazy and Waterman, on the bases; George Wright, as short stop, and Leonard, Harry Wright and McVey in the out-field. In 1870 the title was claimed by the Mutuals and Chicagos, and the disputed claim was never settled.

In 1871 the Professional National Association was organized, and then was begun the first series of championship matches under an official code of rules known in the history of professional ball-playing. From this year to 1876, when the National League was organized, the winning teams were as follows:

1871, Athletic—McBride, pitcher; Malone, catcher; Fisler, Reach and Meyerle on the bases; Radcliff, short-stop, Cuthbert, Sensenderfer and Heubel in the outfield.

1872, Boston—A. G. Spalding, pitcher; C. A. McVey, catcher; Chas. Gould, Ross Barnes and Harry Schafer on the bases; Geo. Wright, short-stop; Andy Leonard, Harry Wright and Fraley Rogers in the outfield.

1873, Boston—A. G. Spalding, pitcher; Jas. White, catcher; James O'Rourke, Barnes and Schafer on the bases; George Wright, short-stop; Leonard, Harry Wright and Manning in the outfield.

1874, Boston—A. G. Spalding, pitcher; McVey, catcher; Jas. White, Barnes and Schafer on the bases; Geo. Wright, shortstop; Leonard, Hall and Jas. O'Rourke in the outfield.

1875, Boston—A. G. Spalding, pitcher; James White, catcher; Latham, Barnes and Schafer on the bases; George Wright, short-stop; Leonard, Jas. O'Rourke and Manning in the outfield.

From 1876 to 1883, inclusive, the winning teams in the League arena were as follows:

1876, Chicago—A. G. Spalding, pitcher; Jas. White, catcher; McVey, Barnes and Anson on the bases; Peters, short-stop; Glenn, Hines and Addy in the outfield.

1877, Boston—Bond, pitcher; Brown, catcher; Jas. White, Geo. Wright and Morrill on the bases; Sutton, short-stop; Leonard, Jas. O'Rourke and Schafer in the outfield.

1878, Boston—Bond, pitcher; Snyder, catcher; Morrill, Burdock and Sutton the bases; Geo. Wright, short-stop; Leonard, Jas. O'Rourke and Manning in the outfield.

1879, Providence—Ward, pitcher; Brown, catcher; Start, McGeary and Hague on the bases; Geo. Wright, short-stop; York, Hines and Jas. O'Rourke in the outfield.

1880, 1881 and 1882, Chicago—Corcoran and Goldsmith, pitchers; Flint, catcher; Anson, Quest and Williamson on the bases; Burns, short-stop; Dalrymple, Gore and Kelly in the outfield.

1883, Boston—Whitney and Buffinton, pitchers; Hines and Hackett, catchers; Morrill, Burdock and Sutton on the bases; Wise, short-stop, and Hornung, Smith and Radford in the outfield.

1884, Providence—Radbourne, pitcher; Gilligan and Nava, catchers; Start, Farrell and Denny on the bases; Irwin, shortstop, and Carroll, Hines and Radford on the outfield.

1885, Chicago—Clarkson and McCormick, pitchers; Flint, catcher; Anson, Pfeffer and Williamson on the bases; Burns, short-stop, and Dalrymple, Gore and Kelly in the outfield.

HINTS TO CLUB MANAGERS.

It has come to be a matter requiring not only considerable experience in a knowledge of the character of men in judging them correctly, but sound judgment in selecting men suitable for the organization of a team which will do team work together effectively. A few hints to young managers of professional club nines will not be out of place in the GUIDE.

In the first place avoid the engagement of players who are in the habit of indulging in the use of intoxicating liquors to excess. Such men are demoralizing agents in any team in which they are allowed to play. Not only is a drunken professional his own enemy, but his presence in a team is also necessarily destructive of its *morale*. In fact, temperate habits among professional ball players are more essential to success than is any special skill they may possess in playing their several positions; for a poor player who is a temperate man and earnest in his work is more serviceable than any man who is a fine player can be who is under the influence of drinking habits.

Secondly.—Quick-tempered, passionate men are unfit to be in a nine made up to play for the side. Hot temper is not only opposed to clear judgment, but it entirely prevents a man under its influence from playing for the side. Such men, when they 'get their mad up' at anything, do not hesitate a moment to indulge their spite at a brother player at the cost of even the loss of the match. A nine who are continually quarreling with one another, or whose special interests clash in some way or other with the general interests of the club they play with so as to prevent them from "playing for the side" as it is called, never can successfully cope with a team who work in harmony together.

Thirdly.—In making up your team bear in mind the importance of "playing for the side" as one of the primary essentials of success. In making up a team for carrying out this policy, you must avoid putting players in it who have any ambitious views for preferment, such as a desire to be made captain of the nine, or manager of the team. It is impossible for such men to play for the side. They are so busy in organizing cliques against the powers that be, and in manœuvering for the desired place, that they think of little else, and they play the game only with this one object in view. This has always been a cause of difficulty in teams in which there are two or more ex-captains or ex-managers. The player who has once tasted the fruit of authority is rarely amenable to control when occupying a subordinate position, unless it be under some ruler whom he knows to be his superior as a captain or a manager.

Fourthly.—The longer players are kept in the service of one club the more they may be relied upon to play for the side, as a general rule; and it is not an unfair conclusion to arrive at that that player who is ready to leave the service of a good club at the temptation of the offer of a couple of hundred dollars a year more salary, is a man whose heart is not in his work sufficiently to make him a good player for his side. In fact, this club feeling—that is, a feeling of special interest in the success of his club outside of any interested motive of a mere personal nature—is one of the foundation stones of the policy of playing for the side. This lack of "playing for the side" is a marked characteristic of nines which are entirely changed season after season. It takes all the summer for a nine to get used to each other's peculiar style of play, and just when they have got to the right point the season closes, and the nine is divided up among a half a dozen other clubs. Here is where the mistake is made. Get rid of your weak men, but retain every man who has worked well for the club, even if he is not quite up to the high mark of playing strength you aim at.

Cliqueism in clubs is something every manager must work out of his team unless he desires failure in his work. When this obstacle to successful management exists, the organization of a well trained and disciplined team is out of the question. When the clique "racket" is not worked in the interests of some selfish aspirant for managerial control, it appears in the form of "clans" in the team who specially favor this or that one of the two "batteries" of the club. Here is a pitcher, for instance, who is really a very effective man in the position, as far as his special skill in the delivery of the ball is concerned; who, not satisfied with legitimately earning the handsome salary paid him, wants to control the entire team; leaving the manager to be a mere figure head in his position, or limiting him to attend only to the outside business of the club. Such a pitcher goes to work to get a clique of "heelers" among the players, who will help him in his "little game," and the result is that each "battery" in the club have their special supporters in the team, and each clique works for the advantage of their pet "battery," at the cost of the general interests of the team as a whole.

One cause of cliqueism and its dissensions in clubs is the interference of some one or other club director with the work of running the team by the regularly appointed manager. Mr. A, for instance, thinks that the pitcher of the club, whom he regards as the most effective man in the position, is not put in the "box" often enough; while Mr. B. thinks that non success of the team is largely due to the fact that his pet pitcher is left out of the nine far too often for its good. The respective pitchers in question are not slow to perceive this difference of opinion which prevails among the governing officials of the club; and utterly disregarding the behests of the manager they go to work to scheme for the advancement of their own special interests, and with this comes the growth of cliques in the team, and a division in the ranks which is fatal to thorough team work. In the face of such barriers to successful field work as these cliques present, how is it possible for a manager to run the team to the best of his ability, or even for a captain to general the nine in the field successfully. The trouble with this business is that the mischief works quietly and beneath the service, the general patrons of the club only being aware that something or other is going wrong without knowing what the cause is. As the business of running a professional club advances with experience, these obstacles to financial success will ultimately disappear. In the interim, however, they tend to ruin the prospects of many a club which starts out at the commencement of a season with every prospect of financial prosperity.

Finally, managers should do their utmost in endeavoring to inspire their team with confidence in their ability to win when they earnestly strive to do so.

Confidence is the one great element of success in a base ball team. It causes batsmen to "bunch their hits," and to punish even first-class pitchers. It inspires a supporting team to help a favorite pitcher to be effective, and it brings about a successful rally in a hard uphill fight. In fact, it is the basis of success in a team's work. Without it good batsmen strike out to poor pitchers; first-class fielders become "rattled" in critical periods of a contest, and a lack of confidence in their team's pitcher causes his supports to fall off in their effectiveness. With confidence to aid them a second-class nine can whip a first-class team which lacks confidence in their work. It was the secret of the old Atlantic's success twenty odd years ago. It was the very basis of the brilliant career of the Cincinnatis of 1869, and it has helped to win every championship pennant since then.

DRUNKENNESS IN THE RANKS.

Prior to the organization of the National League professional ball playing suffered greatly from several then existing evils, prominent among which was "crookedness" among the club players, this evil being almost entirely due to the malign influence of pool gambling, the primary cause of all dishonesty in sports. But this evil was got rid of by the League after a hard fight; and now, pool gambling is prohibited on every respectable professional ball ground in the country; and, moreover, every player found guilty of crooked work is forever debarred from employment in any professional club in the United States, every professional association having adopted the League rules punishing dishonest players.

Next to "crooked" play was the evil of drunkenness in the ranks, and this, we regret to state, is still in existence, it being the most conspicuous evil that was connected with professional ball playing during 1884. This trouble has proved to be not only destructive to the morale of every club team in which it exists, but it is a powerful barrier to the financial success of the club whose team is injured by drunken players among them. Season after season for the past three years, have clubs become bankrupt solely through the failure of their teams to accomplish successful field work, owing to the presence of two or three drunkards in their team. Even one such member demoralizes a nine to such a degree as to offset all the advantages the team possesses in other respects. Club after club has adopted stringent rules against drunkenness in their teams, which have been enforced for a time, but owing to the frequent condoning of offenses the rules have become almost dead letters. Experience plainly points out the fact that there is but one remedy for this evil, and that is total abstinence from the first day of the season to the last, and this rule should be enforced by costly pecuniary penalties, ending with suspension from service for an entire season when the violation is repeated. As for the class of habitual drinkers they should be driven from the ranks of the fraternity forever, just as Jim Devlin, Al Nichols, Craver, and others were for their proved dishonesty. Until this is done our professional clubs will never be free from the trouble drunken players cause them. Honesty in professional ball playing has been given a premium, and no man of questionable integrity of character can find employment in any professional club that is controlled by honorable men. Let temperance also be placed on the premium list by refusing to employ any player in the habit of drinking liquor. It is useless to point out to players of drinking habits the folly of the evil course they are pursuing. Treat them with all the kindly consideration possible by condoning their faults, they will only return it with more indulgence. The example of the folly of their course has no effect in preventing indulgence. Look at the case of young Eagan, the former pitcher of the League Club of Troy, who was taken in hand by the Brooklyn Club and given the means of reformation which would have made a man of him. What was his return for the help given him to rise out of the gutter of dissipation? Let his disgraceful death within prison walls point the moral of his wretched folly, as Devlin's death in low poverty did that of the results of dishonesty on the ball field. Self-preservation by the professional clubs requires that the strong hand of convention law be brought to bear on this existing evil. The hundreds of thousands of dollars invested as capital in base ball stock companies can no longer be placed in jeopardy by the continued trifling with this growing evil. Every base ball city in the land suffered from it in 1885 to a more or less extent, and it undoubtedly bankrupted a third of the clubs which encountered financial failure last season. Whatever may be said about prohibition in political circles, most assuredly it is the only law which should prevail on the subject in the ranks of the professional fraternity, from April to November each base ball year.

THE INTER-COLLEGIATE ASSOCIATION.

The Inter-collegiate Association began its history at the meeting of college delegates on Dec. 6., 1879, when six of the Eastern State Colleges were represented at the convention, viz: Harvard, Yale, Princeton, Amherst, Dartmouth and Brown. As a majority at the convention voted to exclude college players from their nines who took part as players in professional club teams, Yale ultimately withdrew from the Association, and only five clubs entered for the Inter-collegiate Association pennant. Yale afterward arranged a series of eight matches with three of the five clubs, and only lost one game out of the eight. They virtually won the championship honors of the season, though Princeton won the Association pennant of 1880. The official record of the games played under the auspices of the Association, up to 1883 inclusive, is a follows:

1880	Won.	Lost.	1881	Won.	Lost.
Princeton...............	6	2	Yale....................	7	3
Brown...................	5	3	Harvard.................	6	4
Dartmouth...............	4	4	Princeton...............	6	4
Harvard.................	3	5	Brown...................	4	6
Amherst.................	2	6	Dartmouth...............	4	6
			Amherst.................	3	7
	20	20		30	30

BASE BALL GUIDE.

1882.	Won.	Lost.	1883.	Won.	Lost.
Yale............................	8	3	Yale............................	7	1
Princeton.....................	7	4	Princeton.....................	6	2
Harvard.......................	5	5	Amherst.......................	4	4
Amherst.......................	4	6	Harvard.......................	2	6
Brown..........................	4	6	Brown..........................	1	7
Dartmouth....................	3	7			
	31	31		20	20

It will be seen that each of the above seasons saw the Princeton team well up in the front, while only in two seasons was Harvard among the leaders.

In 1880 Yale's record in their contests with the Inter-collegiate clubs was as follows:

May 12	Yale vs. Princeton, at Princeton............................	9—
June 9	Yale vs. Princeton, at New Haven............................	8—
May 15	Yale vs. Harvard, at New Haven............................	21—4
" 29	Yale vs. Harvard, at Cambridge............................	2—1
June 28	Harvard vs. Yale, at New Haven............................	3—1
" 30	Yale vs. Harvard, at Cambridge............................	3—0
May 22	Yale vs. Amherst, at Amherst............................	8—0
June 5	Yale vs. Amherst, at New Haven............................	14—3

The above were, of course, outside games, Yale not being a member of the Inter-collegiate Association that year. But the series were practically championship contests. The full record of the season, including Yale games, was as follows:

RECORD FOR 1880.

	Yale.	Princeton.	Brown.	Dartmouth.	Harvard.	Amherst.	Won.	Lost.	Played.
Yale............................	..	2	0	0	2	2	6	1	7
Princeton.....................	0	..	1	2	2	1	6	4	10
Brown..........................	0	1	..	1	1	2	5	3	8
Dartmouth....................	0	0	1	..	2	1	4	4	8
Harvard.......................	1	0	1	0	..	2	4	7	11
Amherst.......................	0	1	0	1	0	..	2	8	10
Lost............................	1	4	3	4	7	8	27		

In 1881 Yale re-entered the Inter-collegiate Association, and has remained in it ever since. Yale won the honors after a close fight with Harvard and Princeton, as the appended record shows:

RECORD FOR 1881.

	Yale.	Harvard.	Princeton.	Brown.	Dartmouth.	Amherst.	Games Won.	Games Lost.	Games Played.
Yale........................	....	1	1	2	1	2	7	3	10
Harvard.....................	1	....	1	1	2	1	6	4	10
Princeton...................	1	1	....	1	2	1	6	4	10
Brown.......................	0	1	1	....	1	1	4	6	10
Dartmouth...................	1	0	0	1	....	2	4	6	10
Amherst.....................	0	1	1	1	0	....	3	7	10
Games Lost..................	3	4	4	6	6	7	30		

In 1882 the contest between Yale and Princeton was very close, Harvard falling back in the race. Yale finally won, as the appended record shows:

RECORD FOR 1882.

	Yale.	Princeton.	Harvard.	Amherst.	Brown.	Dartmouth.	Games Won.	Games Lost.	Games Played.
Yale........................	....	2	1	2	1	2	8	3	11
Princeton...................	1	....	2	1	1	2	7	4	11
Harvard.....................	1	0	....	2	2	0	5	5	10
Amherst.....................	0	1	0	....	2	1	4	6	10
Brown.......................	1	1	0	0	....	2	4	6	10
Dartmouth...................	0	0	2	1	0	....	3	7	10
Games Lost..................	3	4	5	6	6	7	31		

In 1883 the majority of the clubs acted very unjustly to Dartmouth, and the result was that that club was forced to withdraw from the pennant race of that year; and the Dartmouth Club were not at all disappointed to find Harvard—which Club had been mainly instrumental in driving Dartmouth out of the field—near last in the pennant race of that year. Yale again won the honors, with Princeton once more a good second, as the appended record shows:

RECORD FOR 1883.

	Yale.	Princeton.	Amherst.	Harvard.	Brown.	Games Won.	Games Lost.	Games Played.
Yale........................	....	1	2	2	2	7	1	8
Princeton...................	1	....	1	2	2	6	2	8
Amherst.....................	0	1	....	1	2	4	4	8
Harvard.....................	0	0	1	....	1	2	6	8
Brown.......................	0	0	0	1	....	1	7	8
Games Lost..................	1	2	4	6	7	20		

BASE BALL GUIDE. 79

In 1884 justice was shown Dartmouth, and that Club resumed its proper place in the Association. But in consequence of being out of the arena in 1883 they had lost material strength and consequently had to occupy last place in the race. Last season Princeton fell off badly in the pennant race, while Harvard made quite a good fight of it, they coming in second for the first time since 1881, as will be seen by the appended record:

RECORD FOR 1884.

	Yale.	Harvard.	Amherst.	Brown.	Princeton.	Dartmouth.	Won.	Lost.	Played.
Yale.........	..	1	2	2	2	2	9	2	11
Harvard......	2	..	1	2	2	2	8	3	11
Amherst......	0	1	..	2	1	2	6	4	10
Brown.........	0	1	0	..	2	2	5	5	10
Princeton.....	0	0	1	0	..	1	2	8	10
Dartmouth....	0	0	0	0	1	..	1	9	10
Lost..........	2	3	4	5	8	9	31		

In 1885 Harvard won the pennant in brilliant style, their record of ten victories and no defeats being unprecedented in the annals of the Intercollegiate Association. Yale had nine victories and two defeats in 1884, but that is the nearest record to Harvard's figures for '85.

The record shows that Yale and Princeton tied for second place; Dartmouth was fourth, and Brown and Amherst tied for fifth.

	Harvard.	Yale.	Princeton.	Dartmouth.	Brown.	Amherst.	Won.	Per cent. of Victories.
Harvard......	..	2	2	2	2	2	10	.1000
Yale.........	0	..	1	2	2	2	7	.700
Princeton.....	0	1	..	2	2	2	7	.700
Dartmouth....	0	0	0	..	2	2	4	.400
Brown.........	0	0	0	0	..	1	1	.100
Amherst......	0	0	0	0	1	..	1	.100
Lost..........	0	3	3	6	9	9	30	

Premising that Yale was not a member in 1880 and Dartmouth in 1883, we give below the full record of victories and defeats during each year since the American College Association was organized.

	1880.		1881.		1882.		1883.		1884.		1885.		Totals.	
	W.	L.	W.	L.	W.	L.	W.	L.	W.	L.	W.	L.	W.	L.
Harvard.........	3	5	6	4	5	5	2	6	8	3	10	0	34	23
Yale............			7	3	8	3	7	1	9	2	7	3	38	12
Princeton.......	6	2	6	4	7	4	6	2	2	8	7	3	34	23
Dartmouth......	4	4	4	6	3	7			1	9	4	6	16	32
Brown..........	5	3	4	6	4	6	1	7	5	5	1	9	20	36
Amherst........	2	6	3	7	4	6	4	4	6	4	1	9	20	36
Totals........	20	20	30	30	31	31	20	20	31	31	30	30	162	162

RECORD OF 1885.

The full detailed record of the championship season of 1885 —similar in form to that given exclusively in the Guide of 1885 —is appended. It shows not only the games won and lost by each club, but the date of each game and the scores.

	Harvard.	Yale.	Princeton.	Dartmouth.	Amherst.	Brown.	Won.	Per cent. of Victories.
Harvard......		May 16, 12-4. June 20, 16-2.	May 23, 15-0. June 1, 13-4.	May 27, 12-5. June 6, 9-3.	May 7, 13-4. May 18, 15-5.	May 9, 3-1. June 15, 3-2.	10	.1000
Yale.........	....		May 9, 5-3.	May 2, 15-6. June 10, 6-3.	May 27, 10-9. June 13, 14-2.	May 13, 11-9. June 3, 8-4.	7	.700
Princeton.....		June 6, 11-5.		June 12, 15-5. June 13, 7-5.	May 13, 7-6. June 20, 6-2.	May 11, 12-7. May 16, 14-3.	7	.700
Dartmouth....					Apr. 30, 9-5. June 19, 18-12.	May 25, 8-1. May 29, 23-4.	4	.400
Amherst......						June 6, 12-2.	1	.100
Brown........					May 4, 9-1.		1	.100
Lost.........	0	3	3	6	9	9	30	

SUMMARY.

A summary of the above records gives the appended figures of games played and won each year.

BASE BALL GUIDE. 81

	1880	1881	1882	1883	1884	1885	Won
Yale...........................	6	7	8	7	9	7	44
Princeton.......................	6	6	7	6	2	7	34
Harvard........................	4	6	5	2	8	10	35
Brown..........................	5	4	4	1	5	1	20
Amherst........................	2	3	4	4	6	1	20
Dartmouth......................	4	4	3	0	1	4	16
	27	30	31	20	31	30	169

OFFICIAL RECORD OF AVERAGES—1885.

AMERICAN COLLEGE BASE BALL ASSOCIATION.

	NAME AND CLUB.	Games.	A. B.	R.	B. H.	Bat. Av.	P. O.	A.	E.	Field Av.	Rank.
1	Nichols. H............	10	42	21	21	.500	3	165	27	.862	12
2	Willard. H............	10	43	21	19	.442	74	1	7	.915	8
3	Edwards. P...........	12	52	13	20	.385	33	30	19	.758	25
4	Smith. H.............	10	33	8	12	.364	20	13	7	.825	16
5	Scruton. D...........	7	31	10	11	.355	9	2	3	.786	23
	Shaw. P..............	11	51	10	18	.355	109	31	69	.669	37
	Marsh. Y.............	7	31	11	11	.355	8	0	4	.667	38
6	Terry. Y..............	11	49	18	17	.347	33	36	3	.958	2
7	Allen. H..............	10	45	17	15	.333	129	29	14	.919	7
	VanAusdal. P.........	12	54	10	18	.333	10	2	2	.857	13
	Quackenboss. D......	8	36	7	12	.333	9	4	5	.722	32
8	Stuart. A.............	11	40	8	13	.325	19	32	28	.646	39
9	Winslow. H...........	10	44	7	14	.318	5	1	2	.750	27
10	Shepherd. Y..........	11	45	14	14	.311	19	4	6	.793	21
11	Hutchinson. B........	9	39	6	12	.309	9	33	16	.707	34
12	Beaman. H...........	10	52	9	16	.308	15	12	3	.900	9
13	Merrill. Y............	10	40	7	12	.300	7	2	6	.600	42
14	Kimball. A...........	11	47	9	14	.298	83	1	8	.915	8
15	Springfield. D........	10	48	16	14	.292	10	2	3	.800	18
16	Brill. D..............	7	28	4	8	.286	5	35	15	.727	31
17	Hale. D..............	10	47	9	13	.277	94	1	5	.550	3
18	Weeks. D.............	10	44	13	12	.273	8	4	2	.857	13
19	Tilden. H............	8	39	11	10	.256	2	0	1	.667	38
20	Reynolds. P..........	10	40	15	10	.250	8	2	3	.769	24
21	Toler. P.............	10	41	11	10	.244	86	2	3	.967	1
22	Bickham. P..........	11	46	12	11	.239	7	148	39	.799	19
23	Blossom. P...........	10	42	11	10	.238	5	5	15	.400	48
24	Weistling. H.........	7	26	6	6	.231	1	4	5	.500	47
25	Cooper. P............	12	48	10	11	.229	8	29	5	.381	11
26	Hunt. A.............	11	44	9	10	.227	26	5	14	.889	36
27	Stearns. A...........	11	45	5	10	.222	40	27	29	.598	35
28	Seagrave. B..........	10	43	7	9	.209	63	2	3	.026	6
	Chellis. D............	10	43	9	9	.209	18	30	10	.828	15
29	Dillon. D............	8	29	5	6	.207	8	55	39	.618	41
30	Foster. H............	7	30	7	6	.200	8	2	2	.833	14
31	Marble. A............	11	41	8	8	.195	24	21	11	.790	20

AMERICAN COLLEGE BASE BALL ASSOCIATION—CONTINUED.

	NAME AND CLUB.	Games.	A. B.	R.	B. H.	Bat. Av.	P. O.	A.	E.	Field Av.	Rank.
32	Stagg. Y............	7	31	5	6	.194	7	18	5	.833	14
	Clark. B............	10	36	6	7	.194	72	20	25	.786	23
33	Clarke. P............	12	51	6	9	.176	10	2	6	.667	38
34	Stewart. Y............	11	40	8	7	.175	144	3	8	.948	4
	Tirrell. A............	11	42	5	7	.167	10	33	11	.796	20
35	Artz. D............	7	24	4	4	.167	45	17	25	.713	33
	Coates. A............	9	30	8	5	.167	12	3	2	.882	10
36	Bremner. Y............	11	50	18	8	.160	62	23	46	.641	40
37	Hickox. Y............	11	47	5	7	.149	8	44	18	.743	29
38	Chase. B............	10	35	6	5	.143	58	12	4	.946	5
	Gunderson. B............	9	35	8	5	.143	8	75	19	.813	17
39	McCarthy. D............	10	45	9	6	.133	13	30	14	.754	26
40	Willett. Y............	10	40	4	5	.125	4	83	61	.588	43
41	Rhett. B............	9	36	7	4	.111	16	3	5	.792	22
	Wadsworth. B............	5	18	2	2	.111	6	8	11	.560	45
42	Judson. A............	11	33	3	3	.091	32	15	10	.825	16
43	Lyon. Y............	6	23	1	2	.087	7	4	10	.524	46
44	Cooper. B............	8	29	0	2	.069	11	19	11	.741	30
45	Edgerly. H............	7	30	2	2	.067	2	8	2	.833	14
46	Murphy. B............	10	34	0	2	.059	6	19	18	.581	44
47	Harris. A............	10	36	2	2	.056	13	45	21	.747	28

The above is the official record of averages of the American College Base Ball Association, for the season 1885.

PERLEY WEEKS, Secretary.

Record of those playing less than 5 and more than 2 games.

NAME AND CLUB.	Games.	A. B.	R.	B. H.	Bat. Av.	P. O.	A.	E.	Field Av.
Williams. A..................	3	10	3	3	.300	6	2	2	.800
Cook. B...................	4	11	0	2	.182	4	12	4	.800
Shedd. B...................	3	12	0	2	.167	9	1	3	.769
Johnson. D..................	4	17	3	2	.118	31	9	19	.678
Oldham. A..................	3	12	0	1	.083	5	0	1	.833
Taylor. P...................	4	13	0	1	.071	13	6	10	.655
Brownell. B..................	3	9	0	0	.000	3	0	0	1.000

THE RECORD OF 1885.

The full record giving date, names of clubs and total scores of each game, is appended:

April 30, Dartmouth vs. Amherst, at Amherst...................... 9—5
May 2, Yale vs. Dartmouth, at New Haven...................... 15—6
" 4, Brown vs. Amherst, at Amherst.......................... 9—1

BASE BALL GUIDE. 83

May 7, Harvard vs. Amherst, at Cambridge...................... 13—4
 "   9, Harvard vs. Brown, at Providence....................... 3—1
 "   9, Yale vs. Princeton, at New Haven....................... 5—3
 "   11, Princeton vs. Brown, at Providence..................... 12—7
 "   13, Yale vs. Brown, at New Haven........................... 11—9
 "   13, Princeton vs. Amherst, at Princeton.................... 7—6
 "   16, Harvard vs. Yale, at New Haven......................... 12—4
 "   16, Princeton vs. Brown, at Princeton...................... 14—3
 "   18, Harvard vs. Amherst, at Amherst........................ 15—5
 "   23, Harvard vs. Princeton, at Cambridge.................... 15—6
 "   25, Dartmouth vs. Brown, at Providence..................... 8—1
 "   27, Yale vs. Amherst, at Amherst (12 innings)............. 10—9
 "   27, Harvard vs. Dartmouth, at Cambridge.................... 12—5
 "   29, Dartmouth vs. Brown, at Hanover .... 23—4
June 1, Harvard vs. Princeton, at Cambridge................... 13—4
 "   3, Yale vs. Brown, at Providence.......................... 8—4
 "   6, Harvard vs. Dartmouth, at Cambridge.................... 9—3
 "   6, Princeton vs. Yale, at Princeton....................... 11—5
 "   6, Amherst vs. Brown, at Providence....................... 12—2
 "   10, Yale vs. Dartmouth, at New Haven....................... 6—3
 "   12, Princeton vs. Dartmouth, at Princeton.................. 15—5
 "   13,   "   "   "   "   " .... 7—5
 "   13, Yale vs. Amherst, at New Haven......................... 14—2
 "   15, Harvard vs. Brown, at Cambridge........................ 3—2
 "   19, Dartmouth vs. Amherst, at Hanover...................... 18—12
 "   20, Harvard vs. Yale, at Cambridge......................... 16—2
 "   20, Princeton vs. Amherst, at Amherst...................... 5—2

The record of drawn and exhibition games is as follows:

DRAWN GAMES.

May 30, Princeton vs. Amherst, at Amherst (5 innings)............ 4—4

EXHIBITION GAMES.

May 22, Harvard vs. Princeton, at Cambridge...................... 6—5
June 2,   "   "   "   "   "   .... 13—4
 "   17,   "   "   Brown, at Providence................... 15—2
 "   23, Princeton vs. Yale, at New Haven........................ 15-13

NORTHWESTERN COLLEGE ASSOCIATION.

An increasing interest in base ball has been manifested with each succeeding year since this association was formed. Each year has also, in many respects, been productive of a higher standard of playing. This becomes evident from a study of the records of the different seasons. Such a result is very encouraging, inasmuch as it shows that the prime object for which the association was established, namely, the amelioration of the condition of athletics in the colleges represented, has to a considerable extent been attained, at least in base ball matters. The prospects for the season of 1886 are very good, and close race for the championship may be expected.

At the meeting held in March at the Plankinton House, Milwaukee, officers for 1885 were elected as follows: President, W. D. Fullerton, Northwestern University, Evanston,

Ill.; Secretary and Treasurer, R. K. Welch, Beloit College, Beloit, Wis.

THE CHAMPIONSHIP RECORD FOR 1885.

The championship of the Northwestern College Base Ball Association for 1885, was competed for by four clubs, namely: The University of Wisconsin, Racine College, Beloit College and Northwestern University, the result being the success of the Wisconsin University team again, as will be seen by the appended record:

	Wisconsin.	Racine.	Beloit.	Northwestern.	Games Won.	Games Lost.	Games Played.
Wisconsin......................	....	2	2	2	6	0	6
Racine..........................	0	....	1	2	3	3	6
Beloit...........................	0	1	....	1	2	4	6
Northwestern...................	0	0	1	....	1	5	6

The championship contests began on May 2, at Evanston, and ended on June 13, at Madison, during which time a series of twelve games were played. Four of these games were marked by single figure victories, the best played one of the series being that of May 25, at Racine, between the Wisconsin University nine and the Racine College nine, the former winning by a score of two to one only. The next best game was played at Madison on June 13, between Wisconsin University nine and Beloit College nine, the result being six to five in favor of Wisconsin after ten innings. The other single-figure games were that of May 2, at Evanston, when Racine defeated Northwestern, and May 30, at Evanston, when Northwestern defeated Beloit. The full record is as follows:

May	2, R. C. vs. N. W., at Evanston...............................	10—9
"	9, U. of W. vs. B. C., at Beloit.................................	5—2
"	9, R. C. vs. N. W., at Racine...................................	19—13
"	16, B. C. vs. R. C., at Beloit....................................	13—11
"	18, U. of W. vs. R. C., at Madison.............................	10—2
"	23, U. of W. vs. R. C., at Racine...............................	2—1
"	25, U. of W. vs. N. W., at Evanston...........................	6—3
"	29, R. C. vs. B. C., at Racine...................................	15—7
"	30, N. W. vs. B. C., at Evanston...............................	11—10
June	6, B. C. vs. N. W., at Beloit....................................	15—6
"	8, U. of W. vs. N. W., at Madison.............................	25—2
"	13, U. of W. vs. B. C., at Madison.............................	6—5

BASE BALL GUIDE.

PLAYERS AND POSITION.	CLUB.	Games Played.	Batting Average.	Fielding Average.	Rank in Fielding.
Sibley, c. and 2 b...............	R. C...............	5	.524	.862	15
Parker, r. f......................	U. of W............	6	.409	.750	23
Connolly, p......................	"	6	.344	.875	14
Wright, 1 b.....................	R. C...............	6	.321	.912	10
Canner, l. f.....................	U. of W............	6	.320	1.000	1
Huxford, 2 and 3 b.............	N. W. U...........	6	.310	.700	25
Newton, r. f.....................	R. C...............	6	.276	.444	33
Lunt, p..........................	"	6	.266	.914	8
Powers, c........................	N. W. U...........	3	.266	.923	5
Felker, c. f......................	R. C...............	6	.259	.875	15
Van Tassel, s. s. and c. f......	B. C...............	6	.250	.636	29
Thompson, s. s..................	U. of W............	4	.250	.833	18
Martin, 1 b.....................	B. C...............	6	.240	.859	17
Alderman, 2 b..................	U. of W............	6	.231	.647	28
Zenblin, l. f.....................	N. W. U...........	3	.230	1.000	2
Bannister, c. and 1 b..........	"	5	.227	.800	22
Welsh, 3 b......................	B. C...............	6	.200	.800	20
Whitehead, c. f..................	"	3	.200	1.000	3
Welton, r. f.....................	N. W. U...........	4	.200	.250	36
Sheean, s. s. and r. f...........	B. C...............	6	.185	.611	30
Kramer, 1 b.....................	U. of W............	6	.181	.883	13
Turner, p........................	B. C...............	6	.174	.927	4
Lansing, 2 b.....................	"	6	.166	.800	21
Farr, c...........................	"	6	.160	.887	12
Kreshaw, 3 and 2 b.............	R. C...............	6	.160	.727	24
Parker, s. s.....................	N. W. U...........	3	.154	.838	11
Bass, r. f and 2 b...............	"	3	.154	.400	35
Clark, c. f.......................	U. of W............	6	.148	.400	34
Curtis, 1 b......................	N. W. U...........	3	.143	.914	9
Crow, r. f.......................	B. C...............	3	.143	.000	37
Brown, 3 b......................	U. of W............	6	.120	.666	26
Waldo, c.........................	"	6	.103	.917	7
Garner, s. s.....................	R. C...............	6	.100	.827	19
Ide, p............................	N. W. U...........	6	.087	.920	6
White, l. f......................	B. C...............	4	.062	.666	27
Cook, 3 b........................	N. W. U...........	4	.059	.515	31
Strong, l. f.....................	R. C...............	5	.000	.500	32

Played in less than three games:

Lewis, c. f......................	N. W. U...........	1	.500	1.000	1
Plummer, l. f...................	"	1	.400	.000	13
Crooks, c........................	R. C...............	2	.375	.821	7
Hansen, l. f.....................	N. W. U...........	2	.285	.500	12
Dearborn, 3 b...................	R. C...............	2	.250	1.000	2
Tomlinson, c. f.................	N. W. U...........	2	.222	.000	14
Reed, c. and 2 b................	R. C...............	2	.200	.882	6
Middlekauf, c. f................	N. W. U...........	2	.000	1.000	3
Stocking, 2 b....................	B. C...............	1	.000	1.000	4
Stowe, 1 b.......................	N. W. U...........	2	.000	.933	5
Goldburg, 1 b...................	R. C...............	2	.000	.769	8
Kern, 2 b........................	N. W. U...........	2	.000	.737	9
McKenna, s. s...................	U. of W............	2	.000	.666	10
Fullerton, s. s..................	N. W. U...........	2	.000	.615	11

Yours truly,   R. K. WELSH, Secretary.

INDEX

—TO—

RULES AND REGULATIONS.

	RULE.
The Ground...	1
The Infield..	2
The Bases...	3
The Foul Lines..	4
The Pitcher's Lines...................................	5
The Catcher's Lines...................................	6
The Captain's Lines...................................	7
The Players' Lines....................................	8
The Players' Bench....................................	9
The Batsman's Lines...................................	10
The Three Feet Lines..................................	11
The Lines Must be Marked..............................	12
The Ball..	13
of what composed..........................(1)	13
furnished by Home Club....................(2)	13
replaced if injured.......................(3)	13
" " lost.............................(4)	13
The Bat...	14

FIELD RULES.

Open Betting and Pool Selling Prohibited..............	15
Sale of Liquor Prohibited.............................	16
No Person Allowed on Field During Game	17
Players not to Sit with Spectators....................	18
Penalty for Insulting Umpire..........................	19
Penalty for not Keeping Field Clear...................	20
Restriction as to Addressing Audience.................	21

INDEX TO PLAYING RULES.

THE PLAYERS AND THEIR POSITIONS.

	RULE.
Nine Players on each Side	22
Players' Positions	23
in the Field(1)	23
at the Bat(2)	23
Order of Batting(3)	23
Restriction as to Occupying Catcher's Lines(4)	23

DEFINITIONS.

A High Ball	24
A Low Ball	25
A High or Low Ball	26
A Fair Ball	27
An Unfair Ball	28
A Balk	29
A Dead Ball	30
A Block	31
A Fair Hit	32–34
A Foul Hit	33–34
A Strike	35
A Foul Strike	36
"Play"	37
"Time"	38
"Game"	39
An Inning	40
A Time at Bat	41
Legal or Legally	42

THE GAME.

Number of Innings	43
Drawn Game	44
Forfeited Game	45
"No Game"	46
Substitute, when Allowed	47
Choice of First Innings	48
When Umpire Must Call "Play"	49
Game Must Begin when "Play" is Called	49
When Umpire May Suspend Play	49
" " " Terminate Game	49
Rain, effect of, in Terminating Game(4)	43
" " " " "	44
" " " " "	46
" Definition of	49
" Umpire's Duty in Case of	49
Batsman Must Call for Ball He Wants	**50**

	RULE.
What Umpire Must Count and Call	50
When Batsman is Out	51
" " becomes Base-Runner	52
Base-Runner must touch Bases in Order	53
" " when entitled to hold Base	53
" ' " " take one Base	54
" " " required to return to Base	55
No Substitute Allowed for Base-Runner	56
When Base-Runner is Out	57
When Umpire shall, without appeal, declare player "Out"	58
When Ball is not in Play until Returned to Pitcher	59
Block, effect of	60
Run, when to be Scored	61
Fines on Pitcher	62
" " any Player.....63 (4,) 68,	69
Player not to Address Umpire	63
" " " Audience	21
" " use Improper Language (4)	68
" to Obey Umpire's Orders (4)	68

THE UMPIRE.

Selection of Umpire	64
Disqualification of Umpire (3)	64
Removal of Umpire (4)	64
Duties as to Materials of Game (1)	65
" " Ground Rules (1)	65
" " Reversal of Decision (2)	65
Changing Umpire during Game	66
Expulsion of Umpire	67
Umpire's Jurisdiction and Powers	68
Umpire to give Notice of Fine (5,) (6)	68
" " " " Forfeited Game (6)	68
Special Penalties	69
SCORING REGULATIONS	70

CONSTRUCTION AND AMENDMENTS.

Construction of Rules	71
Amendment of Rules	72

PLAYING RULES

—OF THE—

NATIONAL LEAGUE

—OF—

Professional Base Ball Clubs;

1886.

ADOPTED IN PURSUANCE OF SECTION 51 OF
THE LEAGUE CONSTITUTION.

CLASS I.

THE MATERIALS OF THE GAME.

RULE 1. *The Ground* must be an inclosed field, sufficient in size to enable each player to play in his position as required by these Rules.

RULE 2. *The Infield* must be a space of ground thirty yards square.

RULE 3. *The Bases* must be

(1) Four in number, and designated as First Base, Second Base, Third Base and Home Base.

(2) The Home Base must be of white rubber or white stone, twelve inches square, so fixed in the ground as to be even with the surface, and so placed in the corner of the infield that two of its sides will form part of the boundaries of said infield.

(3) The First, Second and Third Bases must be canvas bags, fifteen inches square, painted white, and filled with some soft material, and so placed that the center of each shall be upon a separate corner of the infield, the First Base at the right, the Second Base opposite, and the Third Base at the left of the Home Base.

(4) All the Bases must be securely fastened in their positions, and so placed as to be distinctly seen by the Umpire.

RULE 4. *The Foul Lines* must be drawn in straight lines from the outer corner of the Home Base, through the center of the positions of First and Third Bases, to the boundaries of the Ground.

RULE 5. *The Pitcher's Lines* must be straight lines forming the boundaries of a space of ground, in the infield, seven feet long by four feet wide, distant fifty feet from the center of the Home Base, and so placed that the six feet lines would each be two feet distant from and parallel with a straight line passing through the center of the Home and Second Bases. Each corner of this space must be marked by a flat iron plate or stone, six inches square, fixed in the ground, even with the surface.

RULE 6. *The Catcher's Lines* must be drawn from the outer corner of the Home Base, in continuation of the Foul Lines, straight to the limits of the Ground back of the Home Base.

RULE 7. *The Captain's Lines* must be drawn from the Catcher's Lines to the Limits of the Ground, fifteen feet from and parallel with the Foul lines.

RULE 8. *The Players' Lines* must be drawn from the Catcher's Lines to the limits of the Ground, fifty feet from and parallel with the Foul Lines.

RULE 9. *The Players' Benches* must be furnished by the home club, and placed upon a portion of the ground outside the Players' Lines. They must be twelve feet in length, and immovably fastened to the ground. At the end of each bench must be immovably fixed a bat-rack, with fixtures for holding twenty bats; one such rack must be designated for the exclusive use of the Visiting Club, and the other for the exclusive use of the Home Club.

RULE 10. *The Batsman' Lines* must be straight lines forming the boundaries of a space on the right, and of a similar space on the left of the Home Base, six feet long by three feet wide extending three feet in front of and three feet behind the center of the Home Base, and with its nearest line distant one foot from the Home Base.

RULE 11. *The Three Feet Lines* must be drawn as follows: From a point on the Foul Line from Home Base to First Base, and equally distant from such bases, shall be drawn a line on Foul Ground, at a right angle to said Foul Line, and to a point three feet distant from it; thence running parallel with said Foul Line, to a point three feet distant from the center of the First Base; thence in a straight line to the center of the First Base, and thence upon the Foul Line to the point of beginning.

RULE 12. *The lines designated* in Rules 4, 5, 6, 7, 8, 10 and 11 must be marked with chalk or other suitable material, so as to be distinctly seen by the Umpire. They must all be so marked their entire length, *except* the Captain's and Players' Lines, which must be so marked for a distance of at least thirty-five yards from the Catcher's Lines, or to the limits of the grounds.

RULE 13. *The Ball.**

(1) Must not weigh less than five nor more than five and one-quarter ounces avoirdupois, and measure not less than nine nor more than nine and one-quarter inches in circumference. It must be composed of woolen yarn, and contain not more than one ounce of vulcanized rubber in mouldings, and be covered with leather. It must be furnished by the Secretary of the League, whose seal shall be final evidence of the legality of the ball.

(2) In all games the ball or balls played with shall be furnished by the Home Club, and become the property of the winning club.

(3) Should the ball become out of shape, or cut or ripped so as to expose the yarn, or in any way so injured as to be unfit for fair use in the opinion of the Umpire, on being appealed to by either Captain, a new ball shall at once be called for by the Umpire.

(4) Should the ball be knocked outside of the inclosure or lost during the game, the umpire shall at once call for another ball.

RULE 14. *The Bat.*

(1) Must be made wholly of wood, except that the handle may be wound with twine, or a granulated substance applied, not to exceed eighteen inches from the end.

(2) It must be round, except that a portion of the surface may be flat on one side, must not exceed two and one-half inches in diameter in the thickest part, and **must not** exceed forty-two inches in length.

CLASS II.

FIELD RULES.

RULE 15. *No Club* shall allow open betting or pool selling upon its grounds, nor in any building owned or occupied by it

---

* The Spalding League Ball has been the official ball of the National League for the past seven years, and has again been adopted for 1886. All games played under League rules this ball must be used.

PLAYING RULES.

Rule 16. *No Club* shall sell or allow to be sold upon its grounds, nor in any building owned or occupied by it, any spirituous, vinous or malt liquors.

Rule 17. *No person* shall be allowed upon any part of the field during the progress of the game, in addition to *the nine players and manager on each side and the umpire, except such officers of the law as may be present in uniform to preserve the peace.*

Rule 18. *Players in uniform* shall not be permitted to seat themselves among the spectators.

Rule 19. *The umpire* is the sole judge of play, and is entitled to the respect of the spectators, and any person offering any insult or indignity to him, must be promptly ejected from the grounds.

Rule 20. *Every Club* shall furnish sufficient police force upon its own grounds to preserve order, and in the event of a crowd entering the field during the progress of a game, and interfering with the play in any manner, the Visiting Club may refuse to play further until the field be cleared. If the ground be not cleared within fifteen minutes thereafter, the Visiting Club may claim, and shall be entitled to, the game by a score of nine runs to none (no matter what number of innings have been played).

Rule 21. No Umpire, Manager, Captain or Player shall address the audience during the progress of a game, except in case of necessary explanation.

CLASS III.

THE PLAYERS AND THEIR POSITIONS.

Rule 22. *The Players* of each club in a match game, shall be nine in number, one of whom shall be the Captain

Rule 23. *The Players' Positions* shall be

(1) When in the field (designated "Fielders" in these Rules) such as may be assigned them by their Captain, *except* that the Pitcher must take his position within the Pitcher s Lines, as defined in Rule 5.

(2) When their side goes to the bat they must immediately seat themselves upon the Players' Bench, and remain there until the side is put out, *except* when batsman or base-runner. All bats not in use must be kept in the bat racks, and the two players next succeeding the Batsman, in the order in which they are named on the Score, must be ready with bat in hand to promptly take position as batsman: *Provided*, That the Captain, and one assistant only, may occupy the space between the Players' Lines and the Captain's Lines, to coach Base-Runners.

(3) The Batsmen must take their positions within the Batsman's Lines, as defined in Rule 10, in the order in which they are named on the Score, which must contain the batting order of both nines and must be followed, except in case of disability of a player, in which case the substitute must take the place of the disabled player in the batting order.

(4) No player of the side at bat, *except* when Batsman, shall occupy any portion of the space within the Catcher's Lines as defined in Rule 6.

CLASS IV.

DEFINITIONS.

RULE 24. *A High Ball* is a ball legally delivered by the Pitcher, over the Home Base, higher than the belt of the Batsman, but not higher than his shoulder.

RULE 25. *A Low Ball* is a ball legally delivered by the Pitcher, over the Home Base, not higher than the Batsman's belt, nor lower than his knee.

RULE 26. *A High or Low Ball* is a ball legally delivered by the Pitcher, over the Home Base, not higher than the Batsman's shoulder, nor lower than his knee.

RULE 27. *A Fair Ball* is a ball delivered by the Pitcher while standing wholly within the lines of his position, and facing the batsman, the ball, so delivered, to pass over the home base, and at the height called for by the batsman.

RULE 28. *An Unfair Ball* is a ball delivered by the Pitcher as in Rule 27, except that the ball does not pass over the Home Base, or does not pass over the Home Base at the height called for by the Batsman.

RULE 29. *A Balk* is

(1) If the Pitcher, when about to deliver the ball to the bat, while standing within the lines of his position, make any one of the series of motions he habitually makes in so delivering the ball to the bat, without delivering it.

(2) If the ball be held by the Pitcher so long as to delay the game unnecessarily; or,

(3) If delivered to the bat by the Pitcher when any part of his person is upon ground outside the lines of his position.

RULE 30. *A Dead Ball* is a ball delivered to the bat by the Pitcher, that touches the Batsman's bat, without being struck at, or any part of the Batsman's person while standing in his position, without being struck at, or any part of the Umpire's person, without first passing the Catcher.

PLAYING RULES.

Rule 31. *A Block* is a batted or thrown ball that is stopped or handled by any person not engaged in the game.

Rule 32. *A Fair Hit* is a ball batted by the Batsman, standing in his position, that first touches the ground, the First Base, the Third Base, the part of the person of a player, or any other object that is in front of or on either of the Foul Lines, or (*exception*) batted directly to the ground by the Batsman, standing in his position, that (whether it first touches Foul or Fair Ground) bounds or rolls within the Foul Lines, between Home and First, or Home and Third Bases, without first touching the person of a player.

Rule 33. *A Foul Hit* is a ball batted by the Batsman, standing in his position, that first touches the ground, the part of the person of a player, or any other object that is behind either of the Foul Lines, or that strikes the person of such Batsman, while standing in his position, or (*exception*) batted directly to the ground by the Batsman, standing in his positson, that (whether it first touches Foul or Fair Ground) bounds or rolls outside the Foul Lines, between Home and First, or Home and Third Bases, without first touching the person of a player

Rule 34. When a batted ball passes outside the grounds, the Umpire shall decide it fair should it disappear within, or foul should it dispaper outside of the range of the foul lines, and Rules 32 and 33 are to be construed accordingly.

Rule 35. *A Strike is*

(1) A ball struck at by the Batsman without its touching his bat; or,

(2) A ball legally delivered by the Pitcher at the height called for by the Batsman, and over the Home Base, but not struck at by the Batsman.

Rule 36. *A Foul Strike* is a ball batted by the Batsman when any part of his person is upon ground outside the lines of the Batsman's position.

Rule 37. *Play* is the order of the Umpire to begin the game, or to resume play after its suspension.

Rule 38. *Time* is the order of the Umpire to suspend play. Such suspension must not extend beyond the day of the game.

Rule 39. *Game* is the announcement by the Umpire that the game is terminated.

Rule 40. *An Inning* is the turn at bat of the nine players representing a Club in a game, and is completed when three of such players have been put out as provided in these Rules.

Rule 41. *A time at bat* is the term at bat of a batsman. It begins when he takes his position, and continues until he is put out, or becomes a base runner.

Rule 42. *Legal, or Legally*, signifies as required by these rules.

CLASS V.

THE GAME.

RULE 43. *A Game* shall consist of nine innings to each contesting nine, except that:

(1) If the side first at bat scores less runs in nine innings than the other side has scored in eight innings, the game shall then terminate.

(2) If the side last at bat in the ninth innings scores the winning run before the third man is out, the game shall then terminate.

(3) If the score be a tie at the end of nine innings to each side, play shall only be continued until the side first at bat shall have scored one or more runs than the other side, in an equal number of innings; or until the other side shall score one more run than the side first at bat.

(4) If the Umpire calls "Game" on account of darkness or rain at any time after five innings have been completed by both sides, the score shall be that of the last equal innings played, *unless* the side second at bat shall have scored one or more runs than the side first at bat, in which case the score of the game shall be the total number of runs made.

RULE 44. *A Drawn Game* shall be declared by the Umpire when he terminates a game, on account of darkness or rain, after five equal innings have been played, if the score at the time is equal on the last even innings played; but (*exception*) if the side that went second to bat is then at the bat, and has scored the same number of runs as the other side, the Umpire shall declare the game drawn, without regard to the score of the last equal innings.

RULE 45. *A Forfeited Game* shall be declared by the Umpire, in favor of the Club not in fault, in the following cases:

(1) If the nine of a club fail to appear upon the field, or, being upon the Field, fail to begin the game within five minutes after the Umpire has called "Play" at the hour appointed for the beginning of the game.

(2) If, after the game has begun, one side refuses or fails to continue playing, *unless* such game has been suspended or terminated by the Umpire.

(3) If, after play has been suspended by the Umpire, one side fails to resume playing within five minutes after the Umpire has called "Play."

(4) If, in the opinion of the Umpire, any one of these Rules is willfully violated.

PLAYING RULES.

RULE 46. "*No Game*" shall be declared by the Umpire if he shall terminate play, on account of rain or darkness, before five innings on each side are completed.

RULE 47. A *Substitute* shall not be allowed to take the place of any player in a game, *unless* such player be disabled in the game then being played, by reason of illness or injury.

RULE 48. *The Choice of First Innings* shall be determined by the two Captains.

RULE 49. *The Umpire* must call "Play" at the hour appointed for beginning a game. The game must begin when the Umpire calls "Play." When he calls "Time," play shall be suspended until he calls "Play" again, and during the interim no player shall be put out, base be run, or run be scored. The Umpire shall suspend play only for an accident to himself, or a player; (but in case of accident to a Fielder, Time shall not be called until the ball be returned to, and held by the Pitcher, standing in his position); or in case rain falls so heavily that the spectators are compelled, by the severity of the storm, to seek shelter, in which case he shall note the time of suspension, and, should such rain continue to fall thirty minutes thereafter, he shall terminate the game. The Umpire shall also declare every "Dead Ball," "Block," "Foul Hit," "Foul Strike," and "Balk."

RULE 50. *The Batsman, on taking his position*, must call for a "High Ball," a "Low Ball," or a "High or Low Ball," and the Umpire shall notify the Pitcher to deliver the ball as required; such call shall not be changed after the first ball delivered. The Umpire shall count and call every "Unfair Ball" delivered by the Pitcher, and every "Dead Ball," if also an "Unfair Ball," as a "Ball;" and he shall also count and call every "Strike." Neither a "Ball" nor a "Strike" shall be called or counted until the ball has passed the Home Base.

RULE 51. *The Batsman is out:*

(1) If he fails to take his position at the bat in his order of batting, unless the error be discovered, and the proper Batsman takes his position before a fair hit has been made, and in such case the balls and strikes called will be counted in the time at bat of the proper Batsman.

(2) If he fails to take his position within one minute after the Umpire has called for the Batsman.

(3) If he makes a Foul Hit, and the ball be momentarily held by a fielder before touching the ground, provided it be not caught in a fielder's hat or cap, or touch some object other than the fielder before being caught.

(4) If he makes a Foul Strike.

(5) If he plainly attempts to hinder the Catcher from fielding the ball, evidently without effort to make a fair hit.

RULE 52. *The Batsman becomes a Base Runner*

(1) Instantly after he makes a Fair Hit.

(2) Instantly after seven Balls have been called by the Umpire.

(3) Instantly after three Strikes have been declared by the Umpire.

RULE 53. *The Base-Runner must touch each Base in regular order*, viz: First, Second, Third and Home Bases, and when obliged to return, must do so on the run, and must retouch the base or bases in reverse order. He shall only be considered as holding a base after touching it, and shall then be entitled to hold such base until he has legally touched the next base in order, or has been legally forced to vacate it for a succeeding Base Runner.

RULE 54. *The Base Runner shall be entitled, without being put out, to take one Base, provided he do so on the run*, in the following cases:

(1) If, while he was Batsman, the Umpire called seven Balls.

(2) If the Umpire awards a succeeding Batsman a base on seven balls, and the Base Runner is thereby forced to vacate the base held by him.

(3) If the Umpire calls a Balk.

(4) If a ball delivered by the Pitcher pass the Catcher and touch any fence or building within ninety feet of the Home Base.

(5) If he be prevented from making a base by the obstruction of an adversary.

(6) If the fielder stop or catch a batted ball with his hat or any part of his dress.

RULE 55. *The Base Runner shall return to his Base*, and shall be entitled to so return without being put out, provided he do so on the run.

(1) If the Umpire declares a Foul Hit, and the ball be not legally caught by a Fielder.

(2) If the Umpire declares a Foul Strike.

(3) If the Umpire declares a Dead Ball, unless it be also the sixth Unfair Ball, and he be thereby forced to take the next base, as provided in Rule 54 (2).

RULE 56. *The Base Runner shall not have a substitute run for him.*

RULE 57. *The Base Runner is out:*

(1) If, after three strikes have been declared against him

while Batsman, and the Catcher fails to catch the third-strike ball, he plainly attempts to hinder the Catcher from fielding the ball.

(2) If, having made a Fair Hit while Batsman, such fair-hit ball be momentarily held by a Fielder, before touching the ground or any object other than a Fielder: *Provided*, It be not caught in the Fielder's hat or cap.

(3) If, when the Umpire has declared three Strikes on him while Batsman, the third-strike ball be momentarily held by a Fielder before touching the ground: *Provided*, It be not caught in a Fielder's hat or cap, or touch some object other than a Fielder before being caught.

(4) If, after three Strikes or a Fair Hit, he be touched with the ball in the hand of a Fielder before such Base Runner touches First Base.

(5) If, after three Strikes or a Fair Hit, the ball be securely held by a Fielder, while touching First Base with any part of his person, before such Base Runner touches First Base.

(6) If, in running the last half of the distance from Home Base to First Base, he runs outside the Three Feet Lines, as defined in Rule 11, *except* that he must do so if necessary to avoid a Fielder attempting to field a batted ball, and in such case shall not be declared out.

(7) If, in running from First to Second Base, from Second to Third Base, or from Third to Home Base, he runs more than three feet from a direct line between such bases to avoid being touched by the ball in the hands of a Fielder; but in case a Fielder be occupying the Base Runner's proper path, attempting to field a batted ball, then the Base Runner shall run out of the path and behind said Fielder, and shall not be declared out for so doing.

(8) If he fails to avoid a Fielder attempting to field a batted ball, in the manner prescribed in (6) and (7) of this Rule, or if he, in any way, obstructs a Fielder attempting to field a batted ball: *Provided*, That if two or more Fielders attempt to field a batted ball, and the Base Runner comes in contact with one or more of them, the Umpire shall determine which Fielder is entitled to the benefit of this Rule, and shall not decide the Base Runner out for coming in contact with any other Fielder.

(9) If, at any time while the ball is in play, he be touched by the ball in the hand of a Fielder, unless some part of his person is touching a base he is entitled to occupy, provided the ball be held by the Fielder after touching him; *but (exception as to First Base)*, in running to First Base, he may overrun said base without being put out for being off said base after

first touching it, provided he returns at once and retouches the base, after which he may be put out as at any other base. If, in overrunning First Base, he also attempts to run to Second Base, he shall forfeit such exemption from being put out.

(10) If, when a Fair or Foul Hit ball is legally caught by a Fielder, such ball is legally held by a Fielder on the base occupied by the Base Runner when such ball was struck (or the Base Runner be touched with the ball in the hands of a Fielder), before he retouches said base after such Fair or Foul Hit ball was so caught. *Provided*, That the Base Runner shall not be out in such case, if, after the ball was legally caught as above, it be delivered to the bat by the Pitcher before the Fielder holds it on said base, or touches the Base Runner with it

(11) If, when a Batsman becomes a Base Runner (*except as provided in Rule 54*), the First Base, or the First and Second Bases, or the First, Second and Third Bases, be occupied, any Base Runner so occupying a base shall cease to be entitled to hold it, until any following Base Runner is put out, and may be put out at the next base or by being touched by the ball in the hands of a Fielder in the same manner as in running to First Base, at any time before any following Base Runner is put out.

(12) If a Fair Hit ball strike him, he shall be declared out and in such case no base shall be run unless forced, and no run be scored.

(13) If, when running to a base or forced to return to a base, he fail to touch the intervening base or bases, if any, in the order prescribed in Rule 53, he may be put out at the base he fails to touch, or by being touched by the ball in the hand of a Fielder, in the same manner as in running to First Base. *Provided*, That he shall not be declared out unless the Captain of the fielding side claim such decision before the ball is delivered to the bat by the Pitcher.

(14) If, when the Umpire calls "Play," after any suspension of a game, he fails to return to and touch the base he occupied when "Time" was called before touching the next base.

RULE 58. *The Umpire shall declare the Batsman or Base Runner out, without waiting for an appeal for such decision*, in all cases where such player is put out in accordance with these rules, *except* as provided in Rule 57, (10), (13) and (14).

RULE 59. *In case of a Foul Strike, Foul Hit not legally caught flying, Dead Ball, or Base Runner put out for being struck by a fair-hit ball,* the ball shall not be considered in play until it is held by the Pitcher standing in his position.

RULE 60. *Whenever a Block occurs*, the Umpire shall declare it, and Base Runners may run the bases without being put out, until after the ball has been returned to and held by the Pitcher standing in his position.

RULE 61. *One Run shall be scored* every time a Base Runner, after having legally touched the first three bases, shall touch the Home Base before three men are put out. If the third man is forced out, or is put out before reaching First Base, a run shall not be scored.

RULE 62. *If the Pitcher causes the ball to strike the Batsman*, and the Umpire be satisfied that he does it intentionally, he shall fine the Pitcher therefor in a sum not less than Ten Dollars, nor more than Fifty Dollars. (See League Contract paragraph 11).

RULE 63. *No Player except the Captain or his assistant shall address the Umpire* concerning any point of play, and any violation of this Rule shall subject the offender to a fine of five dollars by the Umpire.

CLASS VI.

THE UMPIRE.

RULE 64. A staff of four League umpires shall be selected by the Secretary before the 1st day of May.

(1) Applications for such positions will be received by the Secretary until the 1st day of March.

(2) A written contract shall be made with each of the four umpires selected, stipulating for his service from May 1 to Oct. 15, at a salary of one thousand dollars for such period, payable in equal monthly payments, at the expiration of each month of service. He shall also be allowed and paid his actual expenses while absent from his home in the service of the League.

(3) He shall be under the sole control and direction of the Secretary, from whom he will receive all assignments to duty and all instructions regarding the interpretation of the playing rules, and the Secretary shall see that he is proficient in the discharge of his duties, and that he shall appear in proper dress when acting as umpire.

(4) In the event of the failure of such umptre to umpire a game assigned to him, it shall be the duty of the Secretary to provide a substitute to umpire such game, and, in such case, there shall be deducted from the next monthly payment to the League Umpire the sum of twelve dollars for each game as-

signed to him, which, for any reason, he shall have failed to umpire.

(5) It shall be the duty of each League Club to accept as Umpire for any championship game such League Umpire or substitute as the Secretary shall assign to such game, and only in the event of the failure of the League Umpire or substitute so assigned to appear at the hour appointed for the beginning of such game, shall the duty devolve upon the visiting club to designate an Umpire for such game.

(6) Any League Umpire shall be subject to removal by the Secretary at any time, and in the event of the resignation, removal or expulsion of any League Umpire the Secretary shall have power to appoint a suitable person to fill the vacancy thus created.

RULE 65. *The Umpire's Duties*, in addition to those specified in the preceding Rules, are:

(1) Before the commencement of a Match Game, the Umpire shall see that the rules governing all the materials of the game are strictly observed. He shall ask the Captain of the Home Club whether there are any special ground rules to be enforced, and if there are, he shall see that they are duly enforced, provided they do not conflict with any of these Rules. He shall also ascertain whether the fence directly in the rear of the Catcher's position is distant ninety feet from the Home Base. A fair batted ball that goes over the fence at a less distance than two hundred and ten feet from home base shall entitle the batsman to two bases, and a distinctive line shall be marked on the fence at this point.

The Umpire shall not reverse his decision on any point of play upon the testimony of any player engaged in the game, or upon the testimony of any bystander.

(2) It shall be the duty of the Umpire to decide whether the grounds are in proper condition, and the weather suitable for play.

RULE 66. *The Umpire shall not be changed* during the progress of a Match Game, except for reason of illness or injury.

Rule 67. *Any League Umpire who shall in the judgment of the President of the League be guilty* of ungentlemanly conduct or of selling, or offering to sell, a game of which he is umpire, shall thereupon be removed from his official capacity and placed under the same disabilities inflicted upon expelled players by the **Constitution of the League.** (See also Constitution, Sec. 42).

RULE 68. *The Umpire's Jurisdictions and Powers*, in addition to those specified in the preceding Rules, are:

(1) The gentleman selected to fill the position of Umpire must keep constantly in mind the fact that upon his sound discretion and promptness in conducting the game, compelling players to observe the spirit as well as the letter of the Rules,

and enforcing each and every one of the Rules, largely depends the merit of the game as an exhibition, and the satisfaction of spectators therewith. He must make his decisions distinct and clear, remembering that every spectator is anxious to hear such decision. He must keep the contesting nines playing constantly from the commencement of the game to its termination, allowing such delays only as are rendered unavoidable by accident, injury or rain. He must, until the completion of the game, require the players of each side to promptly take their positions in the field as soon as the third hand is put out, and must require the first striker of the opposite side to be in his position at the bat as soon as the fielders are in their places.

(2) The players of the side "at bat" must occupy the portion of the field allotted them, subject to the condition that they must speedily vacate any portion thereof that may be in the way of the ball, or any fielder attempting to catch or field it. The triangular space behind the Home Base is reserved for the exclusive use of the Umpire, Catcher and Batsman, and the Umpire must prohibit any player of the side "at bat" from crossing the same at any time while the ball is in the hands of the Pitcher or Catcher, or is passing between them, while standing in their positions.

(3) Section 9 of the League Constitution makes the League Umpire a member of the League. During the progress of a game he is the sole representative of the League, to see that the game is played and determined solely on its merits, and these Rules invest him with ample powers to accomplish this purpose. In the performance of his duties he must remember that his sole allegiance is due to the League.

(4) The Umpire is master of the Field from the commencement to the termination of the game, and must compel the players to observe the provisions of all the Playing Rules, and he is hereby invested with authority to order any Player to do or omit to do any act, as he may deem it necessary to give force and effect to any and all of such provisions, and power to inflict upon any player disobeying any such order a fine of not less than five nor more than fifty dollars for each offense, and to impose a similar fine upon any player who shall use abusive, threatening or improper language to the Umpire, audience, or other player, and when the Umpire shall have so punished the player, he shall not have the power to revoke or remit the penalty so inflicted. (See League Contract, paragraph 11).

(5) The Umpire shall at once notify the Captain of the offending player's side of the infliction of any fine herein provided for, and the club to which such player belongs shall, upon receipt of a notice of said fine from the Secretary of

PLAYING RULES.   103

the League, within ten days transmit the amount of such fine to the Secretary of the League.

(6) In case the Umpire imposes a fine on a player, or declares a game forfeited, he shall transmit a written notice thereof to the Secretary of the League within twenty-four hours thereafter; and if he shall fail to do so, he shall forfeit his position as League Umpire, and shall forever thereafter be ineligible to umpire any League game.

RULE 69. For the special benefit of the patrons of the game, and because the offenses specified are under his immediate jurisdiction, and not subject to appeal by players, the attention of the Umpire is particularly directed to possible violations of the purpose and spirit of the Rules, of the following character:

1. Laziness or loafing of players in taking their places in the field, or those allotted them by the Rules when their side is at the bat, and especially any failure to keep the bats in the racks provided for them; to be ready (two men) to take position as Batsmen, and to remain upon the Players' Bench, except when otherwise required by the Rules.

2. Any attempt by players of the side at bat, by calling to a fielder, other than the one designated by his Captain, to field a ball, or by any other equally disreputable means seeking to disconcert a fielder.

3. Indecent or improper language addressed by a player to the audience, the Umpire, or any player.

In any of these cases the Umpire should promptly fine the offending player.

4. The Rules make a marked distinction between hindrance of an adversary in fielding a batted or a thrown ball. This has been done to rid the game of the childish excuses and claims formerly made by a Fielder failing to hold a ball to put out a Base Runner, but there may be cases of a Base Runner so flagrantly violating the spirit of the Rules and of the Game in obstructing a Fielder from fielding a thrown ball, that it would become the duty of the Umpire, not only to declare the Base Runner "out" (and to compel any succeeding Base Runners to hold their bases), but also to impose a heavy fine upon him. For example: If the Base Runner plainly strike the ball while passing him, to prevent its being caught by a Fielder: if he hold a Fielder's arms so as to disable him from catching the ball, or if he knock the Fielder down for the same purpose.

5. In the case of a "Block," if the person not engaged in the game should retain possession of the ball, or throw or kick it beyond the reach of the Fielders the Umpire should call

"Time," and require each Base Runner to stop at the last base touched by him, until the ball be returned to the Pitcher, standing in his position.

6. The Umpire must call "Play" at the exact time advertised for beginning a game, and any player not then ready to take the position allotted him, must be promptly fined by the Umpire.

7. The Umpire is only allowed, by the Rules, to call "Time" in case of an accident to himself or a player, or in case of rain, as defined by the Rules. The practice of players suspending the game to discuss or contest a decision with the Umpire, is a gross violation of the Rules, and the Umpire should promptly fine any player who interrupts the game in this manner.

CLASS VII.

Scoring.

RULE 70. *In Order to Promote Uniformity in Scoring* Championship Games, the following instructions, suggestions and definitions are made for the benefit of scorers of League clubs, and they are required to make the scores mentioned in Section 67 of the League Constitution in accordance therewith

Batting.

(1) The first item in the tabulated score, after the player's name and position, shall be the number of times he has been at bat during the game. Any time or times where the player has been sent to base on called balls shall not be included in this column.

(2) In the second column should be set down the runs made by each player.

(3) In the third column should be placed the first base hits made by each player. A base hit should be scored in the following cases.

When the ball from the bat strikes the ground between the foul lines, and out of reach of the fielders.

When a hit is partially or wholly stopped by a fielder in motion, but such player cannot recover himself in time to handle the ball before the striker reaches First Base.

When the ball is hit so sharply to an infielder that he cannot handle it in time to put out a man. In case of doubt over this class of hits, score a base hit and exempt fielder from the charge of an error.

When a ball is hit so slowly toward a fielder that he cannot handle it in time to put out a man.

(4) In the fourth column should be placed to the **credit of** each player the total bases made by him off his hits.

Fielding.

(5) The number of opponents put out by each player shall be set down in the fifth column. Where a striker is given out by the Umpire for a foul strike, or because he struck out of his turn the put-out shall be scored to the Catcher.

(6) The number of times the player assists shall be set down in the sixth column. An assist should be given to each player who handles the ball in a run-out or other play of the kind.

An assist should be given to a player who makes a play in time to put a runner out, even if the player who should complete the play fails, through no fault of the player assisting.

And generally an assist should be given to each player who handles the ball from the time it leaves the bat until it reaches the player who makes the put-out, or in case of a thrown ball, to each player who throws or handles it cleanly, and in such a way that a put-out results or would result if no error were made by the receiver.

An assist shall be given the pitcher when the batsman fails to hit the ball on the third strike, and the same shall also be entered in the summary under the head of "struck out."

(7) An error should be given for each misplay which allows the striker or base-runner to make one or more bases, when perfect play would have insured his being put out.

An error should be given to the pitcher when the batsman is given first base on "called balls."

In scoring errors off batted balls, see (3) of this rule.

Bases stolen by players shall appear to their **credit in the** summary of the game.

CLASS VIII.

CONSTRUCTION AND AMENDMENTS.

RULE 71. No section of these Rules shall be construed as conflicting with or affecting any article of the Constitution of the League.

RULE 72. *No Amendment* or change of any of these **Rules** shall be made, except in the manner provided in the **Constitution of the League.**

OFFICERS AND PLAYERS.

The following is an official list of the Officers of the National League of Professional Base Ball Clubs, and Officers and Players of Clubs, members thereof, for the season of 1886, so far as completed, to March 10th, 1886:

N. E. YOUNG, PRES. and SEC., Box 536, Washington, D. C.

DIRECTORS.

HENRY V. LUCAS, JNO. B. MALONEY, A. H. SODEN, and JNO. B. DAY.

BOSTON BASE BALL ASSOCIATION, OF BOSTON, MASS.

A. H. SODEN, *President*, *116 Water Street.*
J. B. BILLINGS, *Treasurer*, *Box 1756.*

Gunning, Thos. F. Tate, Edward C. Nash, Wm.
Poorman, Thos. Johnston, R. F. Stemmyer, Wm.
Sutton, E. B. Parsons, C. J. Burdock, J. J.
Dealey, P. Radbourn, Chas. Daily, C. F.
Hines, Paul A. Buffinton, C. G. Hornung, Jos.

CHICAGO BALL CLUB, OF CHICAGO, ILL.

A. G. SPALDING, *President*, *108 Madison St.*
JNO. A. BROWN, *Secretary*, *165 Loomis St.*

Ryan, Jas. Dalrymple, A. Flint, F. S.
Williamson, E. N. Pfeffer, Fred. Sunday, W. A.
Burns, Thos. E. Gore, Geo. F. Kelly, M. J.
Anson, A. C. Clarkson, Jno. G. Flynn, Jno.
Moolic, Geo. H. McCormick, Jas.

DETROIT BASE BALL ASSOCIATION, OF DETROIT, MICH.

JOS. A. MARSH, *President*, *94 Griswold St., Room 6.*
ROBT. H. LEADLEY, *Secretary*. *P. O. Box 122.*

Donnelly, J. B. Twitchell, Lawr'nce. Getstein, C. H.
Manning, J. H. Baldwin, C. B. Thompson, Sam'l L.
Brouthers, D. Rowe, J. C. Richardson, H.
White, Jas. L. Hall, Chas. L. McQuery, Wm.
Crane, Sam'l N. Fitzsimmons, O. K. Bennett, C. W.
Lawrence, H. J.

NEW YORK BALL CLUB, OF NEW YORK CITY.

JOHN B. DAY, *President, No. 121 Maiden Lane.*

Corcoran, S. J. Gerhardt, J. J. Conner, R.
Richardson, Dan'l. O'Rourke, J. H. Ward, J. M.

PHILADELPHIA BALL CLUB, OF PHILADELPHIA, PENN.

A. J. REACH, *President,*   JNO. I. ROGERS, *Secretary.*
  23 So. 8th St.   138 So. 6th St.
HARRY WRIGHT, *Manager,* 1941 N. 22d St.

Fogarty, Jas.	Andrews, G. E.	Mulvey, Jos.
Ganzell, C. W.	Siegle, John.	Bignall, Geo.
Titcomb, Ledell.	Guehrer, J. F.	Irwin, A. A.
Clements, John.	Casey, Daniel M.	Farrell, John.
Ferguson, C. J.	McGuire, Jas.	Daily, E. M.

ST. LOUIS ATHLETIC ASSOCIATION, OF ST. LOUIS, MO.

HENRY V. LUCAS, *President.*   G. H. SCHMELZ, *Manager.*
  2527 Cass Ave.

Cahill, Jno. F.	Quinn, Jos.	Bauer, Albert.
Seery, J. E.	Dolan, Thos.	Healy, John.
Howard, Kent.	Boyle, H. J.	Mappes, Geo.
Glasscock, J. W.	Dunlap, Fred.	McKinnon, A.
Denny, Jer.	Kirby, Jno.	Myers, Geo.
Graves, Frank.		

WASHINGTON (NATIONAL) BASE BALL CLUB, OF WASHINGTON, D. C.

ROBT. C. HEWETT, *President,*   WALTER F. HEWETT, *Sec'y.*
  1227 7th St. N. W.

Barr, R. M.	Baker, Philip.	Gladmon, J. H.
Knowles, Jas.	Crane, Ed. N.	Hines, Michael.

KANSAS CITY BASE BALL ASSOCIATION, OF KANSAS CITY, MO.

JOS. J. HEIM, *President.*   JAS. WHITFIELD, *Secretary.*

Record of Championship Games Played During the Season of 1885.

Date 1885.	Names of Contestants.	Winning Club	Runs Scored Winning Club	Runs Scored Losing Club
Apr. 30	St. Louis vs. Chicago	St. Louis	8	2
May 1	" "	Chicago	9	5
" 1	Detroit vs. Buffalo	Detroit	8	3
" 2	" "	"	10	4
" 2	St. Louis vs. Chicago	Chicago	17	1
" 2	New York vs. Boston	New York	2	1
" 2	Philadelphia vs. Providence	Providence	8	2
" 4	New York vs. "	New York	8	5
" 4	St. Louis vs. Chicago	Chicago	7	2
" 4	Detroit vs. Buffalo	Detroit	10	4
" 4	Philadelphia vs. Boston	Boston	2	0
" 5	" "	"	9	8
" 5	New York vs. Providence	Providence	4	3
" 6	Philadelphia vs. "	Philadelphia	9	6
" 6	New York vs. Boston	New York	5	3
" 8	Buffalo vs. Chicago	Chicago	13	4
" 8	Detroit vs. St. Louis	St. Louis	10	3
" 8	Philadelphia vs. Boston	Philadelphia	6	1
" 9	" "	"	15	5
" 9	New York vs. Providence	New York	1	0
" 11	Providence vs. Buffalo	Providence	9	4
" 11	New York vs. Chicago	New York	8	4
" 11	Boston vs. St. Louis	St. Louis	5	4
" 11	Philadelphia vs. Detroit	Philadelphia	10	3
" 12	" "	"	17	8
" 12	Boston vs. St. Louis	St. Louis	8	6
" 12	New York vs. Chicago	Chicago	10	2
" 12	Providence vs. Buffalo	Providence	5	1
" 13	" St. Louis	St. Louis	8	2
" 13	Philadelphia vs. Chicago	Chicago	9	3
" 13	Boston vs. Buffalo	Buffalo	7	3
" 13	New York vs. Detroit	New York	10	7
" 14	" "	"	5	3
" 14	Philadelphia vs. Chicago	Chicago	3	0
" 15	New York vs. "	New York	4	3
" 15	Boston vs. St. Louis	Boston	2	0
" 15	Philadelphia vs. Detroit	Philadelphia	6	3
" 15	Providence vs. Buffalo	Providence	3	0
" 16	" "	"	3	0
" 16	Philadelphia vs. Detroit	Philadelphia	8	7
" 16	Boston vs. St. Louis	St. Louis	4	2
" 16	New York vs. Chicago	New York	13	4
" 18	Philadelphia vs. "	Chicago	7	6
" 18	New York vs. Detroit	New York	12	7
" 19	" "	"	12	4
" 19	Philadelphia vs. Chicago	Chicago	11	9

Record of Championship Games.—*Continued.*

Date 1885.	Names of Contestants.	Winning Club	Runs Scored. Winning Club	Runs Scored. Losing Club
May 19	Boston vs. Buffalo	Boston	11	8
" 19	Providence vs. St. Louis	Providence	10	2
" 20	" "	"	10	4
" 20	Boston vs. Buffalo	Buffalo	6	3
" 21	" vs. Detroit	Boston	4	2
" 21	Philadelphia vs. St. Louis	Philadelphia	9	3
" 21	New York vs. Buffalo	Buffalo	4	3
" 21	Providence vs. Chicago	Chicago	10	8
" 22	" "	"	2	0
" 22	Boston vs. Detroit	Boston	14	1
" 22	New York vs. Buffalo	New York	9	4
" 23	Philadelphia vs. St. Louis	Philadelphia	12	1
" 23	New York vs. "	New York	6	1
" 23	Philadelphia vs. Buffalo	Buffalo	6	2
" 25	" "	Philadelphia	7	6
" 25	New York vs. St. Louis	New York	11	0
" 25	Boston vs. Chicago	Chicago	1	0
" 25	Providence vs. Detroit	Providence	3	1
" 26	" "	"	3	2
" 26	Boston vs. Chicago	Chicago	11	10
" 27	" vs. Detroit	Detroit	6	4
" 27	Philadelphia vs. St. Louis	Philadelphia	4	3
" 27	New York vs. Buffalo	New York	24	0
" 27	Providence vs. Chicago	Chicago	6	1
" 28	" vs. Detroit	Providence	11	5
" 28	New York vs. Buffalo	New York	11	0
" 28	Philadelphia vs. St. Louis	Philadelphia	4	0
" 28	Boston vs. Chicago	Boston	4	3
" 29	Philadelphia vs. Buffalo	Philadelphia	6	4
" 30	" "	"	7	0
" 30	New York vs. St. Louis	New York	10	9
" 30	" "	St. Louis	4	1
" 30	Boston vs. Detroit	Boston	4	8
" 30	Providence vs. Chicago	Providence	4	1
" 30	" vs. Detroit	"	4	3
June 1	Detroit vs. Chicago	Chicago	6	0
" 1	Philadelphia vs. New York	New York	3	2
" 1	Buffalo vs. St. Louis	Buffalo	8	4
" 2	" "	St. Louis	5	2
" 2	New York vs. Philadelphia	Philadelphia	3	1
" 2	Detroit vs. Chicago	Chicago	10	6
" 2	Providence vs. Boston	Providence	2	1
" 3	Boston vs. Providence	"	4	1
" 3	Philadelphia vs. New York	New York	8	7
" 3	Buffalo vs. St. Louis	Buffalo	11	0
" 4	" "	St. Louis	8	4
" 4	Detroit vs. Chicago	Chicago	5	2
" 5	" "	"	7	4

Record of Championship Games.—*Continued.*

Date 1885.		NAMES OF CONTESTANTS.	Winning Club	Runs Scored.	
				Winning Club.	Losing Club.
June	6	Chicago vs. St. Louis	"	9	2
"	6	New York vs. Philadelphia	New York	7	3
"	6	Buffalo vs. Detroit	Buffalo	5	4
"	6	Boston vs. Providence	Providence	6	2
"	8	Providence vs. Philadelphia	"	1	0
"	8	Buffalo vs. Detroit	Detroit	11	5
"	8	Chicago vs. St. Louis	Chicago	9	8
"	9	" "	"	6	1
"	9	Boston vs. New York	New York	10	4
"	9	Buffalo vs. Detroit	Buffalo	10	8
"	9	Providence vs. Philadelphia	Providence	4	1
"	10	" vs. New York	"	2	1
"	10	Buffalo vs. Detroit	Buffalo	7	5
"	10	Boston vs. Philadelphia	Philadelphia	4	2
"	10	Chicago vs. St. Louis	Chicago	13	1
"	11	Boston vs. Philadelphia	Boston	2	1
"	11	Providence vs. New York	New York	4	3
"	12	Boston vs. "	"	6	4
"	12	St. Louis vs. Buffalo	Buffalo	2	0
"	12	Chicago vs. Detroit	Chicago	6	4
"	13	" "	"	17	9
"	13	St. Louis vs. Buffalo	St. Louis	6	2
"	13	Boston vs. New York	New York	7	3
"	13	Providence vs. Philadelphia	Philadelphia	7	4
"	15	" vs. New York	New York	5	3
"	15	Boston vs. Philadelphia	Boston	9	3
"	15	Chicago vs. Detroit	Chicago	13	5
"	16	" "	"	8	6
"	16	St. Louis vs. Buffalo	Buffalo	5	0
"	16	Providence vs. New York	Providence	4	3
"	17	" vs. Philadelphia	"	10	4
"	17	Chicago vs. Buffalo	Chicago	8	1
"	17	Boston vs. New York	New York	10	0
"	17	" vs. Philadelphia	Philadelphia	5	3
"	17	St. Louis vs. Detroit	St. Louis	7	1
"	18	" "	Detroit	4	3
"	18	Chicago vs. Buffalo	Chicago	7	4
"	18	Providence vs. Boston	Providence	8	0
"	19	" "	Boston	9	5
"	19	Chicago vs. Buffalo	Chicago	9	8
"	19	Philadelphia vs. New York	New York	6	3
"	19	St. Louis vs. Detroit	St. Louis	3	0
"	20	" "	"	3	1
"	20	New York vs. Philadelphia	Philadelphia	11	8
"	20	Chicago vs. Buffalo	Chicago	5	0
"	20	Boston vs. Providence	Providence	9	8
"	23	Detroit vs. "	Detroit	11	0
"	23	Buffalo vs. New York	New York	7	6

LEAGUE CHAMPIONSHIP GAMES.

Record of Championship Games.—*Continued.*

Date 1885.	NAMES OF CONTESTANTS.	Winning Club	Runs Scored Winning Club	Runs Scored Losing Club
June 23	St. Louis vs. Boston	Boston	6	2
" 23	Chicago vs. Philadelphia	Chicago	5	3
" 24	" "	"	12	2
" 24	St. Louis vs. Boston	Boston	6	3
" 24	Buffalo vs. New York	New York	4	0
" 24	Detroit vs. Providence	Providence	7	6
" 25	" "	"	7	0
" 25	Buffalo vs. New York	New York	8	3
" 25	St. Louis vs. Boston	Boston	9	1
" 25	Chicago vs. Philadelphia	Philadelphia	2	0
" 26	" "	"	4	3
" 26	St. Louis vs. Boston	Boston	2	1
" 26	Buffalo vs. New York	New York	7	5
" 27	Chicago vs. Boston	Chicago	12	8
" 27	St. Louis vs. Philadelphia	St. Louis	9	4
" 27	Buffalo vs. Providence	Buffalo	5	4
" 29	" "	Providence	12	5
" 29	St. Louis vs. Philadelphia	St. Louis	3	2
" 29	Chicago vs. Boston	Chicago	14	10
" 29	Detroit vs. New York	Detroit	4	1
" 30	" "	New York	1	0
" 30	Chicago vs. Boston	Chicago	13	9
" 30	St. Louis vs. Philadelphia	St. Louis	5	4
" 30	Buffalo vs. Providence	Providence	16	9
July 1	" "	Buffalo	6	5
" 1	St. Louis vs. Philadelphia	Philadelphia	1	0
" 1	Chicago vs. Boston	Chicago	24	10
" 1	Detroit vs. New York	New York	2	1
" 2	" "	Detroit	4	0
" 3	" vs. Boston	"	6	1
" 3	Chicago vs. New York	New York	6	2
" 3	Buffalo vs. Philadelphia	Buffalo	6	5
" 3	St. Louis vs. Providence	Providence	3	2
" 4	" "	St. Louis	4	0
" 4	" "	"	5	2
" 4	Buffalo vs. Philadelphia	Philadelphia	10	5
" 4	" "	"	7	2
" 4	Chicago vs. New York	New York	8	3
" 4	" "	Chicago	6	3
" 4	Detroit vs. Boston	Detroit	8	4
" 4	" "	"	11	6
" 6	Chicago vs. New York	New York	7	4
" 6	Buffalo vs. Philadelphia	Buffalo	9	3
" 6	St. Louis vs. Providence	St. Louis	5	4
" 7	Detroit vs. Boston	Detroit	4	3
" 8	" vs. Philadelphia	"	13	5
" 8	St. Louis vs. New York	St. Louis	8	3
" 8	Buffalo vs. Boston	Boston	9	8

Record of Championship Games.—*Continued.*

Date 1885.		Names of Contestants.	Winning Club	Runs Scored.	
				Winning Club	Losing Club
July	8	Chicago vs. Providence	Chicago	10	3
"	9	" "	"	8	5
"	9	Buffalo vs. Boston	Boston	6	2
"	9	St. Louis vs. New York	St. Louis	6	5
"	9	Detroit vs. Philadelphia	Detroit	3	2
"	10	" "	Philadelphia	4	1
"	10	St. Louis vs. New York	New York	3	2
"	10	Buffalo vs. Boston	Boston	13	6
"	10	Chicago vs. Providence	Providence	5	2
"	11	" "	"	6	1
"	11	Buffalo vs. Boston	Buffalo	7	2
"	11	St. Louis vs. New York	New York	8	2
"	11	Detroit vs. Philadelphia	Detroit	5	4
"	13	" vs. St. Louis	"	9	5
"	13	Philadelphia vs. Boston	Philadelphia	7	1
"	13	Buffalo vs. Chicago	Chicago	6	4
"	13	New York vs. Providence	Providence	4	2
"	14	" "	New York	3	0
"	14	Buffalo vs. Chicago	Chicago	9	1
"	14	Philadelphia vs. Boston	Boston	2	0
"	14	Detroit vs. St. Louis	Detroit	5	0
"	15	" "	"	3	0
"	15	Buffalo vs. Chicago	Chicago	4	2
"	15	New York vs. Providence	New York	7	6
"	16	Philadelphia vs. Providence	Providence	4	2
"	16	Buffalo vs. Chicago	Chicago	9	2
"	16	" "	"	13	9
"	16	New York vs. Boston	Boston	6	5
"	16	Detroit vs. St. Louis	Detroit	13	8
"	17	New York vs. Boston	New York	3	2
"	17	Philadelphia vs. Providence	Providence	6	5
"	18	Providence vs. Buffalo	"	5	4
"	18	New York vs. St. Louis	New York	3	2
"	18	Boston vs. Chicago	Chicago	6	5
"	18	Philadelphia vs. Detroit	Philadelphia	8	4
"	20	" "	Detroit	8	1
"	20	Boston vs. Chicago	Chicago	7	3
"	20	New York vs. St. Louis	New York	3	2
"	20	Providence vs. Buffalo	Buffalo	5	3
"	21	Philadelphia vs. St. Louis	Philadelphia	6	0
"	21	Boston vs. Buffalo	Buffalo	6	3
"	21	New York vs. Detroit	New York	8	7
"	22	" "	"	7	2
"	22	Boston vs. Buffalo	Boston	12	7
"	22	Philadelphia vs. St. Louis	St. Louis	8	1
"	22	Providence vs. Chicago	Providence	6	5
"	23	" vs. Buffalo	"	7	2
"	23	New York vs. St. Louis	New York	15	3

LEAGUE CHAMPIONSHIP GAMES.

Record of Championship Games.—*Continued.*

Date 1885.	Names of Contestants.	Winning Club	Runs Scored. Winning Club.	Runs Scored. Losing Club.
July 23	Boston vs. Chicago	Chicago	12	2
" 23	Philadelphia vs. Detroit	Philadelphia	19	2
" 24	Boston vs. Chicago	Chicago	14	5
" 25	New York vs. St. Louis	New York	3	0
" 25	Boston vs. Buffalo	Buffalo	8	7
" 25	Philadelphia vs. Detroit	Philadelphia	2	1
" 27	" vs. St. Louis	St. Louis	6	1
" 27	Boston vs. Buffalo	Buffalo	9	6
" 27	Providence vs. Chicago	Chicago	4	0
" 27	New York vs. Detroit	New York	6	3
" 28	" "	Detroit	12	6
" 28	Boston vs. Chicago	Chicago	8	7
" 28	Philadelphia vs. St. Louis	St. Louis	6	3
" 28	Providence vs. Buffalo	Providence	11	4
" 29	" vs. Chicago	Chicago	3	2
" 29	Boston vs. Buffalo	Boston	1	0
" 30	" vs. Detroit	"	3	2
" 30	Philadelphia vs. Chicago	Chicago	2	0
" 30	New York vs. Buffalo	New York	3	1
" 30	Providence vs. St. Louis	Providence	4	2
" 31	" "	"	4	1
" 31	Boston vs. Detroit	Detroit	3	2
" 31	New York vs. Buffalo	New York	10	7
" 31	Philadelphia vs. Chicago	Chicago	9	0
Aug. 1	" vs. Buffalo	Philadelphia	6	5
" 1	New York vs. Chicago	New York	7	6
" 1	Boston vs. St. Louis	Tie	0	0
" 1	Providence vs. Detroit	Providence	3	1
" 3	" "	"	11	9
" 3	Boston vs. St. Louis	Boston	7	2
" 4	" vs. Detroit	"	4	2
" 4	Philadelphia vs. Chicago	Chicago	13	3
" 4	New York vs. Buffalo	New York	7	1
" 4	Providence vs. St. Louis	Providence	5	4
" 5	" "	"	4	3
" 5	Boston vs. Detroit	Boston	3	1
" 5	Philadelphia vs. Chicago	Chicago	6	0
" 6	" vs. Buffalo	Philadelphia	9	5
" 6	New York vs. Chicago	New York	1	0
" 6	Boston vs. St. Louis	Boston	5	2
" 6	Providence vs. Detroit	Providence	3	1
" 7	" "	Detroit	3	2
" 7	Boston vs. St. Louis	St. Louis	4	3
" 7	New York vs. Chicago	Chicago	8	3
" 8	Boston vs. St. Louis	St. Louis	7	3
" 8	Philadelphia vs. Buffalo	Philadelphia	7	5
" 10	" "	Buffalo	5	2
" 10	New York vs. Chicago	New York	12	0

Record of Championship Games.—*Continued.*

Date 1885.	Names of Contestants.	Winning Club	Runs Scored Winning Club	Runs Scored Losing Club
Aug. 11	Boston vs. New York	Boston	8	4
" 11	Buffalo vs. Chicago	Chicago	7	2
" 11	Providence vs. Philadelphia	Philadelphia	5	1
" 12	" "	"	2	0
" 12	Buffalo vs. St. Louis	Buffalo	10	3
" 12	Boston vs. New York	New York	3	2
" 12	Detroit vs. Chicago	Chicago	9	7
" 13	" "	"	5	3
" 13	Boston vs. Philadelphia	Philadelphia	4	3
" 13	Buffalo vs. St. Louis	Buffalo	14	3
" 13	Providence vs New York	New York	8	1
" 14	Buffalo vs. St. Louis	Buffalo	6	0
" 14	Detroit vs. Chicago	Chicago	9	4
" 15	" "	"	7	4
" 15	Boston vs. Philadelphia	Boston	7	2
" 15	Buffalo vs. St. Louis	Buffalo	17	6
" 15	Providence vs. New York	New York	12	2
" 17	New York vs. Philadelphia	"	4	2
" 18	" "	"	7	3
" 18	Chicago vs. St. Louis	Chicago	9	4
" 18	Detroit vs. Buffalo	Buffalo	6	4
" 18	Providence vs. Boston	Boston	7	3
" 19	Boston vs. Providence	Providence	10	4
" 19	Detroit vs. Buffalo	Buffalo	3	2
" 19	Chicago vs. St. Louis	Chicago	6	3
" 19	Philadelphia vs. New York	Philadelphia	4	3
" 20	" "	New York	7	1
" 20	Chicago vs. St. Louis	Chicago	7	4
" 20	Detroit vs. Buffalo	Buffalo	6	4
" 20	Providence vs. Boston	Providence	5	4
" 21	Detroit vs. Buffalo	Buffalo	5	3
" 21	New York vs. Philadelphia	New York	7	1
" 22	" "	"	9	0
" 22	Chicago vs. St. Louis	Chicago	5	1
" 22	Detroit vs. Buffalo	Detroit	9	4
" 22	Boston vs. Providence	Boston	7	0
" 24	New York vs "	New York	10	5
" 24	Philadelphia vs. Boston	Boston	2	0
" 25	St. Louis vs. Buffalo	St. Louis	13	7
" 25	Chicago vs. Detroit	Chicago	8	0
" 26	" "	"	2	2
" 26	St. Louis vs. Buffalo	Buffalo	6	5
" 26	New York vs. Providence	New York	6	0
" 26	Philadelphia vs. Boston	Philadelphia	5	1
" 27	" vs. Providence	"	3	0
" 27	New York vs. Boston	New York	2	1
" 27	St. Louis vs. Buffalo	Buffalo	5	1
" 27	Chicago vs. Detroit	Detroit	1	0

LEAGUE CHAMPIONSHIP GAMES.

Record of Championship Games.—*Continued*

Date 1885.	Names of Contestants.	Winning Club	Runs Scored. Winning Club	Losing Club
Aug. 28	St. Louis vs. Buffalo................	Buffalo........	7	4
" 28	New York vs. Boston................	New York....	3	1
" 28	Philadelphia vs. Providence.........	Philadelphia..	2	1
" 29	" "	"	1	0
" 29	New York vs. Boston................	New York....	7	1
" 29	St. Louis vs. Buffalo...............	Buffalo......	6	5
" 31	Philadelphia vs. New York..........	New York. ..	5	1
" 31	Chicago vs. Detroit.................	Chicago......	16	6
" 31	Boston vs. Providence..............	Boston........	6	1
Sept. 1	Providence vs. Boston..............	"	2	0
" 1	St. Louis vs. Detroit...............	Detroit........	8	3
" 1	Chicago vs. Buffalo................	Chicago......	8	4
" 1	" "	Chicago.....	12	9
" 1	St. Louis vs. Detroit...............	Detroit.....	2	1
" 1	Boston vs. Providence..............	Boston	4	3
" 3	" "	"	11	1
" 3	St. Louis vs. Detroit...............	Detroit........	5	2
" 3	New York vs. Philadelphia..........	New York....	18	3
" 3	Chicago vs. Buffalo................	Chicago.......	10	4
" 4	" "	"	12	4
" 4	New York vs. Boston	New York	6	3
" 5	Philadelphia vs. New York..........	Philadelphia..	5	2
" 5	Chicago vs. Buffalo................	Chicago	6	0
" 5	St. Louis vs. Detroit...............	Detroit	2	0
" 5	Boston vs. Providence..............	Boston........	7	2
" 7	" "	"	9	6
" 7	Philadelphia vs. New York..........	Philadelphia..	3	1
" 8	Providence vs. Philadelphia........	"	1	0
" 8	St. Louis vs. Chicago	Tie..........	1	1
" 8	Boston vs. New York...............	New York....	10	4
" 9	St. Louis vs. Chicago	St. Louis......	7	2
" 9	Boston vs. New York...............	Boston........	2	0
" 9	Providence vs. Philadelphia........	Providence ...	3	1
" 10	New York vs. Providence..........	New York....	8	1
" 10	St. Louis vs. Chicago	Chicago	8	1
" 10	Boston vs. Philadelphia............	Philadelphia..	7	5
" 10	Buffalo vs. Detroit.................	Buffalo	5	2
" 11	" "	"	3	1
" 11	St. Louis vs. Chicago	Chicago......	2	0
" 11	New York vs. Providence...........	New York....	9	1
" 12	Boston vs. Philadelphia............	Philadelphia...	2	0
" 12	Buffalo vs. Detroit.................	Buffalo........	6	4
" 12	" "	"	6	3
" 14	St. Louis vs. Chicago	Chicago.......	10	2
" 15	" vs. Providence.......	Providence.. ...	6	0
" 15	Chicago vs. Boston	Boston........	7	2
" 15	Buffalo vs. Philadelphia...........	Buffalo	7	3
" 15	Detroit vs. New York...............	New York....	8	4

Record of Championship Games.—*Continued.*

Date 1885.	NAMES OF CONTESTANTS.	Winning Club	Runs Scored. Winning Club.	Runs Scored. Losing Club.
Sept.16	Detroit vs. New York	Detroit	6	2
" 16	St. Louis vs. Providence	St. Louis	6	4
" 16	Buffalo vs. Philadelphia	Philadelphia	7	3
" 16	Chicago vs. Boston	Chicago	10	4
" 17	" "	"	12	6
" 17	Buffalo vs. Philadelphia	Philadelphia	6	3
" 17	Detroit vs. New York	New York	1	0
" 17	St. Louis vs. Providence	St. Louis	12	2
" 18	" "	St. Louis	7	3
" 18	Chicago vs. Boston	Chicago	10	3
" 19	Buffalo vs. Philadelphia	Philadelphia	12	2
" 19	Detroit vs. New York	New York	6	5
" 19	St. Louis vs. Providence	St. Louis	7	0
" 21	Buffalo vs. New York	New York	10	0
" 22	St. Louis vs. Boston	St. Louis	14	9
" 22	Detroit vs. Philadelphia	Detroit	4	1
" 22	Chicago vs. Providence	Chicago	8	5
" 23	" "	"	16	8
" 23	Detroit vs. Philadelphia	Philadelphia	12	5
" 23	St. Louis vs. Boston	St. Louis	2	1
" 23	New York vs. Buffalo	New York	17	2
" 24	" "	"	11	3
" 24	St. Louis vs. Boston	St. Louis	6	1
" 24	Detroit vs. Philadelphia	Detroit	6	3
" 24	Chicago vs. Providence	Providence	6	3
" 25	" "	Chicago	21	3
" 25	New York vs. Buffalo	New York	15	1
" 26	" "	"	4	1
" 26	St. Louis vs. Boston	Boston	5	2
" 26	Detroit vs. Philadelphia	Detroit	10	6
" 26	Chicago vs. Providence	Chicago	6	0
" 28	Detroit vs. Providence	Detroit	14	2
" 29	" "	"	13	1
" 29	Chicago vs. New York	Chicago	7	4
" 29	Buffalo vs. Boston	Boston	13	2
" 30	" "	"	5	3
" 30	Chicago vs. New York	Chicago	2	1
" 30	St. Louis vs. Philadelphia	Philadelphia	8	3
" 30	Detroit vs. Providence	Detroit	8	5
Oct. 1	" "	"	10	6
" 1	Chicago vs. New York	Chicago	8	3
" 1	Buffalo vs. Boston	Boston	7	3
" 2	St. Louis vs. Philadelphia	Tie	3	3
" 3	" "	Philadelphia	10	4
" 3	Chicago vs. New York	New York	12	8
" 3	Buffalo vs. Boston	Boston	18	0
" 5	St. Louis vs. Philadelphia	Philadelphia	5	2
" 6	" vs. New York	St. Louis	7	4

Record of Championship Games.—*Continued.*

Date 1885.	NAMES OF CONTESTANTS.	Winning Club	Runs Scored. Winning Club.	Losing Club.
Oct. 6	Chicago vs. Philadelphia	Chicago	9	4
" 6	Detroit vs Boston	Boston	3	2
" 7	" "	Detroit	7	1
" 7	St. Louis vs. New York	New York	5	1
" 7	Buffalo vs. Providence	Providence	4	0
" 7	" "	"	6	1
" 8	St. Louis vs. New York	New York	8	3
" 8	Chicago vs. Philadelphia	Philadelphia	5	3
" 8	Detroit vs. Boston	Detroit	7	6
" 9	" "	"	3	2
" 9	Chicago vs. Philadelphia	Philadelphia	12	11
" 9	St. Louis vs. New York	New York	5	0
" 10	Chicago vs. Philadelphia	Philadelphia	10	8
" 10	Providence vs. Buffalo	Providence	8	0
" 10	" "	"	7	3
	Total		3127	1280

BATTING RECORD

Of Players who have taken part in fifteen or more championship games.

SEASON OF 1885.

Rank	NAME.	CLUB.	Games Played.	Times at Bat.	Runs Scored.	Ave. per Game.	First Bases Hits.	Percentage.	Total Bases.	Ave. per Game.
1	Connor	New York	110	455	102	0.92	169	.371	225	2.04
2	Brouthers	Buffalo	98	407	87	0.88	146	.358	220	2.24
3	Dorgan	New York	88	347	60	0.68	113	.325	145	1.64
4	Richardson	Buffalo	96	426	90	0.93	136	.319	195	2.03
5	Gore	Chicago	109	441	115	1.05	138	.312	201	1.84
5	Sutton	Boston	108	457	78	0.72	143	.312	192	1.77
6	Anson	Chicago	112	464	100	0.89	144	.310	212	1.89
7	Ferguson	Philadelphia	59	235	42	0.71	72	.306	89	1.50
8	Ewing	New York	81	342	81	1.00	104	.304	158	1.95
9	Thompson	Detroit	63	254	58	0.92	77	.303	123	1.95
10	Hanlon	"	106	424	93	0.87	128	.301	160	1.50
11	O'Rourke	New York	112	477	119	1.06	143	.299	206	1.83
11	Gillespie	"	102	420	67	0.65	123	.292	152	1.49
12	Lewis	St. Louis	45	181	12	0.26	53	.292	64	1.42
12	White	Buffalo	98	404	54	0.55	118	.292	133	1.35
13	Wood	Detroit	82	362	62	0.75	105	.290	154	1.87
14	Rowe	Buffalo	96	421	62	0.63	122	.289	171	1.74
15	Kelly	Chicago	107	438	124	1.15	126	.287	191	1.78
16	Dorgan	Detroit	89	161	23	0.59	46	.285	56	1.43
17	Wise	Boston	107	424	71	0.66	120	.283	167	1.56
18	Glasscock	St. Louis	111	446	66	0.59	125	.280	152	1.37
19	Start	Providence	99	374	47	0.47	103	.275	122	1.23
20	Dalrymple	Chicago	113	492	109	0.96	135	.274	219	1.93
21	M·Query	Detroit	70	278	34	0.48	76	.273	106	1.51
22	Burns	Chicago	111	445	82	0.73	121	.271	182	1.64
23	Hines	Providence	98	411	63	0.64	111	.270	141	1.43
23	McKinnon	St. Louis	100	411	42	0.42	121	.270	152	1.52
24	Dunlap	"	106	428	70	0.66	114	.269	141	1.33
24	Bennett	Detroit	91	349	49	0.53	94	.269	156	1.71
25	Mulvey	Philadelphia	106	443	74	0.69	119	.268	174	1.64
26	Andrews	"	103	421	77	0.74	112	.266	133	1.29
27	Scott	Detroit	38	148	14	0.36	39	.263	46	1.21
28	Richardson	New York	48	198	26	0.54	52	.262	66	1.37
29	Daly	Providence	59	223	20	0.33	58	.260	63	1.06
	Manning	Philadelphia	107	445	61	0.57	114	.256	155	1.44
30	Deasley	New York	52	207	22	0.42	53	.256	60	1.15
	Esterbrook	"	88	359	48	0.54	92	.256	120	1.36
31	Nash	Boston	26	94	9	0.34	24	.255	28	1.07
31	Sunday	Chicago	42	172	36	0.85	44	.255	59	1.40
32	Lillie	Buffalo	112	430	49	0.43	107	.248	129	1.15
33	Ringo	Detroit	16	65	12	0.75	16	.246	19	1.18
34	Farrar	Philadelphia	111	420	49	0.44	103	.245	139	1.24

BATTING RECORD.—Continued.

Rank.	NAME.	CLUB.	Games Played.	Times at Bat.	Runs Scored.	Ave. per Game.	First Base Hits.	Percentage.	Total Bases.	Ave. per Game.
35	Radford........	Providence.....	105	371	55	0.52	90	.242	110	1.04
36	Baldwin.......	Detroit........	31	124	12	0.38	30	.241	42	1.35
	Crowley.......	Buffalo........	92	344	29	0.31	83	.241	101	1.09
	Poorman	Boston........	55	224	44	0.80	54	.241	73	1.32
37	Pfeffer.........	Chicago........	112	469	90	0.80	113	.240	152	1.35
38	Buffinton......	Boston........	82	338	26	0.31	81	.239	102	1.24
39	Johnston......	"	26	109	17	0.65	26	.238	41	1.57
	Williamson...	Chicago........	112	407	87	0.77	97	.238	137	1.22
40	Whitney......	Boston........	72	290	35	0.48	68	.234	82	1.13
41	Carroll........	Providence. ...	104	426	62	0.59	99	.232	117	1.12
	Radbourne....	"	65	249	34	0.52	58	.232	71	1.09
	Donnelly.....	Detroit........	55	211	24	0.43	49	.232	61	1.10
42	Fogarty.......	Philadelphia...	111	427	49	0.44	99	.231	118	1.06
43	Dealey........	Boston........	34	130	18	0.52	30	.230	39	1.14
44	Ward.........	New York.....	111	446	72	0.64	101	.226	125	1.12
45	Force..........	Buffalo	71	253	20	0.28	57	.225	65	0.91
	Morrill, ...	Boston........	111	394	74	0.66	89	.225	131	1.18
46	Denny........	Providence.....	83	318	40	0.48	71	.223	103	1.24
47	Wood.........	Buffalo.......	28	104	10	0.35	23	.221	29	1.03
48	Hines.........	Bos. and Prov..	15	59	11	0.73	13	.220	17	1.13
49	Purcell........	Boston	21	87	9	0.42	19	.218	22	1.04
	Manning......	Bos. and Det...	104	384	49	0.47	84	.218	124	1.19
	M'Cormick....	Prov. and Chi..	29	119	15	0.51	27	.218	37	1.27
50	Clarkson......	Chicago........	72	283	34	0.47	61	.215	94	1.30
51	Gilligan	Providence....	69	252	24	0.64	54	.214	67	0.97
52	Quinn.........	St. Louis......	97	343	27	0.27	73	.212	85	0.87
53	Getzein.......	Detroit........	39	137	9	0.23	29	.211	32	0.82
54	Phillips.......	"	33	139	13	0.39	29	.208	34	1.03
	Flint..........	Chicago........	67	249	27	0.40	52	.208	67	1.00
55	Sweeney......	St. Louis......	73	270	28	0.38	56	.207	64	0.87
56	Farrell	Providence.....	67	257	27	0.40	53	.206	65	0.97
	Daily.........	Philadelphia...	49	184	22	0.44	38	.206	53	1.08
	Welch........	New York.....	55	199	28	0.50	41	.206	54	0.98
57	Myers.........	Buffalo........	89	326	40	0.44	67	.205	78	0.87
58	Myers.........	Philadelphia..	93	357	25	0.26	73	.204	93	1.00
59	Boyle.........	St. Louis......	72	258	24	0.33	52	.201	66	0.91
	Hornung	Boston........	25	109	14	0.56	22	.201	32	1.28
60	Stearns	Buffalo........	30	105	7	0.23	21	.200	29	0.96
61	Briody........	St. Louis......	61	215	14	0.22	42	.195	54	0.88
	Quest.........	Detroit........	55	200	24	0.43	39	.195	47	0.85
62	Shaffer........	St. Louis......	69	257	30	0.43	50	.194	64	0.92
63	M'Cauley.....	Chi. and Buffalo	27	98	5	0.18	18	.193	22	0.81
64	Clements......	Philadelphia...	52	188	14	0.27	36	.191	56	1.07
	Crane.........	Detroit........	68	245	23	0.33	47	.191	67	0.98
65	McGuire......	"	34	121	11	0.32	23	.190	31	0.91
66	Galvin........	Buffalo........	32	122	14	0.43	23	.188	34	1.06
67	Whiteley	Boston..... .	33	135	14	0.42	25	.185	31	0.94
68	Gunning......	"	48	174	17	0.35	32	.184	35	0.73
	Hackett, W. H.	"	35	125	8	0.22	23	.184	26	0.74
69	Hackett, M. M.	"	33	115	9	0.27	21	.182	30	0.90
	McCarthy.....	"	40	148	16	0.40	27	.182	29	0.72

BATTING RECORD.—Continued.

Rank.	NAME.	CLUB.	Games Played.	Times at Bat.	Runs Scored.	Ave. per Game	First Base Hits.	Percentage.	Total Bases.	Ave. per Game.
70	Caskins........	St. Louis.......	70	262	31	0.44	47	.179	50	0.71
	Irwin..........	Providence.....	59	218	16	0.25	39	.179	43	0.73
71	Cusick.........	Philadelphia...	39	141	12	0.30	25	.177	26	0.66
	Morton.........	Detroit.........	22	79	9	0.40	14	.177	20	0.90
72	Ganzel.........	Philadelphia...	33	125	15	0.45	21	.168	26	0.78
73	Bastian.........	"	104	285	63	0.60	65	.167	98	0.94
74	Sutcliffe........	Chi. and St. L..	26	91	7	0.27	15	.164	19	0.73
75	Keefe...........	New York.....	46	166	20	0.43	27	.162	35	0.76
	Seery..........	St. Louis.......	58	216	20	0.34	35	.162	45	0.77
76	Rowe...........	"	16	62	8	0.50	10	.161	13	0.81
77	Knight.........	Providence	25	81	8	0.32	13	.160	13	0.52
78	Weidman.......	Detroit	43	153	7	0.16	24	.156	31	0.72
79	Gerhardt	New York......	112	399	43	0.38	62	.155	78	0.69
80	Serad..........	Buffalo.........	29	104	8	0.27	16	.153	19	0.65
81	Bassett.........	Providence.....	81	285	21	0.25	41	.143	52	0.64
82	Burdock........	Boston.........	45	169	18	0.40	24	.142	30	0.66
83	Shaw...........	Providence....	48	165	17	0.35	22	.133	23	0.47
84	Halpin.........	Detroit.........	15	54	3	0.20	7	.129	8	0.53
85	Baker..........	St. Louis.......	39	131	5	0.12	16	.122	16	0.41
86	Conway........	Buffalo........	29	90	7	0.24	10	.111	18	0.62

FIELDING AVERAGES

Of Players who have taken part in fifteen or more championship games,
SEASON OF 1885.

FIRST BASEMEN.

Rank	NAME	CLUB	Games Played	Number Put Out	Times Assisting	Fielding Errors	Total Chances	Percentage Accepted
1	McKinnon	St. Louis	100	1102	26	25	1153	.978
2	McQuery	Detroit	70	707	28	18	753	.976
3	Brouthers	Buffalo	98	996	25	26	1047	.975
3	Conner	New York	110	1178	42	31	1251	.975
4	Farrar	Philadelphia	111	1153	41	31	1225	.974
5	Start	Providence	99	1036	35	31	1102	.971
6	Morrill	Boston	92	952	32	31	1015	.969
7	Scott	Detroit	38	394	18	14	426	.967
8	Buffinton	Boston	15	159	2	6	167	.964
9	Anson	Chicago	112	1253	39	57	1349	.957

SECOND BASEMEN.

Rank	NAME	CLUB	Games Played	Number Put Out	Times Assisting	Fielding Errors	Total Chances	Percentage Accepted
1	Dunlap	St. Louis	106	314	374	49	787	.933
2	Morrill	Boston	17	56	48	9	113	.920
3	Burdock	"	45	99	134	21	254	.917
4	Gerhardt	New York	112	314	352	65	731	.911
5	Crane	Detroit	68	179	197	38	414	.908
6	Richardson	Buffalo	49	163	169	35	367	.904
7	Farrell	Providence	67	158	194	30	391	.900
7	Bassett	"	39	84	123	23	230	.900
8	Quest	Detroit	39	107	122	26	255	.898
9	Hackett, W. H.	Boston	20	42	50	11	103	.893
10	Pfeffer	Chicago	109	325	391	86	802	.892
11	Myers	Philadelphia	93	201	287	64	552	.884
12	Force	Buffalo	42	113	134	33	280	.882
13	Wise	Boston	22	56	67	18	141	.872

THIRD BASEMEN.

Rank	NAME	CLUB	Games Played	Number Put Out	Times Assisting	Fielding Errors	Total Chances	Percentage Accepted
1	Richardson	New York	21	15	43	3	61	.950
2	Bassett	Providence	21	27	50	6	83	.927
3	Williamson	Chicago	111	113	258	45	416	.891
4	White	Buffalo	98	118	198	40	356	.887
5	Esterbrook	New York	84	111	159	35	305	.885
6	Caskins	St. Louis	67	82	139	29	250	.884
7	Sutton	Boston	90	132	168	43	343	.874
8	Denny	Providence	83	128	157	43	328	.868
9	Nash	Boston	18	24	27	8	59	.864
10	Donnelly	Detroit	55	73	102	31	206	.849
11	Mulvey	Philadelphia	106	144	201	62	407	.847
12	Quinn	St. Louis	31	33	64	19	116	.836
13	Morton	Detroit	18	20	37	19	76	.750

122 LEAGUE FIELDING AVERAGES—CONTINUED.

SHORT STOPS.

Rank	NAME.	CLUB.	Games Played.	Number Put Out.	Times Assisting.	Fielding Errors.	Total Chances.	Percentage Accepted.
1	Glasscock	St. Louis	109	156	397	50	603	.917
2	Bassett	Providence	21	29	75	10	114	.912
2	Force	Buffalo	23	28	66	9	103	.912
3	Ward	New York	111	167	350	55	572	.903
4	Bastian	Philadelphia	104	164	337	62	563	.889
5	Sutton	Boston	15	12	50	8	70	.885
6	Phillips	Detroit	33	35	120	21	176	.880
7	Irwin	Providence	58	70	209	40	319	.874
8	Wise	Boston	79	135	270	67	472	.855
9	Radford	Providence	16	13	43	10	66	.848
10	Burns	Chicago	111	151	370	96	617	.844
11	Quest	Detroit	15	10	46	11	67	.835
12	Rowe	Buffalo	64	71	186	51	308	.831
13	Hackett, W. H.	Boston	15	17	36	11	64	.828
14	Stearns	Buffalo	18	32	46	17	95	.821
15	Halpin	Detroit	15	13	59	17	89	.809
16	Manning	Boston and Detroit	21	18	52	20	90	.777

FIELDERS.

Rank	NAME.	CLUB.	Games Played.	Number Put Out.	Times Assisting.	Fielding Errors.	Total Chances.	Percentage Accepted.
1	Knight	Providence	24	39	6	2	47	.957
1	Lewis	St. Louis	45	71	18	4	93	.957
2	Richardson	New York	18	35	3	2	40	.950
3	Gillespie	"	102	133	12	9	154	.941
4	Fogarty	Philadelphia	89	227	26	16	269	.940
5	O'Rourke	New York	112	162	10	11	183	.939
6	Boyle	St. Louis	28	62	2	5	69	.927
7	Andrews	Philadelphia	98	175	11	16	202	.920
8	Hornung	Boston	25	33	1	3	37	.919
9	Shaffer	St. Louis	69	106	28	12	146	.917
10	Rowe	"	16	28	1	3	32	.906
11	Dorgan	New York	87	142	11	16	169	.905
12	Richardson	Buffalo	46	120	6	14	140	.900
13	Manning	Boston and Detroit	83	164	21	21	206	.898
14	Manning	Philadelphia	107	134	21	18	173	.896
15	Whitney	Boston	17	31	2	4	37	.891
16	Thompson	Detroit	63	84	24	14	122	.885
16	Wood	"	70	112	11	16	139	.885
16	Carroll	Providence	104	207	10	28	245	.885
17	Gore	Chicago	109	204	17	29	250	.884
18	Dalrymple	"	113	180	16	27	223	.878
19	Quinn	St. Louis	55	83	8	13	104	.875
20	Crowley	Buffalo	92	152	8	23	183	.874
20	Seery	St. Louis	58	95	16	16	127	.874
21	Kelly	Chicago	67	95	29	19	143	.868
22	Poorman	Boston	55	82	9	14	105	.866
23	McCarthy	"	40	69	8	12	89	.865
24	Hines	Providence	92	199	18	34	251	.864
25	Hanlon	Detroit	105	220	19	38	277	.862
26	Lillie	Buffalo	108	183	23	33	239	.861

LEAGUE FIELDING AVERAGES—CONTINUED.

FIELDERS' AVERAGES—Continued.

Rank	NAME.	CLUB.	Games Played.	Number Put Out.	Times Assisting.	Fielding Errors.	Total Chances.	Percentage Accepted.
27	Dorgan	Detroit	39	55	5	10	70	.857
	Bennett	"	19	10	2	2	14	.857
28	Radford	Providence	87	141	26	29	196	.852
29	Johnston	Boston	26	40	8	9	57	.842
30	Purcell	"	21	19	2	4	25	.840
31	Sweeney	St. Louis	38	62	5	14	81	.827
32	Sunday	Chicago	42	46	6	11	63	.825
33	Myers	Buffalo	20	36	1	8	45	.822
34	Whitely	Boston	32	42	8	14	64	.781
35	Buffinton	"	16	21	1	8	30	.733

CATCHERS' AVERAGES.

Rank	NAME.	CLUB.	Games Played.	Number Put Out.	Times Assisting.	Fielding Errors.	Passed Balls.	Total Chances.	Percentage Accepted.
1	Bennett	Detroit	63	347	87	38	18	490	.885
2	McGuire	"	31	249	52	26	21	348	.864
3	Rowe	Buffalo	22	123	30	13	12	178	.859
4	Flint	Chicago	67	356	100	36	41	533	.855
5	Ewing	New York	60	337	102	39	40	518	.847
6	Deasley	"	51	281	80	25	44	430	.839
7	Deasley	Boston	27	162	42	22	23	249	.819
8	Hackett, M. M	"	33	194	53	27	30	304	.812
9	Ganzell	Philadelphia	32	175	39	27	26	267	.801
10	Gilligan	Providence	62	305	84	57	40	486	.800
11	Briody	St. Louis	59	243	83	39	44	409	.797
12	Myers	Buffalo	69	305	95	45	57	502	.796
13	Daily	Providence	47	220	70	41	37	368	.788
14	Gunning	Boston	48	252	68	45	46	411	.778
15	Clements	Philadelphia	41	181	47	28	44	300	.760
16	Kelly	Chicago	33	146	64	30	36	276	.760
	Baker	St. Louis	34	148	31	28	30	237	.755
17	Cusick	Philadelphia	38	180	60	57	34	331	.725
18	McCauley	Chi. and Buffalo	23	96	40	17	37	190	.715
19	Sutcliffe	Chi. and St. Louis	23	109	26	24	37	196	.688

124 LEAGUE PITCHERS' RECORD.

PITCHERS' RECORD IN ALPHABETICAL ORDER.

NAME.	CLUB.	Games Played.	Times at Bat of Opponents.	Runs Scored by Opponents.	Average per Game.	Runs Earned by Opponents.	Average per Game.	First Base Hits Made by Opponents.	Percentage.	Number Put Out.	Times Assisting.	Fielding Errors.	Wild Pitches.	Total Chances.	Percentage Accepted.
Baldwin	Detroit	20	699	85	4.25	27	1.35	141	.201	9	176	35	9	229	.807
Boyle	St. Louis	42	1433	226	5.38	95	2.26	367	.245	26	209	109	24	368	.638
Buffinton	Boston	50	1742	237	4.74	95	1.90	423	.242	16	279	91	27	413	.714
Conway	Buffalo	27	904	173	6.40	71	2.63	251	.277	3	147	48	20	218	.688
Clarkson	Chicago	70	2420	254	3.62	103	1.45	502	.207	25	489	114	12	640	.803
Daily	Philadelphia	49	1691	209	4.26	68	1.38	372	.219	15	228	103	37	384	.635
Ferguson	Philadelphia	46	1555	202	4.39	81	1.76	345	.221	26	259	87	16	418	.753
Galvin	Buffalo	32	1226	205	6.40	97	3.03	247	.201	18	172	50	14	254	.748
Getzein	Detroit	37	1363	222	6.00	76	2.05	283	.221	17	198	100	16	331	.749
Keefe	New York	45	1472	154	3.42	49	1.09	361	.264	29	315	111	31	476	.722
Radbourn	Providence	49	1765	209	4.26	69	1.40	297	.201	21	270	88	34	413	.704
Shaw	Providence	47	1549	205	4.36	72	1.53	423	.259	21	275	105	28	420	.683
Serad	Buffalo	28	1013	191	6.82	76	2.71	337	.284	12	131	91	35	267	.531
Sweeney	St. Louis	33	1106	163	4.94	86	2.60	288	.246	10	148	65	16	248	.673
McCormick	Prov. & Chi	28	973	129	4.60	44	1.57	273	.231	19	161	66	9	259	.710
Weidman	Detroit	38	1373	201	5.29	98	2.58	225	.255	28	210	73	15	310	.716
Welch	New York	55	1842	170	3.09	54	0.98	351	.200	12	325	138	35	514	.663
Wood	Buffalo	22	834	160	7.27	68	3.09	269	.271	16	85	73	17	183	.508
Whitney	Boston	50	1852	286	5.72	130	2.60	500	.269	8	321	54	33	426	.795

BATTING AND FIELDING.

Record of Clubs, Members of the National League of Professional B. B. Clubs.

SEASON OF 1885.

Rank.	NAME OF CLUB.	Games Played.	Games Won.	BATTING.						FIELDING.				
				Times at Bat.	Runs Scored.	Average per Game.	Runs Earned.	Average per Game.	First Base.	Percentage.	Total Bases.	Average per Game.	Number Put Out.	Times Assisting.	Fielding Errors.	Total Chances.	Percentage Accepted.
1	Chicago...	113	87	4096	835	7.39	334	2.95	1034	.264	1582	14.00	3033	2049	834	5916	.859
2	New York..	112	85	4038	691	6.17	263	2.34	1085	.269	1429	12.76	2992	1881	749	5622	.866
3	Philadelphia	111	56	3895	519	4.62	180	1.62	895	.229	1180	10.63	2806	1763	895	5496	.849
4	Providence.	111	53	3729	442	4.01	168	1.53	820	.219	1001	9.10	3675	1785	850	5510	.845
5	Boston......	113	46	3943	528	4.67	206	1.82	915	.232	1218	10.77	2940	1918	852	5710	.850
6	Detroit.....	108	41	3771	421	4.76	221	2.04	920	.243	1256	11.63	2858	1853	800	5511	.854
7	Buffalo.....	112	38	3904	494	4.41	229	2.04	978	.250	1292	11.53	2950	1687	906	5553	.836
8	St. Louis...	111	36	3753	390	3.51	140	1.26	829	.220	1008	9.08	2896	1799	861	5556	.845
	Total	890	442	31119	4407	4.95	1741	2.06	7594	.241	9986	11.23	23462	14735	6677	44874	.851

TIE GAMES.

Aug. 1, St. Louis 0, Boston 0; Sept. 8, St. Louis 1, Chicago 1; Oct. 2, St. Louis 3, Philadelphia 3.

SCHEDULE OF LEAGUE GAMES FOR 1886.

CLUBS.	At Detroit.	At Chicago.	At St. Louis.	At Kans's C'y.	At Philadelp'a.	At New York.	At Boston.	At Washington.
Detroit		May 6 " 7 " 8 July 8 " 9 " 10 Sept. 9 " 10 " 11	April 29 " 30 May 1 July 15 " 16 " 17 Sept. 16 " 17 " 18	May 3 " 4 " 5 July 12 " 13 " 14 Sept. 13 " 14 " 15	June 5 " 7 " 8 July 31 Aug. 2 " 3 Oct. 7 " 8 " 9	May 31 " 31 June 1 Aug. 7 " 9 " 10 Sept. 30 Oct. 1 " 2	May 27 " 28 " 29 Aug. 4 " 5 " 6 Sept. 25 " 28 " 29	June 2 " 3 " 4 July 28 " 29 " 30 Oct. 4 " 5 " 6
Chicago	June 19 " 21 " 22 Aug. 20 " 21 " 23 Sept. 20 " 21 " 22		May 3 " 4 " 5 July 12 " 13 " 14 Sept. 13 " 14 " 15	April 29 " 30 May 1 July 15 " 16 " 17 Sept. 16 " 17 " 18	May 31 " 31 June 1 Aug. 7 " 9 " 10 Sept. 25 " 27 " 28	June 5 " 7 " 8 July 31 Aug. 2 " 3 Oct. 7 " 8 " 9	June 2 " 3 " 4 July 28 " 29 " 30 Oct. 7 " 8 " 9	May 27 " 28 " 29 Aug. 4 " 5 " 6 Sept. 30 Oct. 1 " 2
St. Louis	June 11 " 12 " 14 July 22 " 23 " 24 Aug. 16 " 17 " 18	June 15 " 16 " 17 July 19 " 20 " 21 Aug. 12 " 13 " 14			June 2 " 3 " 4 Aug. 4 " 5 " 6 Sept. 30 Oct. 1 " 2	May 27 " 28 " 29 July 28 " 29 " 30 Oct. 7 " 8	May 31 " 31 June 1 July 31 Aug. 2 " 3 Oct. 4 " 5 " 6	June 5 " 7 " 8 Aug. 7 " 9 " 10 Sept. 25 " 28 " 29
Kansas City	June 15 " 16 " 17 July 19 " 20 " 21 Aug. 12 " 13 " 14	June 11 " 12 " 14 July 22 " 23 " 24 Aug. 16 " 17 " 18	May 6 " 7 " 8 Aug. 20 " 21 " 23 Sept. 20 " 21 " 22		May 27 " 28 " 29 July 28 " 29 " 30 Oct. 4 " 5 " 6	June 2 " 3 " 4 Aug. 4 " 5 " 6 Sept. 25 " 28 " 29	June 5 " 7 " 8 Aug. 7 " 9 " 10 Sept. 30 Oct. 1 " 2	May 31 " 31 June 1 July 31 Aug. 2 " 3 Oct. 7 " 8 " 9

Philadelphia	May 18, 19, 20, June 23, 24, Aug. 24, 25, 26	May 21, 22, 24, June 26, 25, 29, Aug. 27, 28, 30	May 14, 15, 17, July 5, 5, 6, 6, 7, 8	May 11, 12, 13, July 1, 2, 3, Sept. 1, 2, 4	. . . .	June 14, 15, 16, 20, 21, 22, Sept. 18, 20, 21	June 17, 18, 19, 24, 26, 27, Sept. 15, 16, 17	April 29, 30, May 1, July 16, 17, 19, Sept. 10, 11, 13
New York	May 10, 11, 12, July 5, 5, 6, Sept. 1, 2, 4	May 13, 14, 15, July 1, 2, 3, Sept. 6, 7, 8	May 21, 22, 24, June 23, 24, Aug. 25, 27, 30	May 18, 19, 20, June 26, 28, 29, Aug. 24, 25, 26	May 3, 4, 5, 9, July 10, 12, Aug. 19, 20, 21	. . . .	. . . .	July 13, 14, 15, 24, 26, 27, Aug. 16, 17, 18
Boston	May 13, 14, 15, July 1, 2, 3, Aug. 27, 28, 30	May 10, 11, 12, July 5, 5, 6, Aug. 24, 25, 26	May 21, 22, 23, 24, 25, Sept. 6, 7, 8	May 18, 19, 20, June 23, 24, 25, 26, Sept. 11	May 7, 8, July 13, 14, 15, 16, 17, 18	April 29, 30, May 1, July 16, 17, 19, Sept. 13, 14	. . . .	May 3, 4, 5, 9, July 10, 12, Aug. 19, 20, 21
Washington	May 21, 22, 24, June 26, 28, 29, Sept. 6, 7, 8	May 18, 19, 20, June 23, 24, 25, Sept. 2, 4	May 11, 12, 13, July 1, 2, 3, Aug. 24, 25, 26	May 14, 15, 17, July 5, 5, 6, Aug. 27, 28, 30	June 10, 11, 12, Aug. 12, 13, 14, Sept. 22, 23, 24	May 6, 7, 8, June 17, 18, 19, Sept. 15, 16, 17	June 14, 15, 16, 21, 22, 23, Sept. 18, 20, 21	. . . .

AMERICAN ASSOCIATION SCHEDULE.

	At St. Louis.	At Louisville.	At Cincinnati.	At Pittsburg.	At Baltimore.	At Phila.	At New York.	At Brooklyn.
St. Louis...		May 7 " 8 " 9 " 11 June 6 " 7 " 8 Sept. 3-4 " 5	April 29 May 13 " 14 " 15 June 21 " 25 " 26 Aug. 23-24 " 25	May 1 " 3 " 4 " 5 June 22 " 23 " 24 Sept. 7-8 " 9	June 1 " 2 " 3 " 4 July 26 " 27 " 28 Sept. 17-18 " 20	May 27 " 29 " 31 " 31 July 29 " 30 " 31 Sept. 21-22 " 23	May 20 " 21 " 25 " 26 July 17 " 20 " 23 Sept. 10-13 " 16	May 18 " 19 " 22 " 23 July 18 " 22 " 24 Sept. 11-14 " 15
Louisville...	April 21 " 22 " 24 " 25 June 9 " 10 " 12 Aug. 27-28 " 29		April 17 " 30 May 1 " 4 June 15 " 16 " 17 Sept. 7 8	May 13 " 14 " 15 " 17 June 18 " 19 " 21 Aug. 31 Sept. 1-2	May 23 " 24 " 25 " 26 July 29 " 30 " 31 Sept. 10-11 " 13	May 18 " 19 " 20 " 21 July 26 " 27 " 28 Sept. 14-15 " 16	May 27 " †31 June 1 " 4 July 19 " 22 " 24 Sept. 18-21 " 23	May 29 " †31 June 1 " 3 July 17 " 20 " 23 Sept. 17-19 " 22
Cincinnati...	April 26 " 27 " 28 May 16 June 18 " 19 " 20 Aug. 31 Sept. 1-2	April 18 " 20 May 13 June 13 " 14 " 22 " 23 Aug. 19-21 " 22		May 7 " 8 " 10 " 11 June 5 " 7 " 8 Sept. 3-4 " 6	May 18 " 19 " 20 " 21 July 22 " 23 " 24 Sept. 21-22 " 23	May 22 " 24 " 25 " 26 July 17 " 19 " 20 Sept. 17-18 " 20	May 29 " †31 June 2 " 4 July 26 " 28 " 30 Sept. 11-14 " 15	May 27 " *31 June 2 " 4 July 27 " 29 " 31 Sept. 10-12 " 16
Pittsburg...	April 17 " 18 " 19 " 20 June 13 " 15 " 16 Aug. 19-21 " 22	April 26 " 27 " 28 " 29 June 25 " 26 " 27 Aug. 23-24 " 25	April 21 " 22 " 23 " 24 June 9 " 10 " 12 Aug. 27-28 " 30		May 27 " 28 " 29 July 16 " 17 " 19 " 20 Sept. 14-15 " 16	June 1 " 2 " 3 " 4 July 22 " 23 " 24 Sept. 10-11 " 13	May 18 " 19 " 22 " 24 July 27 " 29 " 31 Sept. 17-20 " 22	May 20 " 21 " 25 " 26 July 25 " 28 Aug. 1 Sept. 18-21 " 23

Baltimore........	July 7 " 8 " 10 " 11 Aug. 11 " 12 " 13 Sept. 25 " 26 " 28	July 12 " 13 " 14 " 15 Aug. 14 " 15 " 16 Sept. 30 Oct. 2 " 3	June 28 " 29 " 30 July 1 Aug. 3 " 4 " 5 Oct. 8 " 9 " 11	May 31 " " July 1 " 2 " 3 Aug. 5 " 6 " 7 Oct. 9 " 5 " 6	....	April 24 " 26 May 15 June 17 " 18 " 19 Aug. 24 " 25 " 26	May 3 " 4 " 13 " 14 June 21 " 22 " 23 Sept. 3 " 4 " 6	April 22 " 23 May 5 " 6 June 24 " 25 " 26 Aug. 27 " 28 " 29
Philadelphia.....	July 12 " 13 " 14 " 15 Aug. 6 " 7 " 8 Oct. 4 " 5 " 6	July 7 " 8 " 10 " 11 Aug. 3 " 4 " 5 " 8 " 9 " 10	July 2 " 3 " 5 Aug. 13 " 14 " 16 Sept. 29 " 30 Oct. 2	June 28 " 29 " 30 July 10 " 11 " 12 Sept. 25 " 27 " 28	April 27 " 28 May 7 " 8 June 14 " 15 " 16 Aug. 19 " 21 " 23	....	April 22 " 23 May 5 " 6 June 10 " 11 " 12 Aug. 27 " 28 " 30	May 3 " 4 " 10 " 12 June 5 " 6 " 8 Sept. 3 " 4 " 5
New York........	July 3 " 4 " 5 Aug. 6 " 7 " 8 Sept. 25 " 26 " 28	July 3 " 4 " 5 Aug. 6 " 7 " 8 Sept. 25 " 26 " 28	July 7 " 8 " 10 Aug. 11 " 12 Oct. 4 " 5 " 6	July 12 " 13 " 14 " 15 Aug. 14 " 16 " 17 Oct. 8 " 9 " 11	April 20 " 21 May 10 June 5 " 7 " 8 Sept. 7 " 8 " 9	April 17 " 19 " 29 May 1 June 24 " 25 " 26 Aug. 31 Sept. 1 " 2	....	....
Brooklyn........	July 3 " 4 " 5 " 5 Aug. 14 " 15 " 16 Oct. 8 " 9 " 10	June 28 " 29 " 30 July 1 Aug. 10 " 11 " 12 Oct. 4 " 5 " 6	July 12 " 13 " 14 " 15 Aug. 6 " 7 " 9 Sept. 25 " 27 " 28	July 7 " 8 " 9 " 10 Aug. 3 " 4 " 5 Sept. 30 Oct. 1 " 2	April 17 " 19 " 29 May 10 June 11 " 12 Aug. 31 Sept. 1 " 2	April 20 " 21 May 13 " 14 June 21 " 22 " 23 Sept. 7 " 8 " 9	April 26 " 28 May 15 June 15 " 17 " 19 Aug. 21 " 24 " 26	April 24 " 27 May 7 June 8 " 13 " 16 " 18 Aug. 19 " 22 " 25

*A. M.   †P. M.

CLIFTON HOUSE,

CHICAGO.

The Proprietors of the CLIFTON would respectfully solicit the patronage of the League and other traveling Base Ball Clubs for the season of 1886. We offer a special rate of

$2.00 Per Day,

And refer to all the League Clubs for the past three seasons, who have made their home with us, also to Messrs. A. G. SPALDING & BROS. 108 Madison St.

WOODCOCK & LORING,

PROPRIETORS.

THE CHICAGO TRIBUNE.

The Western Sporting Authority.

THE SUNDAY EDITION OF THE CHICAGO TRIBUNE, and the Daily Edition throughout the playing season of 1886, will be found, as heretofore, indispensable to those who desire accurate, reliable, and comprehensive base ball records and reports.

Every club and club-room should keep THE SUNDAY TRIBUNE on file.

THE TURF DEPARTMENT

of THE TRIBUNE is universally admitted to be without an equal, and during 1886 it will be still further improved. Special telegraphic reports of the principal running and trotting meetings will be furnished, and particular attention be given to the performances of the American horses in England.

In other departments of sport THE TRIBUNE will maintain the superiority it has so long enjoyed.

TERMS:

SUNDAY EDITION, 16 Pages, per year, - $ 2.00
DAILY TRIBUNE, including Sunday, - - 12.00

Address,

THE TRIBUNE,
CHICAGO, ILL.

"The Niagara Falls Route."
The Way the League Clubs Travel.

The cities that have representative clubs contesting for the championship pennant this year are—Chicago, Boston, New York, Washington, Kansas City, Detroit, St. Louis and Philadelphia. All of these cities are joined together by the **MICHIGAN CENTRAL** Railroad. This road has enjoyed almost a monopoly of Base Ball travel in former years, by reason of its quick time and first-class accommodations, first-class implying all possible comfort and elegance in Sleeping Cars, Day Coaches and Smoking Cars, and particularly its sumptuous Dining Cars. It is luxury to eat and fly, which must be experienced in order to be appreciated.

The trains of the **MICHIGAN CENTRAL** pass through Detroit, and run in full view of Niagara Falls. **IT IS THE ONLY ROAD THAT DOES THIS**, and the only road that runs trains to Niagara Falls, N. Y., and Niagara Falls, Ont. It is the only road under a single management from Chicago to Niagara Falls and Buffalo, and runs Palace Cars through without change between Chicago and Toronto, Buffalo, Syracuse, Albany, Boston and New York. It is not only the **"NIAGARA FALLS ROUTE"** and the Great East and West Highway, but also the route that insures the greatest degree of comfort and safety, and possesses **THE MOST COMPLETE AND PERFECT THROUGH CAR SERVICE BETWEEN CHICAGO AND THE EAST.**

Information in regard to Rates, Routes, Accommodations, etc., will be furnished by any of the Company's Agents on application.

H. B. LEDYARD,   **O. W. RUGGLES,**
Pres. and Gen'l Manager,   *Gen'l Pass. and Ticket Agent.*
DETROIT.   CHICAGO.

The Chicago Herald

H AS THE LARGEST MORNING CIRCULATION in Chicago because it gives *all the News for*

2 Cents

The Sunday Herald

I S LARGELY DEVOTED TO SPORTS AND THE DRAMA, and is the Favorite Sunday Paper of Chicago.

BY MAIL, ONE YEAR, $2.

Address—

THE CHICAGO HERALD,
120 and 122 FIFTH AVE.,
CHICAGO, ILL.

JAMES W. SCOTT, Publisher.

✳—— SEASON OF 1886 ——✳

BASE BALL POSTERS,

WINDOW HANGERS,

Colored Score Cards,

Again Adopted by the National League and all Principal Associations.

Inclose 25 Cents in Stamps for Sample Set of Twenty-Four Designs.

JOHN B. SAGE,
BUFFALO, N. Y.

• SPORTSMEN'S WEAR.

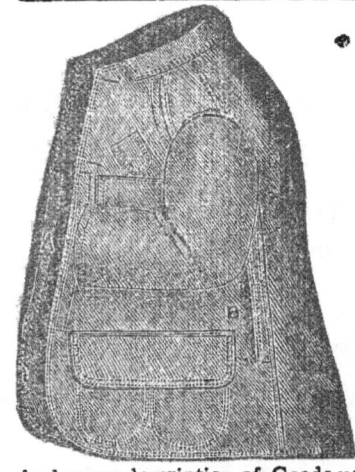

No. A 1 Barnard Canvas Shooting Coat............................$5.00
No. 1 Barnard Canvas Shooting Coat............................ 4.00
No. 2 Barnard Canvas Shooting Coat............................ 2.50
No 3 Barnard Canvas Shooting Coat............................ 1 75

For sale by all Gun and Sporting Goods Dealers. Ask for them. See that our trade-mark is on the lining. They are the best. Take no other. We also manufacture

Hats, Caps, Leggings, Pants, Vests, Waterproof Horsehide Boots and Shoes, Carryall Bags, Gun Cases, Cartridge Bags, Shell Boxes,

And every description of Goods used by Sportsmen, made from Canvas, Corduroy and Waterproof Leather. Illustrated Catalogue, Samples and Measurement Blanks sent free upon application.

GEO. BARNARD & CO.,
108 Madison St., CHICAGO, ILL.
Eastern Agency—241 Broadway, NEW YORK.

TO BASE BALL PLAYERS.

Ten years ago we issued a notice to Base Ball Players, announcing that we had engaged in the business of furnishing Base Ball Supplies, and solicited their patronage. That our efforts to furnish satisfactory implements and paraphernalia have met with success, is evidenced by the remarkable increase in our business since that time. Having been for ten years prior to that date intimately identified with the game, we had acquired a practical knowledge of the wants of ball players; and it has always been our aim, instead of flooding the market with cheap, worthless goods that might please the trade but displease the player, to manufacture and sell articles of genuine merit only, and such as would give the most perfect satisfaction to players. With our practical experience in the game, and being the largest manufacturers of everything that is necessary in the base ball player's outfit, we are now in a position to anticipate the wants of players, and furnish a better grade of goods than any other house in the trade.

Manufacturers who have no reputation to sustain are continually offering inferior goods, which are readily sought after by the average dealers in base ball supplies, who, not being acquainted with the practical wants of players, are apt to regard only the low prices, and not the quality of the goods. It is our constant endeavor to manufacture only the very best goods, and to sell them at fair prices. To illustrate, take one article, Catcher's Masks. We have seen some made by other manufacturers, which, while cheaper than ours in price, were yet so utterly worthless as protectors, that no ball player could afford to take the chance of being disfigured by using them.

As our business is largely by mail, we would urge upon our patrons the importance of writing plainly the names of their town, county and State; and in order to save return express charges on money, to accompany their orders with draft, post-office order, express money order, or currency for the amount due. In all cases where the goods are not satisfactory and exactly as represented by us, they may be returned, and the money will be refunded. We desire to sell all the goods we can, but we wish also to do more than this, and that is to please our customers in every instance. The established reputation of our goods, and the record we have made by the fair and liberal treatment of our customers, is the best guarantee that can be offered for the future.

Our patrons will no doubt be pleased to note that we have established in New York a store fully as large as our Chicago house. We shall carry duplicate and complete lines of Base Ball and all Sporting Goods in either house, and our Eastern customers can now order direct from the New York establishment.

A. G. SPALDING & BROS.,

108 Madison St.,   241 Broadway,
CHICAGO.   NEW YORK.

COMPLETE UNIFORMS.

Our facilities for manufacturing Base Ball, Cricket, Lawn Tennis, and all kinds of athletic uniforms are the very best. This department is under the supervision of a practical tailor and shirt cutter, who is an expert in designing and cutting base ball and athletic uniforms. We would urge clubs not to make the mistake of intrusting the making of their uniforms to local dealers, whose experience in this kind of work is necessarily small, but send direct to us, and get a good, cheap, and satisfactory outfit. We make complete base ball uniforms at prices ranging from $5.00 to $30.00 per man. Measurement blanks sent free upon application. Send ten cents for samples of flannel and belt webbing, and receive a handsome engraved fashion plate, showing the different styles and prices. At the following very low prices it is economy to order complete uniforms:

Prices of Complete Uniforms.

No. 0. League Club outfit consisting of Pants and Shirt of extra heavy flannel, made expressly for our trade. Extra quality Stockings, Cap, Belt, Chicago Club Shoe, Steel Shoe Plates, and Necktie to match trimmings. Price complete, each...................$15.00

No. 1. Outfit, first quality twilled flannel for Pants and Shirts, first quality Cap, best English Web Belt, first quality Stockings, Amateur Shoe, Steel Shoe Plates. Price complete, each........................... 11.00

No. 2. Outfit, second quality twilled flannel (same as most dealers put into their first quality uniform), second quality Cap, English Web Belt, second quality Stockings, Amateur Shoes, malleable iron Shoe Plates. Price complete, each............................ 9.00

No. 3. Outfit, third quality flannel, third quality Cap, American Web Belt, third quality Stockings, Amateur Shoes, malleable iron Shoe Plates. Price complete, each..................................... 7.00

No. 4. Boy's uniform, fourth quality material, consisting of Shirt, Pants, Cap, Belt, Shoes and Shoe Plates complete, each................................... 5.00

Measurement blanks and Lithographic Fashion Plate showing different styles of uniforms, furnished upon application.

A. G. SPALDING & BROS.,

108 Madison Street,   241 Broadway,
CHICAGO.   NEW YORK.

BASE BALL SHIRTS.

FANCY SHIELD SHIRT.

LACED SHIRT FRONT.

No.
0. Extra quality Shirt, of extra heavy flannel, made expressly for our League Club trade, any style, White, Blue or Gray.......... Each. $5 00 Per Doz. $54 00
1. First quality twilled flannel, White, Blue or Red   4 00   42 00
2. Second quality twilled flannel, White, Blue or Gray................................   3 25   36 00
3. Third quality, Shaker flannel, White only....   2 25   24 00
4. Boys' size only, of fourth quality...........   1 50   18 00

To MEASURE FOR SHIRT.—Size Collar worn. Length of Sleeve, bent, from center of back. Size around Chest. Length of Yoke from shoulder to shoulder.

BASE BALL PANTS.

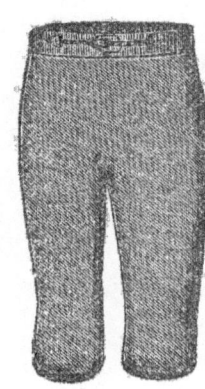

No.   Each.   Dozen.
0. Extra quality flannel Pants, White, Blue or Gray....... $5 00 $54 00
1. First quality twilled flannel, White, Blue or Red......   4 00   42 00
2. Second quality twilled flannel, White, Blue or Gray......   3 25   36 00
3. Third quality, Shaker flannel, White only...............   2 25   24 00
4. Fourth quality, white only..   1 50   18 00

To MEASURE FOR PANTS.—Size around waist. Length of outside seam from waist to eight inches below the knee (for full length pants measure to the foot). Length of inside seam. Size around hips.

A. G. SPALDING & BROS.,

108 Madison Street,   241 Broadway,
CHICAGO.   NEW YORK.

Base Ball Shoes.

No. 1.   No. 2.

No. 1. **League Club Shoe.** Same as used by League Clubs. Made of selected leather, hand sewed, and warranted. Per pair $5.50

No. 2. **Chicago Club Shoe.** Extra quality canvas, foxed with French calf. The Standard Screw Fastener is used. Price per pair. 4.00

No. 3.   No. 4.

No. 3. **Amateur, or Practice Shoe.** Good quality canvas, strap over instep. Price per pair.. $2 00

No. 3X. **Amateur Base Ball Shoe for Boys.** Second quality canvas. Price per pair.. 1 50

No. 4. **Oxford Tie Base Ball Shoe.** Low cut, canvas. Price per pair 2 00

SPALDING'S SHOE PLATES.

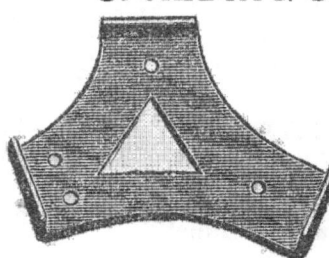

Our new design League Steel Shoe Plate has become the favorite plate among League players during the past season, and we have this year added it to our regular line of shoe plates. It is made by hand of the best quality English steel, and so tempered that it will not bend or break. The peculiar shape of the plate is shown in the adjoining cut. The majority of League players use this plate on the toe, and our No. 1, or Professional Plate, on the heel. Each pair of plates—right and left—are put up with screws.

                                  Per   Per
                                  Pair. Doz.

No. 0. Spalding's League Shoe Plate, $ 50 $5 00

No. 1. **Spalding's Professional Shoe Plate**, as shown in the adjoining cut, is made of first quality steel. It is lighter and smaller than the No. 0 plate, but will render good service. Each pair put up with screws, complete................. 25   2 50

No. 2. **Spalding's Amateur Steel Shoe Plate**, light and durable, with screws........................... 15   1 50

Any of the above Shoe Plates mailed upon receipt of price. Address

BASE BALL CAPS AND HATS.

		1st. qual.	2d qual.	3d qual.
No. 1.	League Parti-colored Cap	$12 00	....	....
No. 3.	Base Ball Hat, any color	18 00	15 00	....
No. 5.	Base Ball Cap, Chicago style, any color, with or without stripes	9 00	7 50	....
No. 7.	Base Ball Cap, Boston shape, without star, any colors	9 00	7 50	6 00
No. 7.	Ditto, all white only	9 00	7 50	6 00
No. 11.	Base Ball Cap, Jockey shape, any color	9 00	7 50	6 00
No. 11.	Ditto, all white only	9 00	7 50	6 00
No. 13.	Base Ball Cap, Boston shape, with star	9 00	7 50	6 00
No. 19.	Base Ball Skull Cap, any color	9 00	7 50	6 00
No. 19.	Ditto, white only	9 00	7 50	6 00
No. 21.	College Base Ball Cap, any color	9 00	7 50	6 00
No. 21.	Ditto, white only	9 00	7 50	6 00

Boys' Flannel Caps, per dozen.............................$4 00
" Cotton Caps, Red, White, or Blue..................... 3 00

In addition to the styles above mentioned, we are prepared to make any style of Cap known, and will furnish at prices corresponding to above.

BAT BAGS.

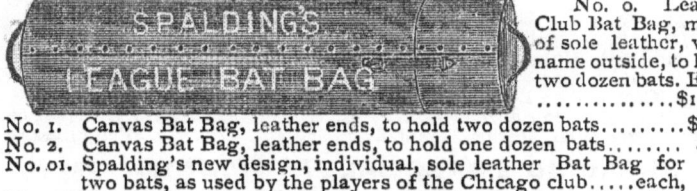

No. 0. League Club Bat Bag, made of sole leather, with name outside, to hold two dozen bats. Each...........$15 00
No. 1. Canvas Bat Bag, leather ends, to hold two dozen bats........$5 00
No. 2. Canvas Bat Bag, leather ends, to hold one dozen bats........ 2 00
No. 01. Spalding's new design, individual, sole leather Bat Bag for two bats, as used by the players of the Chicago club.....each, 4 00
No. 02. Same size and style as above, made of strong canvas... "   1 50

BASES.

No. 0. League Club Bases, made of extra canvas, stuffed and quilted complete, with straps and spikes, without home plate....Per set of three $7 50
No. 1. Canvas Bases, with straps and spikes, complete without home plate............................. 5 00
Marble Home plate................. ..... 3 00
Iron   "   " 1 00

A. G. SPALDING & BROS.,

108 Madison Street,   241 Broadway,
CHICAGO.   NEW YORK.

SPALDING'S BASE BALL BELTS—Worsted Web Belts.

Our No. 0, or League Club Belt is made of best Worsted Webbing, 2½ inches wide, mounted in best manner, with large nickel plated buckle, the finest belt made. Our No. 1 belt is made of same webbing, leather mounted. We use the following colors of webbing. In ordering, please state the color wanted, and size around waist.

Style A. Red.
" B. Blue.
" C. Navy Blue.
Style D. Brown.
" E. Black.
" F. White.
Style G. Red, White Edge.
" H. Blue, "

No. 0. League Club Belt, of any of the above colors, nickel plated buckle as shown in above cut. Per Dozen.................... $6.00

No. 1. Worsted Web Belt, same colors as above, mounted in leather, with two broad straps and buckles as shown in above cut. Per doz.. $4.50

SPALDING'S COTTON WEB BELTS.

Our Cotton Web Belts are made of best quality Cotton Webbing, in the following fast colors. In ordering please state color, and size around waist.

Style L. Red.
" M. Blue.
" N. Red, White Edge.
Style O. Blue, White Edge.
" P. Red, White and Blue.
" Q. White.
Style R. Red and White, Narrow Stripe.
" S. Blue and White, Narrow Stripe.
" T. Yellow & Black, Wide Stripe.

No. 3. Cotton Web Belts, any of above colors, large patent nickel. plated buckle. Per dozen... $4.00
No. 4. Cotton Web, Leather Mounted......................Per doz. $2.50

SPALDING'S BASE BALL STOCKINGS. PER DOZ.

No. 0. League Regulation, made of the finest worsted yarn. The following colors can be obtained: White, Light Blue, Navy Blue, Scarlet, Gray, Green, Old Gold, Brown............................$18.00
No. 1. Fine Quality Woolen Stockings, Scarlet, Blue or Brown.... 12.00
No. 2. Good   "   "   "   "   "   " 9.00
No. 3. Second "   "   "   "   " or Blue............. 6.00
No. 4. Cotton... 3.50
No. 5.   " 2.50

A. G. SPALDING & BROS.,
108 Madison Street,　　　　　　　241 Broadway,
　　CHICAGO,　　　　　　　　　　NEW YORK.

Spalding's Trade-Marked Catcher's Mask.

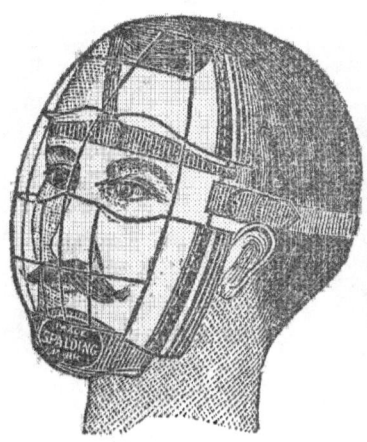

The first Catcher's Mask brought out in 1875, was a very heavy, clumsy affair, and it was not until we invented our open-eyed mask in 1877 that it came into general use. Now it would be considered unsafe and even dangerous for a catcher to face the swift underhand throwing of the present day unless protected by a reliable mask. The increased demand for these goods has brought manufacturers into the field who, having no reputation to sustain, have vied with each other to see how *cheap* they could make a so-called mask, and in consequence have ignored the essential qualification, *strength*. A cheaply made, inferior quality of mask is much worse than no protection at all, for a broken wire or one that will not stand the force of the ball without caving in, is liable to disfigure a player for life. We would warn catchers not to trust their faces behind one of these *cheap* made masks. Our trade-marked masks are made of the very best hard wire, plated to prevent rusting, and well trimmed, and every one is a thorough face protector. We shall make them in three grades as described below, and with our increased facilities for manufacturing, are enabled to improve the quality, and at the same time reduce the price.

Beware of counterfeits. *None genuine without our Trade Mark stamped on each Mask.*

No. 00—**Spalding's Special League Mask**, used by all the leading professional catchers, extra heavy wire, well padded with goat hair, and the padding faced with the best imported dogskin, which is impervious to perspiration, and retains its pliability and softness .... Each $3 00

" 0.—**Spalding's Regulation League Mask**, made of heavy wire, well padded, and faced with horsehide, warranted first-class in every respect .... Each.. 2 50

" 1.—**Spalding's Boys' League Mask**, made of heavy wire, equally as heavy in proportion to size as the No. 00 mask. It is made to fit a boy's face, and gives the same protection as the League Mask .... Each 2 00

CHEAP MASKS.

To meet the demand for good masks at a low price, we have manufactured a line of cheap masks, which are superior to any masks in the market at the same price. We do not guarantee these masks, and believe that our Trade Marked Masks are worth more than the difference in price.

No. A.—**Amateur Mask**, made the same size and general style as the League Mask, but with lighter wire, and faced with leather (we guarantee this Mask to be superior to so-called League or professional masks sold by other manufacturers) $1 50

" B. **Boys' Mask**, similar to the Amateur Mask, only made smaller to fit a boy's face .... Each 1 25

☞ Any of the above masks mailed postpaid on receipt of price.

SPALDING'S TRADE MARKED CATCHERS' GLOVES.

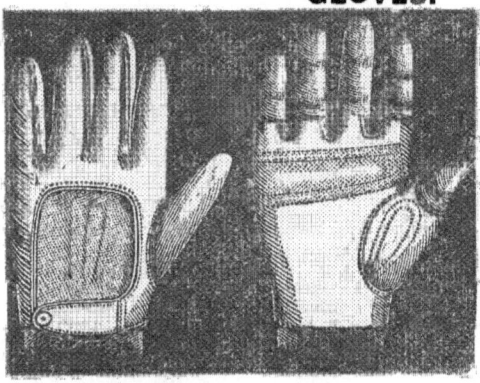

After considerable expense and many experiments, we have finally perfected a Catchers' Glove that meets with general favor from professional catchers.

The old style of open backed gloves introduced by us several years ago is still adhered to, but the quality of material and workmanship has been materially improved, until now we are justified in claiming the best line of catchers's gloves in the market. These Gloves do not interfere with throwing, can be easily put on and taken off, and no player subject to sore hands should be without a pair. We make them in ten different grades, as follows:

No. 000.—**Spalding's Special League Catchers' Gloves.** Full left hand, back stop glove, made of the heaviest Indian-tanned buckskin, the very best that can be procured. The full left hand glove is extra padded, and sole leather finger tips, to prevent the low curved balls from breaking or otherwise injuring the fingers. The right hand glove is made with open back and fingerless, thoroughly padded......................Price per Pair, $ 5 00

No. 00.—**Spalding's League Regulation Catchers' Gloves,** made of extra heavy Indian-tanned buck, and carefully selected with reference to the hard service required of them. This Glove has full left hand, as shown in the illustration, with fingerless right hand, well padded, and warranted..........................Price per Pair, 3 50

No. 0.—**Spalding's League Catchers' Gloves,** made of extra heavy Indian-tanned buck, and carefully selected with special reference to the hard service required of them, open back, both hands fingerless, well padded, and fully warranted......................Price per Pair, 2 50

No. 1.—**Spalding's Professional Gloves,** made of Indian-tanned buckskin, open back, well padded, but not quite as heavy material as the No. 0.............Price per Pair 2 00

The above Gloves are Trade Marked and fully warranted.

AMATEUR CATCHERS' GLOVES.

To meet the demand for a cheaper grade of Gloves, we have added the following line:

No. A.—**Full Left Hand Catchers' Gloves,** equal to most professional gloves in the market..............Price per Pair, $ 2 50
No. B.—**Amateur Gloves,** made of buckskin, open back, well padded, and adapted for amateur players..........Per Pair 1 50
No. C.—**Practice Gloves,** made of light material, open back, well padded...Per Pair 1 00
No. D.—**Junior Gloves,** open back, a good glove at the price " 75
No. E.—Cheap open back glove............................ " 50
No. F.— " " " " .... " 25

☞ Any of the above Gloves mailed postpaid on receipt of price. In ordering, please give size of ordinary dress gloves usually worn.

A. G. SPALDING & BROS.,
108 Madison St., CHICAGO.   241 Broadway, NEW YORK.

MORTON'S
PERFECT SUPPORTER.

The best fitting, most comfortable and effective supporter yet devised. Made of best quality canton flannel, with laced front, cool and pleasant to wear. Prices each, 50 cents.

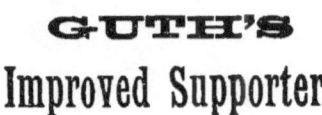

---o---

GUTH'S
Improved Supporter,

Well known to Professional Ball Players. Price, Chamois Skin, $1.50; Muslin, 50c. each.

SPALDING'S AUTOMATIC UMPIRE INDICATOR.

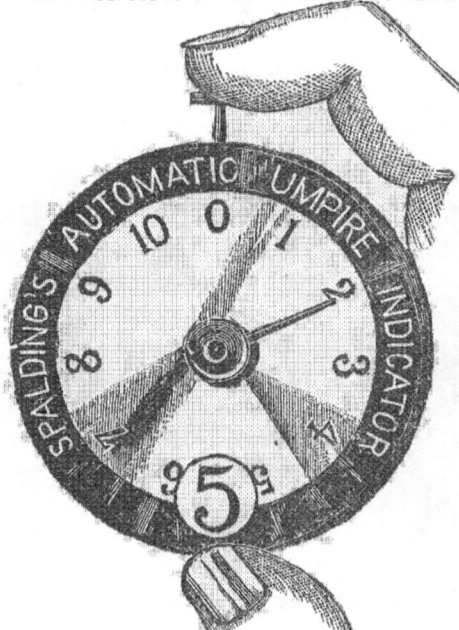

As the name implies, this little apparatus is intended for umpires of base ball matches, and is the best thing of the kind ever brought out; in fact, it is the only really practical umpire's indicator, or guide, on the market. The illustration, which represents the exact size of the indicator, gives a good idea of its construction and mode of handling. By touching the spring at the top of the indicator the number of balls called from 1 to 6 or 7 are registered, and so remain until the spring is touched again. The index hand upon the dial serves to record the number of strikes on the batter. It works automatically, and can be carried in the palm of the hand unobserved by the spectators. It is recommended and is in general use by all the prominent League and Association umpires. It is neatly packed in a pasteboard box, and will be mailed to any address upon receipt of price. **Price, 50 Cents.**

BRIGHT'S AUTOMATIC REGISTERING TURN STILE.

Is acknowledged to be the most reliable, durable and simple Turn Stile made. It is designed especially for Base Ball and Fair Grounds, Expositions, etc., and is an almost indispensable assistant in making a correct division of receipts and avoiding all possibility of the gate-keeper's appropriating any portion of them, by accurately counting and registering each person passing through it.

The movement registers from 1 to 10,000, and can easily and almost instantly be reversed to zero by any person having the key, without the necessity of removing from the Stile to which it is securely attached and locked. It is provided with all necessary stops, etc., to prevent its getting out of order through being handled by meddlesome persons, and is shipped complete and in readiness to be placed beside a doorway or other suitable entrance to inclosure, either permanent or temporary, and used without delay.

They have been in use during the past season by the Cleveland and Philadelphia League Clubs and by all of the Clubs of the N. W. League, without an instance of failure or dissatisfaction, but have since been greatly improved by the addition of several valuable features, making it unquestionably the best adapted and most durable Turn Stile in the market.

Orders from Base Ball Clubs should be sent in as early as possible, insuring their being filled before the beginning of the season.

Price complete...$50 00

GRAND STAND CUSHIONS FOR BASE BALL GROUNDS.

The Chicago Club have for several seasons furnished cushions to ther patrons at a nominal rental of 5 cents per game. It is a feature highly appreciated by base ball spectators. We are now manufacturing these cushions, and can supply them to clubs at 50 cents each. Special prices made when ordered in hundred lots.

A. G. SPALDING & BROS.,

108 Madison Street,
CHICAGO.

241 Broadway,
NEW YORK.

Gray's Patent Body Protector.

The most useful device ever invented for the protection of catchers or umpires, and renders it impossible for the catcher to be injured while playing close to the batter. Made very light and pliable, and does not interfere in any way with the movements of the wearer, either in running, stooping or throwing. No catcher should be without one of these protectors.

Price,............each, $10.00.

MORTON'S Patent Sliding Pad.
A NECESSITY TO BALL PLAYERS.

The Sliding Pad protects the side and hip of the player when undertaking to slide for a base.

Its use increases a player's confidence, and renders the act of sliding free from danger.

It is worn and recommended by all leading professional ball players.

No. 0. Chamois lined, price each by mail............ $2 50
No. 1. All Canvas, price each by mail............ 1 50

TESTIMONIALS.

"I have examined and used Morton's Sliding Pad, and can say that I would not go on the ball field without one of them on, and think every ball player should have them." M. J. KELLY,
Chicago B. B. C.

"I have examined Morton's Sliding Pad, and have ordered them for our team." CHAS. COMISKEY,
Capt. St. Louis Browns B. B. C.

A. G. SPALDING & BROS.,
108 Madison St., CHICAGO.   241 Broadway, NEW YORK.

SPALDING'S SCORE BOOK.

Spalding's new design Pocket and Club Score Book continues to be the popular score book, and is used by all the leading scorers and base ball reporters. They are adapted for the spectator of ball games, who scores for his own amusement, as well as the official club scorer, who records the minutest detail. By this new system, the art of scoring can be acquired in a single game.

Full instructions, with the latest League rules, accompany each book.

WHAT AUTHORITIES SAY OF IT.

Messrs. A. G. SPALDING & BROS., Chicago, Ill.

Gentlemen:—I have carefully examined the Spalding Score Book, and, without any hesitation, I cheerfully recommend it as the most complete system of scoring of which I have any knowledge.

Respectfully,
N. E. YOUNG, Official Scorer Nat'l League P. B. B. Clubs.

The new system of score books just issued by A. G. Spalding & Bros. of Chicago, are the neatest thing of the kind we ever saw. Every lover of the game should have one. They are simple in their construction, and are easily understood.—*Cincinnati Enquirer*.

THE TRIBUNE has received from A. G. Spalding & Bros., 108 Madison Street, a copy of their new score book for use this year. The book or system is so far in advance of anything ever before brought out in the way of simplicity, convenience and accuracy, that it seems wonderful that it was not thought of years ago. The new style will be in universal use before the season is half through.—*Chicago Tribune*.

A. G. Spalding, Captain of the Chicago White Stockings, has just brought out a new score book, which will meet with the unqualified indorsement of everybody who has ever undertaken to score a game of base ball. They are of various sizes, to meet the requirements both of the spectator who scores simply for his own satisfaction, and for official scores of clubs. The novel and commending feature of the book is the manner in which each of the squares opposite the name of the player is utilized by a division which originated with Mr. Spalding. Each of these squares is divided into five spaces by a diamond in its center, from the points of which lines extend to each of the four sides of the square. Each of these spaces is designed for the use of the scorer according to marks and signs given in the book. By thus dividing the squares into spaces he scores without the liability to make mistakes. The League rules of scoring are printed in the book.—*N. Y. Clipper*.

PRICES:
POCKET.

			EACH.
No. 1.	Paper Cover,	7 games	$ .10
No. 2.	Board Cover,	22 games	.25
No. 3.	Board Cover,	46 games	.50
Score Cards			.05

CLUB BOOKS.

No. 4.	Large Size,	30 games	$1.00
No. 5.	Large "	60 games	1.75
No. 6.	Large "	90 games	2.50
No. 7.	Large "	120 games	3.00

Mailed upon receipt of price.

A. G. SPALDING & BROS.,

108 Madison Street,　　　　　　241 Broadway,
CHICAGO.　　　　　　　　　　NEW YORK.

No. 10.—**Spalding's Boss Ball.** Size, 7½ inches; weight, 3 oz. Packed one dozen in a box. The best juvenile five-cent ball on the market.................... Each $ 5   Per doz. $ 50

Spalding's Sample Case of Balls. We have manufactured a new Sample Case of an original design, which is particularly attractive. It contains one each of the above balls, and is suitable for traveling salesmen or show window. Also handsome, four color lithographic show cards for advertising, and miniature samples of all Spalding's Trade Marked Base Ball Bats, will be furnished dealers. Prices given on application.

	To Clubs,	
No. 8.—Spalding's Eureka Ball, white. A trifle under the regulation size and weight. The best cheap ball for the money on the market.	Each.	Per doz.
	$ 20	$ 2 00

	To Clubs.	
No. 9.—Spalding's Rattler Ball, white. Size, 8⅝ inches; weight, 4½ ounces. The best and largest ten-cent ball made.	Each.	Per doz,
	$ 10	$1 00

No. 7.—Spalding's Boys' Favorite, white. Regulation size and weight, horschide cover. A good boys' ball. Each ball put up in a separate box, and sealed with white band showing the Spalding trade mark. The best ball for the money ever offered. Mailed upon receipt of price........... Each $ 25   To Clubs, Per doz. $2 75

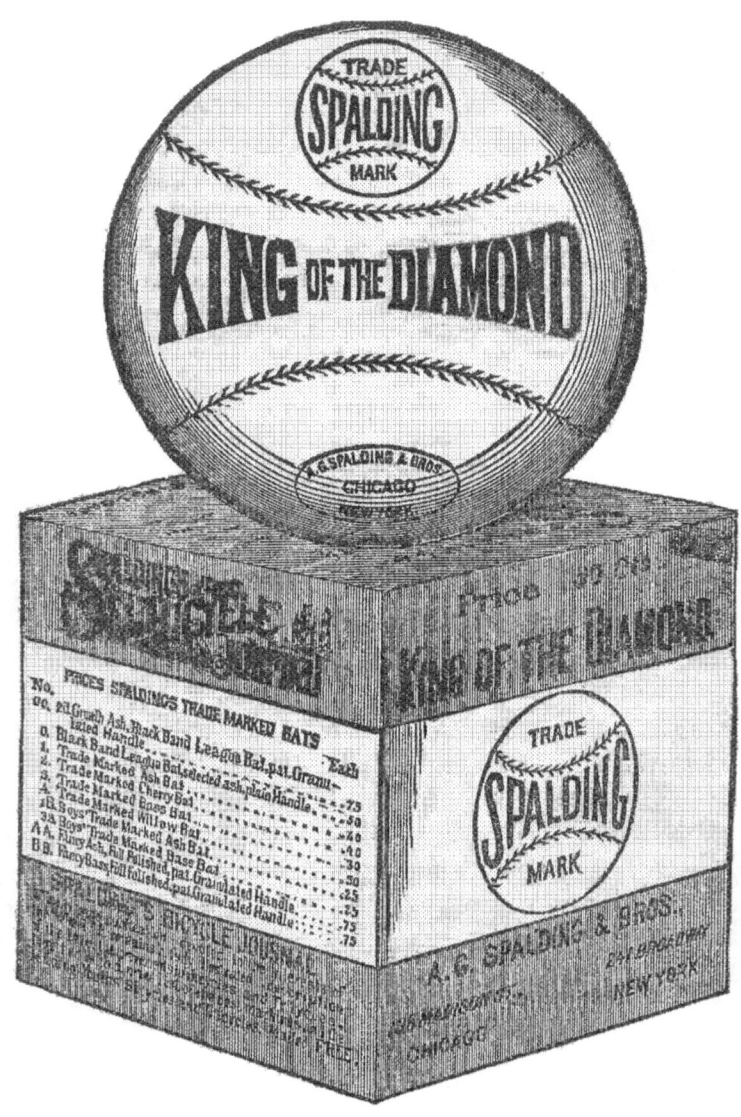

No. 5.—Spalding's King of the Diamond Ball, white. Covered with horsehide, regulation size and weight. A good ball for catching and throwing. Each ball put up in a separate box as shown above, and sealed with label showing the Spalding trade mark. Mailed upon receipt of price............... $ 50 $5 00

To Clubs,
Each. Per doz.

No. XX. — Spalding's Amateur Lively Ball, white. Covered with horsehide. Each ball put up in a separate box as shown above, and sealed with label showing the Spalding trade mark. To meet the growing demand for a good lively ball, at a medium price, we introduced this ball last season, and finding that it met with such a ready sale will continue it this season. Mailed upon receipt of price ....

To Clubs,
Each. Per doz.

$ 75 $8 00

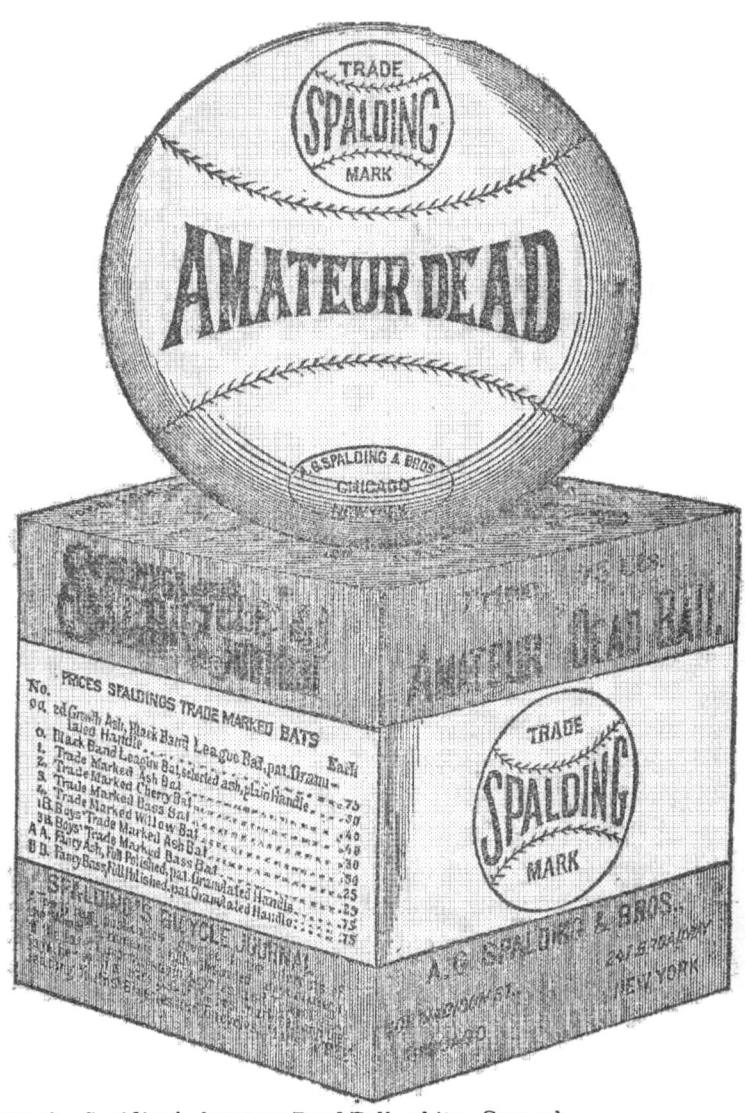

No. 3.—Spalding's Amateur Dead Ball, white. Covered with horsehide, and especially adapted for practice games. Each ball put up in a separate box as represented in the above illustration, and sealed with a white label, on which is shown the Spalding trade mark. Every ball warranted............................

No. 3R.—Spalding's Amateur Dead Ball, red. Same as No. 3, only colored red, with white label, on which is shown the Spalding trade mark in red. Mailed upon receipt of price..

	To Clubs,
Each.	Per doz.
$ 75	$8 50
75	8 50

No. 2.—Spalding's Professional Dead Ball, white. The best Dead Ball made, covered with selected horsehide. Every ball warranted to last a game of nine innings. Each ball put up in a separate box as represented in the above illustration, and sealed with a white label, on which is shown the Spalding trade mark, Mailed upon receipt of price..

To Clubs,
Each.   Per doz.
$1 00 $11 00

No. 1B.—Spalding's Boys' League Ball. To meet the growing demand for a first class ball for boys, we introduce this season our Boys' League, which is made exactly like the official League Ball, but smaller in size, each ball wrapped in tin foil, and put up in a separate box as represented in the above illustration, and sealed in accordance with the latest League regulations. Warranted to last a full game without ripping or losing its elasticity or shape. Mailed upon receipt of price.................................

To Clubs, Each. Per doz.

$1 00 $11.00

No. 1A.—Spalding's Association Ball, similar to the ball used by the American Association, each ball wrapped in tin foil, and put up in a separate box and sealed, as represented in the above illustration. Warranted to last a full game without ripping or losing its shape. Mailed upon receipt of price..........................   To Clubs, Each. $1 25   Per doz. $13 50

SPALDING'S
Official League Ball.

Spalding's League Ball is now recognized as the STANDARD in every part of the world where base ball is played. It was first introduced in 1876, and made under specifications designed by A. G. Spalding, whose long connection with the game had given him a knowledge of the requirements of a first-class ball not possessed by any other manufacturer. Every pains was taken with its manufacture, and it soon became very popular among professional players on account of its uniformity, elasticity and durability, which resulted in its being adopted as the official ball of the National League in 1878, and has been readopted every year since by the leading associations, including 1886.

The large sale and great demand for this ball has brought out many imitators, who would pirate on our trade and reputation by offering an inferior article at a lower price, and endeavor to create the impression that these inferior low grade balls are the same, or are equal to Spalding's Official League. We would caution ball players against infringements, and urge them not to be misled by the misrepresentations of dealers whose increased profits on the cheap goods may have something to do with their statements.

Our League Ball can be obtained of any first-class dealer in base ball supplies, to whom a liberal trade discount is allowed.

The following base ball leagues and associations have adopted the Spalding League Ball as the official ball of their associations for 1886, and by their regulations, all championship games played during the season, this ball MUST be used:

THE NATIONAL LEAGUE.
Composed of the following Clubs:
Chicago, New York, Boston, Detroit, Philadelphia, St. Louis, Kansas City and Washington.

THE NEW ENGLAND LEAGUE.
Composed of Boston, Haverhill, Newburyport, Lawrence, Portland, and Brockton.

THE EASTERN LEAGUE.
Composed of Newark, Jersey City, Waterbury, Bridgeport, Hartford, Providence and Troy.

THE INTERNATIONAL LEAGUE.
Composed of Utica, Rochester, Syracuse, Binghamton, Oswego, Buffalo, Hamilton and Toronto, Ont.

THE NORTHWESTERN LEAGUE,
THE WESTERN LEAGUE,
THE AMERICAN COLLEGE ASS'N,
THE NORTHWESTERN COLLEGE ASS'N.
THE NEW YORK INTER STATE COLLEGE ASS'N

We refer with considerable pride to the following Resolution unanimously adopted at the recent annual meeting of the American College Association, held at Springfield, Mass., March 12, 1886.

"*Resolved,* that the American College Association in unanimously adopting Spalding's League Ball for 1886, express their great satisfaction which this ball gave the Association last year, aad also cheerfully indorse it as the best ball they have ever used."

No. 1.—Spalding's Official League Ball, as adopted by the National League for 1886; each ball wrapped in tin foil, and put up in a separate box as represented in the above illustration, and sealed in accordance with the latest League regulations. Warranted to last a full game without ripping or losing its elasticity or shape. Mailed upon receipt of price..........

	Each.	To Clubs, Per doz.
	$1 50	$15 00

THE REVISED EDITIONS OF
Spalding's Hand Books
For 1886. Price 25c.

NUMBER THREE will be the revised book on
THE ART OF PITCHING AND FIELDING,

A work containing instructive chapters on all the latest points of play in base ball pitching, including special methods of delivery, the philosophy of the curve, the tactics of a strategist, headwork in pitching, the effects of speed, throwing to bases; and the revised book on The Art of Fielding, containing special articles on battery work in fielding, the pitcher and catcher as fielders, the infield, first base play, the second baseman's work, third base play, short fielding, the outfielder's work, backing up, throwing to first base, the captain of the nine, how to captain a team, together with the best pitching and fielding records of the National League, American Association, Eastern League, and Southern League, for 1885. The combined books of the Art of Pitching and Fielding mailed upon receipt of price, 25 cents.

NUMBER FOUR of the revised works for 1886, comprising the
ART OF BATTING AND BASE RUNNING,

Containing special chapters on scientific batting, facing for position, placing the ball, sacrifice hitting, waiting for balls, the batsman's position, standing in good form, fungo batting, home run hitting, base hits, earned runs, etc.. and the Art of Base Running, containing points of play in running bases, the rules for base running, etc., together with the leading batting averages of 1885, in all the National Associations. Mailed on receipt of price, 25 cents.

BY HENRY CHADWICK,
Base Ball Editor New York Clipper, Author of Routledge's Book of American Sports, and of Hand Books of Games, Etc.

What Competent Authorities say of these Hand Books.

Walter C. Camp, the athletic instructor, and noted ball player of Yale College, says: I have looked over your works on "Pitching," "Batting," "Fielding," etc., published in Spalding's Library of Athletic Sports, and I am sure from the remembrance of my own experience, that they will be of inestimable value to lovers of sports; particularly your book on "Pitching," which I consider as thorough and satisfactory an explanation of the various curves as any I have read. The whole series will be of service to our younger players, especially of our colleges, and interesting to the older players.

The veteran, Harry Wright, says: For years I have read your books on the game of base ball, and I have always found them both instructive and interesting. Your latest works on "The Art of Pitching," "Batting," "Fielding," etc., should be in the hands of all base ball players desiring to perfect themselves in the knowledge of the game. The scientific points of play, so clearly explained, should be carefully studied, and practice will eventually demonstrate their truthfulness. To quote, I will add, "whatever may be said about luck, it is skill that leads to fortune."

That skillful and experienced strategist in pitching, T. S. Keefe, of the League team of New York, says: I have given your books on "Pitching," "Batting," and "Fielding," etc., a close perusal in every particular, and I can safely say that there is no work in the market so complete in all its details as your book on "The Art of Pitching." You have taken the game from its past low standing and placed it before the public in a manner that has greatly aided it in reaching its present high position among the sports of the day. The books on "Batting" and "Fielding," as well as on "Pitching," are not only valuable to the beginner, but they offer a great deal of food for reflection for the expert class of players. In fact, you have dealt with the game, in all its details in such a manner that every person can readily comprehend the full meaning of the points laid down in each book. Were the advice you offer followed by the professional class of players, it would have a great tendency to advance the game as far as science can command.

John M. Ward, the Captain of the New York League team, says: I have carefully read your book on "The Art of Pitching." You have treated the subject with an understanding possible only to one of your extended experience. I take pleasure in recommending the book as a most complete work of instruction in pitching.

SPALDING'S
Trade Marked Bats.

THE PROMINENT LEAGUE PLAYERS
WHO USE THEM.

We point with considerable pride to the many testimonials and high indorsements we have received from nearly all the prominent base ball players of the country, who recognize the superior merits of Spalding's Trade Marked Bats, and show their appreciation by using them in all their match games. Space will not permit us to publish their letters of indorsement in full, but we refer to any of the following League players who have used Spalding's Bats for the greater part of their professional careers:

ROGER CONNER, of the New York Club,
                                  Champion League Batter of 1885.
JAMES O'ROURKE, of the New York Club,
                                  Champion League Batter of 1884.
DENNIS BROUTHERS, of the Detroit Club,
                                  Champion League Batter of 1882 and 1883.
A. C. ANSON, of the Chicago Club,
                                  Champion League Batter of 1879 and 1881.
GEO. F. GORE, of the Chicago Club,
                                  Champion League Batter of 1878.
JAMES WHITE, of the Detroit Club,
                                  Champion League Batter of 1877.

—ALSO—

Ewing, Deasley, Welch, Keefe, Gerhardt, Esterbrook, Ward, Gillespie, Dorgan, Richardson. Flint, Clarkson, McCormick, Pfeffer, Williamson, Burns, Dalrymple, Kelly, Sunday. Dealy, Gunning, Buffinton, Radbourn, Morrill, Burdock, Sutton, Hornung, Wise, Johnston. Bennett, Rowe, Getzein, Baldwin, Richardson, White, Manning, Hanlon, Thompson. Clements, Ferguson, Casey, Farrar, Farrell, Mulvey, Irwin, Andrews, Fogerty, Wood. Dolan, Myers, Sweeney, Boyle, McKinnon, Dunlap, Denny, Glasscock, Seery. Gilligan, Hines, Shaw, Barker, Knowles, Gladmon, Bassett, Kennedy. Briody, Weidman, Conway, McQuery, Force, Bastian, Rowe, Crowley, Lillie, Whitney, Hackett.

These goods can be obtained from any of our Depots of Supplies, or from any first-class dealers in base ball goods.

A. G. SPALDING & BROS.,
108 Madison St., CHICAGO.   241 Broadway, NEW YORK.

SPALDING'S TRADE MARKED BATS.

Spalding's Trade Marked Bats were first introduced in 1877, and they have gradually grown into popularity, until now they are used almost exclusively by all prominent professional and amateur players. All the timber used in these bats is allowed to season from one to two years before being made up, and the result is we are enabled to make much lighter and stronger bats than where the timber is hastily "kiln-dried," as done by nearly all manufacturers of cheap goods. Each bat is turned by hand, after the most approved and varied models, and if found to answer the requirements as to weight, size, length, etc., the *Trade Mark* is stamped on each bat to insure its genuineness. The success and popularity of these bats, which is due to the very great care that has been taken in their manufacture, have brought out many cheap imitations and we would caution the trade to see that the *Spalding Trade Mark* is stamped on each bat.

	Each.	To Clubs, per doz.
No. 00.—Spalding's Special Black Band League Bat, made out of the choicest white selected, second growth ash, on the most approved models, as recommended and used by League players. Each bat is carefully weighed, and the weight stamped in ounces under the Trade Mark. Each Bat is encased in a strong paper bag, lathe polished, and guaranteed to be the finest bat made. Having purchased the patent of Wm. Gray, of Hartford, Conn., covering the use of a granulated handle, and believing it to have great merit in preventing the hand from slipping, we have decided to use it on this grade of bats	$ 75	$8 00
No. 0.—Spalding's Black Band League Bat, made on the most approved model, as recommended by prominent League players. These bats are made from the best selected ash, lathe polished, weighed and stamped, each bat encased in a strong paper bag	50	5 50
No. 1.—Spalding's Trade Marked Ash Bat, made on three different models, finished with two coats of the best orange shellac, and lathe polished, 35 to 38 inches. Each bat weighed and stamped with weight in ounces under the Trade Mark	40	4 00
No. 2.—Spalding's Trade Marked Cherry Bat, made on three different models, finished with two coats of the best orange shellac, and lathe polished, 35 to 38 inches. Each bat weighed and stamped with weight in ounces under the Trade Mark	40	4 00
No. 3.—Spalding's Trade Marked Basswood Bats, light weight, clear, white selected timber, lathe polished, 36 to 39 inches. Each bat weighed and stamped with weight in ounces under the Trade Mark	30	3 50
No. 4.—Spalding's Trade Marked Willow Bat, light weight, large handles, lathe polished, each bat encased in a strong paper bag. The best light wood bat made, 36 to 39 inch. Each bat weighed and stamped with weight in ounces under the Trade Mark	50	5 00
No. 1B.—Spalding's Trade Marked Boys' Ash Bat, finished same as No. 1, 30 to 34 inches	25	2 50
No. 3B.—Spalding's Trade Marked Boys' Basswood Bats, finished same as No. 3, 30 to 34 inches	25	2 50
No. AA.—Spalding's Trade Marked Fancy Ash Bats, finished in a light mahogany color, with patent granulated handle. Very highly polished, put up in strong paper cases. Each bat weighed and stamped	75	7 50
No. BB.—Spalding's Trade Marked Fancy Basswood Bats, finished in a handsome mahogany color. Each bat weighed and stamped. Very highly polished, put up in strong paper cases	75	7 50

PLAIN FINISHED BATS.

	Each.	Per doz.
No. 6.—Men's Ash, Plain finish, ass'd length, 36 to 39 in.	$ 25	$1 50
" 7.— " Basswood, " " " " 36 to 39 in.	20	1 50
" 8.—Boys' Ash, " " " " 28 to 32 in.	15	1 00
" 9— " Basswood, " " " " 28 to 32 in.	15	1 00

SPALDING'S TRADE MARKED BATS.

Probably no class of Sportsmen are more particular about their weapons than a professional ball player is about his bat, for it is a recognized fact, that no player can excel as a batsman, unless he uses a first-class, well-proportioned, thoroughly seasoned bat. A cheap, poor bat is worthless at any price. Recognizing that ball players would appreciate a good article, and would willingly stand the slight additional expense, about eight years ago we introduced "Spalding's Trade Marked Bats," and they proved so popular, and were so far ahead of anything else ever put upon the market, that for a time it seemed impossible to keep up with the demand. We have improved these bats from year to year, until now they are the bat *par excellence*, and are used by every prominent professional player in America.

No. 00.　No. 0.　No. 1.　No. 3.　No. 4.　No. AA.

For testimonials and indorsements, we refer to all professional ball players in America.

www.ingramcontent.com/pod-product-compliance
Lightning Source LLC
Chambersburg PA
CBHW030301170426
43202CB00009B/828